Woman
Aboard

Books by Janet Stevenson

WEEP NO MORE
THE ARDENT YEARS
SISTERS AND BROTHERS
WOMAN ABOARD
THE UNDIMINISHED MAN:
  A POLITICAL BIOGRAPHY OF ROBERT WALKER KENNY

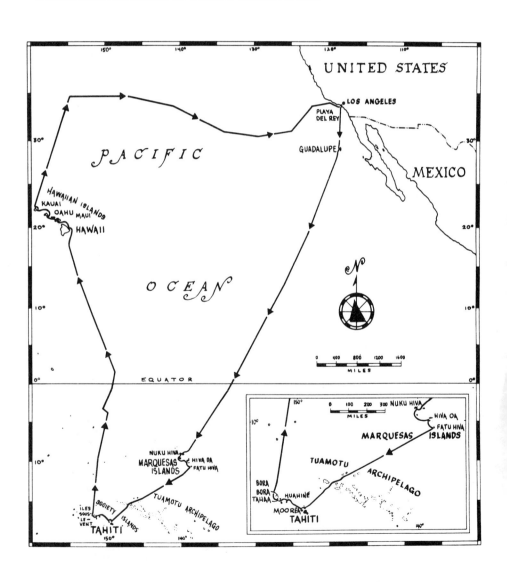

Woman Aboard

Janet Stevenson

CHANDLER & SHARP PUBLISHERS, INC.
NOVATO, CALIFORNIA

To the men

Photographs by Jack Baskin and Janet Stevenson

Library of Congress Cataloging in Publication Data

Stevenson, Janet.
    Woman aboard.

    Reprint. Originally published: New York:
Crown Publishers, 1969. With new pref.
    Includes indexes.
    1. Islands of the Pacific—Description and
travel. 2. Stevenson, Janet. 3. Boats and
boating—Islands of the Pacific. 4. Aikane (Sloop)
I. Title
DU23.S8   1981   909'.09164   81-14537
ISBN 0-88316-545-7 (pbk.)   AACR2

International Standard Book Number: 0-88316-545-7
Library of Congress Catalog Card Number: 81-14537
Printed in the United States of America.

First Chandler & Sharp edition published in 1981, by arrangement
with Janet Stevenson. First edition published in 1969 by Crown
Publishers, Inc.

Contents

The *Aikane* under sail.

Preface to the 1981 Edition

The decision to republish this book was taken one humid evening on the deck of a trimaran, moored in one of the small bays near the great harbor of Pago-Pago in American Samoa.

The occasion was a farewell dinner for two couples who have been for several years past circumnavigating in tandem, in two small sloops. One of the women was a fan of *Woman Aboard*. She had been given a copy as a going-away present when she and her husband pulled up stakes in Nebraska to spend the rest of their active lives at sea. Over the years, she assured me, the book has been useful, consoling, even entertaining. She loaned it out many times and eventually lost it. Did I have a spare copy?

I did not. Principally because I have replaced so many copies lost or worn out in similar circumstances. I had been thinking for some time that there was a "felt need" for another edition, but I had been shy about republishing without retracing the voyage of the *Aikane* to see for myself what, if anything, had changed in the interim—an alluring notion, but quite an impossible one.

The owner of the trimaran is of the opinion that there have been great changes, particularly in the Marquesas, and none of them for the better. "You were there at the best of times. Now there are too many visiting 'yachties.' People are not so cordial as they were to you."

This is disputed by every other set of recent visitors with whom I have talked since that evening.

But there is one startling change in that quarter: an air strip on Nuku Hiva (and another a-building) and one on Hiva Oa. According to recent visitors, this has made less difference than one might suppose. For one thing, both landing strips are on the windward side, far from the good anchorages and centers of population, with no roads leading overland between them. For another, there is only one plane a week, bearing mail and other inanimate freight, but few people.

Papeete is, I am reliably informed, about as we found it, only more so. There are no longer so many French Foreign Legionnaires in evidence, but there are more tourists. The roads are better, the bars are less boisterous, but the mix is made of the same ingredients. The same applies to Bora Bora. Huahine has been "discovered" but not yet subdued.

I could find no one who has touched recently at the Dangerous Islands, and that leads me to hope that they are still off the main routes, and still much the same.

At any rate, as my host and his guests agreed that evening, the sea has not changed, and neither have the problems of living and moving on it. "And your recipes are still good because the ingredients are still available, free for the picking or the fishing."

On the subject of the off-shore cuisine, I have explored the possibility that there are better preserved foods and better equipment available to those who hope to cruise the same latitudes. One expert assures me there are now deep freezers and microwave ovens that will work on the kind of current a small boat's engine can generate. But the preponderance of opinion is that these improvements are neither necessary or practical.

One small but significant piece of up-dating may serve to end this preface. Paul Gauguin is no longer the only illustrious occupant of the little Calvary on the mountainside above Atuona. Near his grave is that of Jacques Brel, who spent his last years on Hiva Oa and insisted on being buried there. His song, *Les Marquises*, hums in my head whenever I think of the islands:

"... et la mer se déchire,
   infinitment brisée
par les rochers qui prirent
des prénoms affolés ...
et par manque de brise
le temps s'immobilise
aux Marquises."

("... and the sea is torn up,
   infinitely smashed
by the rocks that have taken on
mad names ...
and for want of a wind
time lies motionless
in the Marquesas.")

JANET STEVENSON
June 1981

Prolog

What follows is a record (slightly condensed and lightly censored) of a recent six-month sea journey of nearly 10,000 miles: from Los Angeles to the Marquesas—a distance of roughly 2500 miles; from the Marquesas through the Tuamotus to the Society Islands—a distance of over 1000 miles as we sailed it; from the Societies to the Hawaiian Islands—about 2400 miles; and from the Hawaiian Islands back to Los Angeles—about 2500 miles. A journey undertaken by four people all of whom had had some experience sailing in small boats (experience that varied from considerable to very little), but no one of whom had ever been deep-sea sailing before.

It was not an expedition or an exploit. There was nothing to be proved; no record was to be set, no discovery looked for. Each of us had his own unique quota of expectations, and one —my husband—had a sort of auxiliary purpose. But the governing purpose of the voyage of the *Aikane* was recreation. We were all going on vacation, the best vacation of our lives.

Perhaps that is only a superficial view, and perhaps it is presumptuous of me to speak for the others. Perhaps each did have some secret, self-made challenge to meet, something he hoped to prove to himself about himself. But I had no such secret—until two or three days before we sailed. It came to me quite accidentally, and as an unpleasant surprise.

The *Aikane* was moored in a slip at the Del Rey Yacht Club in Playa del Rey harbor (near Los Angeles). The four of us were spending our daylight hours down there, making last-minute changes in gear or stores: adding "absolutely necessary" items, subtracting "not absolutely necessary" ones, multiplying

1

the safety devices, and dividing the cargo into various bilge, berth, and lazarette stowage spaces—coming and going along the dock on hundreds of small but vital errands. In the slip next to ours was a large powerboat belonging to a retired businessman who spent a good deal of time puttering about the deck watching us.

One afternoon he stopped me. "Say! I see you down here all the time. You're not going on this cruise, are you?"

I said yes.

He looked aghast. "Well! What do you think you're going to be? A woman aboard?"

I said yes. But I thought of a better answer an hour or so later. And an even better one in the middle of the night. I was too green to know the sailors' superstition about a woman (or a preacher) aboard bringing bad luck to a ship. I took the question at face value—as an impertinence.

But it stuck in my mind like a snag on which my thoughts kept catching, and very pertinent questions began rising to the surface around it. What was it going to mean to be a woman aboard a small boat surrounded by the open sea and the limitless horizon for as long as a month at a time? Was it going to be different from being a man under the same circumstances? In what way? Better or worse? Was it going to matter that I was outnumbered, three to one?

When the trip was first talked of nearly three years before, I had said I didn't want to go as a seagoing housekeeper. If I went, it would be on the same basis as the others. I would navigate, take my turn at the wheel, change sails, polish brass, varnish, etc.—whatever "etc." turned out to be. The men agreed. They would take care of their own laundry and mending, etc., just as they would with an all-male crew. Dishwashing and cleanup would be divided as wheel watches were.

Each crew member was to have a special province. I like to cook, so I was glad to take the galley as mine. But I wasn't going to be a galley slave. On the other hand, I wanted no preferential treatment. I would do my share of all jobs except those few for which I was too short or too feeble, for example, hauling up a heavy sail, making a line fast against a strong pull, or reaching farther than my short arm's length.

And so I had seen no reason why being a woman aboard should be a special assignment or a problem. But now that the question had been put in so belligerent a tone, I felt myself going on the defensive, betting myself that I could make it, and just as well as a man.

It was because of this bet with myself that I kept the journal from which this record is taken—especially the "sea legs." My answers to my own questions and the winning (or losing) of the bet may have no application to the case of other women aboard other vessels. But then, again, they may. And not only to women, but to other novice sailors setting out on an adventure in which untested powers are to be severely tried, an adventure from which there is no backing out once the land drops away astern.

My particular experience was formed in a mold made of three ingredients: the physical situation—winds, seas, sun, rain, feast, famine, insects, microbes, and viruses; the psychological situation—the personalities and relationships of the four human beings aboard; and the *Aikane* herself—her size, shape, design, and character.

The weather was the most important ingredient of the physical situation. All that needs to be said of it in a preface is that the voyage was timed to avoid all the predictable storms in the parts of the South Pacific we were to visit and to take full advantage of all predictable winds. The plan worked well overall, not so well in detail.

The ingredients of the psychological situation were a crew consisting of: (1) Jack, the skipper and owner of the *Aikane*, a successful builder and engineer who decided several years in advance that he would retire when he was forty-five and take a real vacation—embark on a full-scale adventure of the sort one can hardly manage if one waits till the age when most Americans are willing or able to give up "gainful employment." (Incidentally, this decision seemed to many of Jack's friends a most unusual one for a man in his position, but one of the things we learned on the voyage was that it was not. The Pacific—and, for all we know, every other ocean—supports an international population of boat bums, men who have opted out, temporarily or permanently, and who sail—some single-handed, some with their wives and children, teen-agers or toddlers, some in loose partnerships with other like-minded males or females. There are Australians, New Zealanders, Britishers, Belgians, Austrians, even Spaniards! But the majority is American.) Jack began to sail about four years before the start of our voyage, mostly up and down the California coast and mostly in a forty-foot Kettenburg sloop. He began seriously to plan this voyage two years in advance, and bought the *Aikane*, after a long, frustrating search, only two months before the date set for departure. He was trained in celestial navigation during World War II but never used the training, so he brushed up for this trip in an intensive tutoring course. As cautious and conservative as a man could be (the sort of man, that is, who could conceive of such a project in the first place), Jack prepared himself by reading, study, consultation with experts, and a series of trial runs. He was sure in his own mind that he and the *Aikane* could make it when the time came.

Numbers (2) and (3) were my husband and myself, old friends of Jack's who had spent a good many vacations with him in wilderness situations, so that the three of us knew what to expect of one another under various sorts of physical strain. I was a writer with fifty years of experience at being a woman ashore but with only a few weeks of sailing experience strung out over many years and all of it within sight of an island or coastline. I speak Spanish and once spoke French. I was brushing up on the latter as we went along in expectation of acting as interpreter when we put in to French-speaking ports. I had accepted the posts of Chief Steward (that is, planner, purchaser, and stower of all stores of edibles and potables) and of Chief Cook.

Benson, my husband, was the same age and in the same state of generally good health, but bigger, stronger, and better able to stay awake at the wheel. He had had a good deal of experience with powerboats, mostly on rivers and lakes, but had sailed even less than I. His field is educational psychology, and he planned to test and observe certain aspects of adolescent behavior in the societies we visited. For this reason he was armed with an impressively official letter of introduction from the French consul of the city where we live, to *Messieurs les Inspecteurs d'Acadé-mie des Archipels des Marquises et de la Société*, a document that was to open many nonacademic doors as well as a few traps. Benson's major responsibility was that of Chief Engineer in charge of the *Aikane*'s diesel-burning engine. (He was also Medical Officer, but since he turned out to be the only really interesting medical case of the voyage and to be very negligent at self-treatment, he has been stripped of his stripes in retrospect.) Neither Benson nor I knew anything about celestial navigation and not a great deal about dead reckoning, either, but we expected to learn.

The fourth was Norris, a stranger to the rest of us when we sailed. He was a last-minute replacement for a twenty-four-year-old graduate student who had to regret when his draft board informed him that he would be reclassified 1A the day

The four—Jack, Norris, Benson, Janet.

he left his carrel in the library. Norris was in his late thirties, an electrical draftsman by profession, a world traveler by inclination. He had sailed less than any of us, but he had once studied navigation, and was brushing up on it as I was brushing up on French. He was equipped to act as interpreter in Danish and to some degree in German—neither of which we expected to have to use. And he turned out to be a natural linguist who picked up a smattering, or a working pidgin, of each of the Polynesian languages to which we were exposed.

Finally, the vital statistics on the vessel that was to be home to this oddly assorted foursome for six months: the *Aikane* was one of the first of the new line of K-43's, a lovely, sturdy sloop with a hull of solid mahogany planking, sawn oak ribs, and a 50-foot mast. She was 11½ feet at the beam and 43 feet long. That length referred to the deck measured from bow to stern; living quarters were about 30 feet by 10—roughly the size of one of the popular models of house trailer one sees by the thousands in state and national parks every summer. Every inch of that space had been put to good use in the *Aikane*'s design, and there was plenty of air and light belowdecks—a feature that is rare in oceangoing craft of this size, and very important for cruising in comfort within twenty degrees of the equator.

Nevertheless, the layout posed real problems of *Lebensraum* for four adults: problems of simple claustrophobia and of "interpersonal tensions," as they are called in good pedaguese. There was only one "cabin sole"—which means a room on which a door can be closed for privacy. That was assigned to Benson and me, and it consisted of a long, pie-shaped bunk (most of it under the nose of the bow), two small hanging lockers, two drawers, and a standing space less than four feet square.

The "head" (toilet and washroom) had even less standing space. It had built-in cabinets for drugs, towels, paper goods, and so on, a washbowl to which fresh water could be pumped (by hand), and a very efficient seagoing toilet, which could be flushed with salt water (also by hand pump). The luxury feature of the K-43 head was that it could be reached by *two* doors. One led directly into the forward cabin, which gave Benson and me a private entrance. As things worked out, this was less of a boon than one would have thought, and if I were designing a boat I would sacrifice that extra door in favor of some sort of shower—even a cold saltwater shower, which we did not have.

The rest of the space belowdecks was one large room, divided by use rather than by partitions, into a galley, a dining area (which also served as a chart, writing, or game table), and bunks. There were two of these along the starboard side: the quarter berth Jack used most of the time; the other was used for sleeping only when we were heeled over on a port tack, and served as a sitting place or a dumping ground the rest of the time. On the port side was a transom berth above and behind the benches that went around three sides of the table. There was a way of converting this bench-table unit into a double bed, but we used it only once on the trip—when we had overnight guests. Also in the main cabin were two hanging lockers, two deep drawers, one set of shallow drawers like a chiffonier, and assorted shelves for radios, tape recorder, direction finder, compass, and the ship's library. The galley was furnished with a small double sink, a two-burner propane stove with a small oven, and a work counter under which was a fair-sized refrigerator. The latter was run by the auxiliary motor, which also recharged the *Aikane*'s batteries and, of course, turned the prop and moved us along when the wind wouldn't. The motor could do all three chores at once, or one—any one—or two. Half an hour of motoring night and morning would keep the batteries up and the refrigerator temperature down, and when we were using the prop anyway, charging and cooling were "free."

Special equipment aboard included labor- and brain-saving devices, but no frills. There were a ship-to-shore radio telephone, a high-seas radio that brought in the time-tick by which we checked our chronometer, an automatic pilot, roller-reefing, and an electric power winch for the bow anchor.

The *Aikane* was named without thought of how difficult it was going to be to convey to the marine operator in Oakland, California (not to mention foreign ports), but the name was appropriate for a boat in which human relationships were to be tested. Jack found it in a passage from Richard Henry Dana's *Two Years Before the Mast*:

Every [Hawaiian] has one particular friend whom he considers himself bound to do everything for, and with whom he has a sort of contract—an alliance, offensive and defensive —and for whom he will often make the greatest sacrifices. . . . This friend they call AIKANE. . . .

Such a contract—such an alliance—all of us made with our *Aikane* and, through her, with one another.

Shakedown

Playa del Rey Harbor to San Diego to Guadalupe

There was a large, noisy, confused farewell party, half aboard, half on the dock: visitors clogging the cabins, children swarming on the bow and the narrow decks amidships, parents ordering them off or on or in or out, and warm beer for all hands, courtesy of the yacht club, which was honoring its first member to venture "deep sea."

Out of the chaos order came as quietly as dawn. Jack told Norris and me to unbag the jib and get ready to raise it while he took the sail cover off the main, and Benson lowered the gay dress flags. Children were collected and counted. Farewells began in earnest, but before they could get tearful, we were away, gliding so silently that many on the dock didn't know we had cast off till they saw the widening water between us and them.

The main went up, and we began to tack back and forth down the narrow harbor entrance. A few determined good-bye wavers followed us as far as they could drive on the breakwater. One latecomer threw a gift—a can of smoked albacore—which we did not catch. Then we came about for the last time and made it out the harbor mouth. We caught the afternoon westerlies and a big swell at the same time. The *Aikane* heeled to port.

The trip was real at last.

Belowdecks a number of things we had not secured properly began to slide, roll, or topple, and for a while we were all kept busy making things fast. Then the stove, which had leveled itself on its gimbals, was lit, and I began to cook supper.

There is something disquieting (to one accustomed to land living) about frying hamburgers in a pan into which one is

9

constantly on the verge of falling. Benson had invented a harness into which I was to buckle myself to keep from lurching into or away from the stove. I tried it out for the first time, and discovered that the pressure on my midriff increased the disquiet. Before the hamburgers were brown, I was as close to seasick as I had ever been. Not an auspicious beginning for a hitch as Chief Cook!

I went above and offered to take the wheel for a while. Everyone else wanted the same assignment for the same reason. Benson broke out the Dramamine, and no one ate the hamburgers after all.

The sudden quiet after all the noise on the dock had the effect (on me, at least) of a door shutting. Shutting us all in together for an indefinite sentence, instead of out into the big adventure we had looked forward to. We needed something small and definite to do, to keep spirits up and Dramamine down. Jack set a navigation problem, a preview of the classes that were

Taking on supplies at Playa del Rey.

to start as soon as we were really at sea. By the time we were finished and our papers corrected, it was dark and the first night watch began. It was mine.

The original idea for dividing the night was that everyone was to stand a three-hour watch except me. I was offered a bribe: I could get off with only one hour in exchange for "supervising" all the meals and cooking the "most important" ones. I ought to have refused indignantly, but I was afraid that I might not be able to stay awake for three hours in the middle of the night all by myself. So I had compromised and accepted a two-hour watch and the cooking chore. I felt a little better about it when Jack announced that he too was going to stand only two hours, since he was on call during all night watches, if needed.

The wind had dropped at sundown and we were motoring, which meant that the automatic pilot was doing the steering and the man on watch had nothing to do but watch. There was nothing to see most of the time, and looking *for*, rather than *at*, lights in the darkness has the same effect on me as counting sheep. Besides that, it was cold—a slow-to-penetrate, hard-to-shake-off cold. The only way I could keep warm was to wrap myself in a blanket and huddle in the forward cockpit, under the canvas canopy. From that position I could see nowhere but dead astern.

Periodically I unwound myself from the cocoon and checked the compass (which read the same every time) and the engine gauges (which also read the same every time) and had a look forward, to port, and to starboard for the lights of an approaching vessel. In the beginning I performed these rites every quarter of an hour, but some time in the second hour of my ordeal I fell asleep. The next time I opened my eyes there were the lights of a large vessel not half a mile off the starboard beam! It took me about five minutes to be sure that she was heading away from, not right at, us. I never did figure out whether she had crossed our bow or our stern or how close.

But I had no trouble staying awake after that.

The channel approach to San Diego's harbor was spooky in the dawn. No wind, a light haze of fog, very little sound except that of our discreet British diesel. We met two sleek submarines, several landing craft, and a weird-looking vessel with long metal arms, which the men decided must be a missile launcher. To starboard there was an acre or so of superannuated Catalina flying boats, the mothball fleet of the air, which reminded me of a scene in *On the Beach*, everything silent, as if frozen by some atomic catastrophe.

It was comforting to put in to the busy Kettenburg yard, where we were hauled out on ways to have our bottom inspected and painted with algae-repellent paint.

While the men supervised (or studied under) the skilled workmen at Kettenburg's, I did our last big provision shopping in San Diego's supermarkets: frozen meats, chilled fruit and vegetables, and carefully wrapped whole-wheat bread. Everything else in the ship's stores was either dried or canned and had been stowed according to a card-file system. Eggs (144 of them), which had been dipped in mineral oil to preserve them, were stowed under one of the dining-table benches. Onions, which must be kept dry, were under the floor of the forward cabin. Green vegetables and citrus fruit, which were to be kept damp, were packed into crates covered with gunnysacks and stacked on the fantail. Meats went into the lowest level of the refrigerator, where they would thaw as slowly as possible. Everything else had been stowed under the floor of the main cabin or one or another of the bunks. The card file was keyed to a floor plan on which each hiding place was lettered. The system was designed not only to guide the cook to needed supplies but also to expedite reprovisioning. Every time a can, package, or bottle was removed from its resting place, the item was to be checked off on the card in the file.

We had supplies for thirty-two days and expected to make our first landfall in twenty-eight (maximum). It might be ninety days before we made a port where we could restock some items, like paper towels, powdered milk, canned meats, and luxury items like chocolate and wine. But the worst problem I foresaw in the steward's department was that we had all the fresh meat we were going to have till we made landfall at the same time we were sailing in waters where fishing was good. Many deep-sea sailors have reported that they got no strikes on the long haul through the latitudes that stretched ahead of us. Were we going from glut to famine with no transition?

We left the Kettenburg dock in the late afternoon, February 17, cleared Point Loma, and sighted a gray whale astern before the breeze and the sunset died. The moon came up behind the coast we were leaving, huge and cheddar colored. The air was full of Coast Guard helicopters buzzing angrily and blinking colored lights.

I went to sleep soon after we cleared the Coronados to be rested in case I was called for my night watch. There was some doubt about it because we were motoring, and if no breeze sprang up by 10:00 P.M., Jack was going to cut the motor and heave to until dawn. (He was already worried about wasting diesel before the doldrums.)

By ten o'clock there was not only a slight breeze but also a large freighter on our tail, so it seemed inadvisable to park our vehicle on the highway. I was called at 3:00 A.M., by which time I was in great shape for staying awake at the wheel till dawn.

This was the day the navigation classes began. Jack prefaced his first lecture by reminding us that as things stood, if anything were to happen to him, none of us would know how to get where we were going (or back home). Having scared us into full attention, he assured us that after a week of daily classes any of us would be able to navigate alone.

I took down all the directions for finding where we were "latitude-wise" by "shooting the sun" at noon. It didn't sound beyond my powers, and I could hardly wait for my turn at the crew's sextant. Jack had an old-fashioned mariner's sextant, a fine instrument that no one but he was permitted to handle, much less use. For the rest of us there was a war-surplus bubble sextant from which Benson had removed the bubble (and several other appurtenances). He and Norris were very enthusiastic about it, insisting that it was as simple to read as a child's primer, even without its astigmatizer "which would flatten the sun out like a pancake on the horizon."

I let myself be led to an appropriate spot on deck, listened to the directions for "bringing the sun down," followed them to the best of my ability—and failed even to find the sun. For a while I admitted my failure, but eventually I began to lie. It was too humiliating, with one or another of the men always standing over me, asking me if I didn't see it now. The only way to escape was to say yes, sneak a look at someone else's reading, add a couple of seconds, and do the calculations. I could manage the *Nautical Almanac* and 249 tables pretty well, and had some hope of mastering the problem of translating my arithmetic into geometry on the empty space of a universal plotting sheet. But I had a disheartening suspicion that I would never be able to bring us safely into port because I would never find, much less "bring down," the sun.

After thirty-six hours—including two nights—we sighted land right when and where our navigators had predicted, and spent our second day coasting along the south shore of Guadalupe Island, a wildly contorted volcanic outcrop a couple of hundred miles west of Baja California in the latitude of Bahía Sebastiano Vizcaíno.

It was afternoon when we anchored in a sheltered bay that served as the dooryard of a Mexican garrison. We went ashore in the dinghy (christened *Lili Aikane*, Little Friend) and met the authorities, a ragged but extremely courteous group of young soldiers, most of them married and already the fathers of numerous children.

We asked about abalone and lobsters, and were told there were plenty of both. Lobsters were for sale, but the traps were at some distance. But abs were free for the picking, in the water right under us.

There were only two neoprene diving suits aboard. One fitted me and the other fitted no one very well, but Jack could come closest to zipping it up. So he and I suited up, and inflated our rubber life raft to "buddy" the pair of us. We had two scuba rigs aboard, but Jack wanted to save the air for use in emergencies, so we were going to skin dive with snorkels only. As we rowed into the part of the bay that was shallow enough for that, a couple of the soldiers passed us on their way to the lobster traps, and shouted something that sounded like "*elefante.*" We thought it was some kind of joke, so we laughed, waved, and got into the water.

It was about fifty-five degrees, and terrible bands of cold clamped on every exposed part of me, the most painful being my forehead and my neck. I could stand it just about as long as I could hold my breath (which wasn't long, as I was out of practice). As a result, I hardly had time to get down, turn over rocks or peer into grottoes, and locate an ab, before it was time to surface again.

Once, when I came up for air, I found Jack waiting for me. He said something excitedly, but without taking the snorkel out of his mouth, and pointed down. I dived. There on the bottom was what looked like a grotesque exaggeration of a seal! An enormous creature at least thirty feet long, fat and goggle-eyed, staring at me as if she found me every bit as alarming as I found her!

I shot up to the surface like a cork. Jack was still there; together we struck out at a fast crawl and nearly swamped the life raft by trying to climb into it at the same time.

Jack explained, when he got enough breath to make words,

Aikane at anchor off Guadalupe.

that he had turned around down there and found himself mask to eyeball with the lady monster. He had been telling me to stay away, not to go down and have a look. We compared notes and tried to tell Benson how big she really was, allowing for the fact that everything looks a third larger under water. Benson didn't believe us. But just then Enrique (the captain of the garrison) and one of his friends swam up to dump some pink abs into the raft. We told them what we had seen, and they said "*Elefante!*" and struck out for shore.

It turns out that Guadalupe is a preserve—the only breeding ground in the Americas—for the nearly extinct species of seal called the "sea elephant." The male has a short trunk and a very bad temper during the mating season—which this was. One old bull had just bitten a hole in a small boat, and Enrique had a scar on his heel to show for his encounter with another irritable lover.

Our new friends had pried loose about two dozen abs before the alarm was sounded, so we had more than enough. We shucked two of the largest and marinated them to make *céviche*.

ABALONE CÉVICHE

   **Raw abalone (preferably the pink or yellow kind) sliced
      paper thin**
   **Raw onions (preferably Bermudas or red) sliced equally
      thin**
   Lime or lemon juice
   Oregano or tarragon
   Tabasco or taco sauce (optional)

Clean the abalone and slice it vertically or on the bias. Slice the onions and mix the two together in a deep dish. Pour lime juice over the mixture and turn it occasionally to be sure that all the abalone is exposed to the action of the juice. Sprinkle in the herb after about 10 minutes. Add the piquante (if any) just before serving. This is best served chilled. The minimum marinating time is 20 minutes; an hour is not too much.

Norris, who had never tasted seafood of any kind raw, was sure he was not going to like this dish, but he ate his whole portion as hors d'oeuvre with an apéritif of white wine.

Enrique and the *medico*, who is not a real doctor, came out in a launch with a gift of small lobsters for our supper. They were the official representatives of the Republica Mexicana here, and had the responsibility of examining and stamping passports and the papers of all ships that put in. Also, they really wanted to inspect the interior of the *Aikane*. After going through the motions with the papers (which they couldn't read, since they were all in English), they accepted a *copita*, took their look around the boat, and invited us to do them the honor of a visit to their homes when we had eaten.

BROILED LOBSTER ON SHIPBOARD

Lobsters (small, one apiece)
Sauce of melted margarine (or butter) with garlic, and parsley or tarragon

Split the lobsters by hammering through them, backside up, with a heavy knife. If you have no charcoal broiler aboard, pan-fry them in oil or margarine. Start with the shell up. A crust will form and hold the juice in. After 10 minutes (or less for very small lobsters) turn them and let the heat work through the shell. Another 10 minutes should be enough for the medium-sized. Pour the sauce into the shell or serve it in a paper cup for dipping.

We didn't offer to pay for these lobsters but we took presents in when we paid our call: a box of instant powdered milk for Enrique's baby, chocolate and bananas for the other children and the wives, and a bottle of wine for the men. We also contracted to buy two dozen lobsters for the ship's stores at regular Ensenada prices: $6 a dozen for mediums; $8 for large; to be delivered to us just before we sailed.

After a full day ashore, during which we explored the island, fished (unsuccessfully), and paid more visits, we got an unbroken night's sleep—the last we could look forward to for some time. By 10:30 A.M. the next day, we had the lobsters aboard and were ready to weigh anchor, when a fog rolled in.

A moment before, everything had been brilliantly clear. I was at the wheel while the men prepared to raise the main. Jack saw the fogbank, yelled at me to take a bearing of our course, which lay between two great rocks that guard the southern entrance to the little bay. I had just time to note the compass reading before it became impossible to see as far as the bow.

We nosed our way out under power, with Norris and Benson keeping bow watch. Stories of cruises that had taken years of preparation meeting disaster before they had really got under way popped up from the worry locker in my mind. Minutes dragged by. We had not run afoul of either Scylla (El Zapato) or Charybdis (El Toro), and I began to believe we were safe.

There was nothing in our way for the next 2300 miles.

The First Sea Leg
Guadalupe to Nuku Hiva

Our course was 200 degrees, and the wind was stiff enough to move us ahead at seven knots for two days in succession, but it did not blow from the quarter Jack expected. He had a set of very large charts showing the prevailing winds in each part of the Pacific each month of the year. Little arrows with tails of varying length indicate how many days (on the average) the winds blow from each point of the compass. Jack spent hours studying these oracles and calculating the chances of our "unusual" wind persisting. The answer was always zero, but the wind went right on, and finally we had to change our course to 230 degrees to compensate for the "westerly error."

Navigation classes were held every morning after "washup" (a chore we all shared at the start, but which became increasingly Norris's, by his own choice). I began to see a glimmer of light on the sextant front. Once I actually saw the sun and had almost brought it down before I lost it. My progress might have been more rapid if I had had a sextant all to myself, but both Norris and Benson wanted it at the same time I did, especially at noon when the latitude shot was taken, and I felt I had no right to keep the instrument from people who knew how to use it.

Meanwhile Jack had given his second lecture: on the more difficult "line-of-position" operation, which yields, not one's longitude, as I had expected, but a line extended on the blankness of a universal plotting sheet, "somewhere along which the ship is." To make anything useful of this, one has to achieve a "fix" by plotting two different l.o.p.'s (either obtained from observing the same celestial body at different times or two celestial bodies at the same time) and marking their intersection. That gives a point that places the ship.

Since we were using only the sun at this point in our navigational careers, we had to "shoot" it twice, and "advance" the earlier l.o.p. to meet the later one. The formula for this (known as a "running fix") is complicated, and the possibilities of error are almost infinite. Benson and I chose freely among them. He was very good with the sextant and reasonably accurate with his arithmetic (neither of which things I was), but very weak on the mathematical operations. It took several weeks for us to discover why: he had been seasick during both of Jack's lectures, and had hardly understood a word of either.

Meanwhile Jack and Norris spent half their waking hours getting and comparing fixes and persuading each other that we were going to have to make a sail change.

One of the things that make deep-sea sailing different from (and easier than) day sailing is that one isn't always having to change tacks. It's quite possible to go from North to South Pacific and across a dozen longitude lines without raising or lowering a sail. But after three days Jack decided we ought to take advantage of our following wind and sail wing and wing. That meant substituting the ballooner (a swollen-bellied sail of very light Dacron) for the Genoa, and rigging the spinnaker pole. Neither the pole nor the crew had been used for this purpose before, so the maneuver was not accomplished with grace or speed, and when it was done, it turned out to be no easier to hold the course. We tried 190 degrees to compensate for previous errors, and the navigators' muttering died down a little.

A full week out of Los Angeles (and our last real showers), we decided it was time to wash clothes and selves. For the former, we used a laundry detergent that was supposed to rinse out, even in salt water, and leave no scum, but although we dragged the clothes in a nylon net bag for almost a whole hour, the results were not very impressive. Then Benson soaped himself all over with liquid Lux, and I scooped buckets of water out of the sea and poured them over his head. His gasps and shudders disheartened the rest of us, and we settled for "European" or "spit" baths with a tumblerful of fresh water in the washbowl in the "head." The sea was warming steadily at the rate of a degree every twelve hours, and we all promised ourselves a "Benson bath" when it got up to seventy-five degrees.

The gastronomic climax of the first week at sea was an abalone chowder, made by Norris (against his will) out of the black abs from Guadalupe. I was at the wheel during the preparation, giving directions and advice with a tolerant authoritarianism that partly compensated for the beating my *amour propre* had taken from Norris in the matter of running fixes.

ABALONE CHOWDER

1 lb. (approx.) of shucked raw abs (black will do)
2 medium-size onions, sliced
6 slices of bacon, chopped
1 cup (½ regular pkg.) dehydrated potatoes
1 can evaporated milk
1 cup white wine (dry)
Oregano (or marjoram or basil or tarragon)
Salt and pepper

Having thoroughly cleaned the abs, put them through a meat grinder. Chop the bacon and fry it till it's crisp. Remove it and lay it aside. Fry the onion slices till clear, in the bacon fat. (Note: dehydrated onion bits will do, and don't need to be fried.) Then add the ground abalone and juice, and cook till the ab is tender (about 20 minutes) in a heavy vessel with a tight-fitting lid. (Another note: pressure cookers do this well, in less time.)

When everything is reduced to the state of tenderness desired, add the dehydrated potatoes with enough water—part salt, if you like—and the wine and all the seasonings. Keep adding water as the potatoes absorb it until the chowder is as thick or as thin as desired. Only then add the milk and bring the mixture to just below the boiling point. Add bacon crisps and serve.

If you use raw potatoes, they must be chopped fine, will take a little longer to cook, but will use less water. *Caution:* Don't boil the chowder after adding the milk. It will curdle. It tastes almost as good curdled, but it doesn't look appetizing.

This chowder is even better the second day. It can be

kept up to 3 days in a refrigerator that stays at 40 degrees.
It makes an excellent main dish, with bread or hardtack, a
raw salad, and a canned fruit dessert.

There was, by this time, a developing problem about our
lobster-and-ab pound on the fantail. We had been watering the
gunnysacks full of shellfish whenever we watered the crates of
fruit and vegetables. The lobsters seemed to be surviving, but
abs need rushing water to keep healthy. Ours were beginning to
look a bit limp, so we decided to shuck all the pink ones, make
céviche out of some, and slice the rest into steaks, to be pounded
later. We stored the latter in foil, as close to the cooling coils of
the refrigerator as we could manage. The rest of the abs (black)
and the shells of the pinks, which would make fine trading goods
in the South Pacific, we tied in one of the sacks, and threw overboard, trailing at the end of a twenty-foot nylon line. The idea
was that it would not only keep the abs in good heart but also
act as a drogue, and steady us. (The *Aikane* was switching her
stern around like a fresh filly.)

It seemed a very clever arrangement, but during the first
night the nylon line got snarled with the taffrail log, and fouled
up all our "distance-covered" calculations. Also, the shells
worked a hole in the sack. When we pulled it in, everything
was gone but one small black ab and two inferior shells.

Before we had recovered from that setback, real tragedy
struck. Death stalked through Lobsterville!

The first notice we had was by nose, and it came too late
because the smell had to get pretty high before we could believe
it. The sack had been kept carefully out of the sun and well
watered, and now and again I had peered into the darkness
within. I couldn't see much, but there was certainly movement
in the tangle of legs, feelers, and fat, spine-armed tails. I knew
better than to put a hand in to test the health of any particular
specimen, and the only other way to check would have been to
dump the whole colony into the cockpit, after which each irritable crustacean would have had to be caught and put back in
the sack—a perilous pursuit on dry land and worse than that at
sea.

So I put it off. The smell grew gradually more menacing, until at last all four of us agreed that it was no longer "a good lobstery smell."

We emptied the sack into the cockpit. There were twenty-five lobsters—one more than we had paid for—and all but five were dead.

I should have thrown the twenty corpses into the sea and cooked the living five for lunch. Instead I sorted through the whole hideous pile, breaking each in half at the "waist." Those that were soft I did throw overboard. But many seemed quite firm. Of these, I discarded only the head, which contains the parts that spoil most easily. I saved the tails and turned them over to Jack, who sorted through my pile and discarded two more. We ended up with thirteen recently deceased and five limp but still living lobsters.

I steamed the whole lot (in relays) in our aluminum pot, with an inch of white wine and another inch of fresh water, which I kept replenishing as it boiled away. The liquor that was left after the last tail was removed was the stock from which the following gourmet soup was made:

IT-SHOULDN'T-BE-A-TOTAL-LOSS BISQUE

    Pot liquor (cf. above)
    Leftover Abalone Céviche
    Leftover lobster bits (whatever clung to the shell after
      they were shucked)
    Cornstarch for thickening
    Evaporated milk

We picked all the meat we could out of the tails, and cooked the bits with the céviche until the onions in the latter were soft. Then we thickened the liquor with cornstarch and seasoned it with herbs (same choice as in Abalone Chowder) and pepper. No salt! Finally we added the evaporated milk, a little more water and wine (white, dry) to bring it to the desired consistency. A great delicacy, anytime you happen to have the ingredients.

When we had cleaned up the cockpit and shucked the

lobster tails (using tin snips to cut down the tough underside), we wrapped them in foil, four tails to a package, and prepared to stow them near the abalone steaks: that is, under the cooling coils of the refrigerator.

At that point the second nasal disaster warning came through. As we moved things around to make room, a suspicious odor began to rise from the depths of the refrigerator. Taking no more chances, I dove (Benson had to hold me by the knees) to the very bottom and brought up all the meat.

None of it was spoiled, but the paper in which it was wrapped was soggy with blood and water, and smelled vile. We threw all the wrappings overboard (the sea is such a great garbage disposal!), rinsed the meat, and scrubbed the whole refrigerator with a solution of baking soda. This took nearly an hour, and no one had much appetite for lunch.

We put everything back, started the motor to cool things, and tried to decide what to do with the meat. There was one superb slab of beef, a leg of lamb, and two cut-up frying chickens. All of it thawed and ready to be cooked! I finally decided to marinate the chickens in soy sauce, ditto the beef, and to roast the lamb for dinner. (I wonder if the Japanese invented the *teriyaki* marinade because they had no refrigeration. Soy not only gives you an extra day but also covers any faint trace of gaminess.)

Third crisis: the leg of lamb. By the time I was ready to light the oven, the wind had picked up, and the boat was not only rolling but pitching as well. Gimbals counteract roll, but not pitch. It didn't occur to me that this could make trouble. I seasoned the lamb with marjoram, salt, and pepper, and stuck it full of splinters of garlic. Then I jammed it into the only baking dish we had, which was no longer or wider than the leg of lamb, and only three inches deep. It didn't occur to me that this could make trouble either. I was totally preoccupied with the challenge of lighting the oven for the first time.

There was a big movable chunk of lead in our oven to slow the pendulum action when the going got rough. It was normally placed right over the hole through which a match had to be poked. In a bad sea the stove swung wildly the instant the weight was removed. My efforts to follow the moving target with a lighted match were fruitless, and soon there was so much butane in the cabin that I had to run the bilge blower and wait for it to clear.

In the end I had to call Benson to hold the stove while I lit it and replaced the weight. I volunteered for wheel duty to get rested up.

(Wheel duty always relieved me of all feeling of other responsibility. Ashore I am stove-oriented: no matter what else I may be doing, I feel responsible to whatever is on the fire. But at sea, the wheel took precedence. The moment I glued my eyes to the white numbers bobbing gently in the black globe of the compass, everything else went out of focus.)

About an hour after I took the wheel, someone said something about there being smoke in the cabin. I don't believe I said anything, but I dimly remember thinking it was probably because the oven hadn't been used before. Or because a little lamb fat had splashed out and was burning. But the problem was not mine to solve; I was steering the ship.

Quite a long time after that, Benson appeared, rubbing his eyes and choking, and insisted on relieving me. "You go down and see how things are coming," he said.

I went.

The galley was so full of smoke that I had to grope my way to the stove. I opened the oven and looked in. At least a cup of melted fat had overflowed or been sloshed out of the baking pan. The walls as well as the floor of the oven were covered with smoking grease, and there was a puddle of the stuff congealing on the floor under the stove.

I cleaned it up.

I used nearly a whole roll of paper towels, smelled of tallow until I could get a real bath, and bore the mark of Cain on my brow. That last, because I had to take the weight out of the oven again to sop up the fat. Naturally, it started swinging, and naturally the edge that hit me in the forehead was hot enough to brand.

I kept my temper up to the minute when Jack and Norris materialized. They had been up on the bow where the air was clear, and they wanted to know what I was doing down there on my knees. Was something wrong? Why hadn't I called for help?

Then I blew.

The roast lamb was very good, and the lobster made great cold supper salads—which became more and more popular as we approached the Line. I decided to turn the beef into *suki-yaki*. (There was a package of bean thread in the goodies locker. With a can of mushrooms, fresh onions, celery, and half the beef sliced thin, we came pretty close to the real thing.) So nothing but a dozen lobsters had been lost.

The real crisis came on at sundown.

Norris was at the wheel. I was on my stomach, fishing for things in the bilge compartment under the center aisle, getting out the ingredients of breakfast, which I planned, but didn't cook. Whatever I wanted was always at the bottom of what-ever compartment it was in, and I was using a flashlight, trying to see into the dark V below, when I caught a glint of some-thing wet. The bilges had been inspected daily and had been marvelously dry, till this moment. I was concerned enough to move a whole case of canned goods to get a better look. Sure enough! There was what looked like two inches of tomato juice sloshing around below.

At first I thought one of the juice cans had split, and I was testing them to find the bad one when Jack came along and asked what I was up to. I told him. He lay down and reached between the boards till his fingers touched the red stuff. He sniffed them and looked worried. Benson had joined us, and he took a sniff. The two of them looked at each for a moment, and then, without a word, they began pulling up sections of the cabin floor.

For the next three-quarters of an hour, I was marooned in the forward end, in a box seat for observing and worrying about what was going on.

I understood without being told that the red liquid was not tomato juice, but that was about all I did understand. From the way Jack and Benson were behaving I deduced that they suspected a leak somewhere in the vitals of the boat. But what?

It was not water. Nor gasoline. Nor anything we had brought along to drink.

It occurred to me that we had passed the point of no return. There was no land nearer than Nuku Hiva toward which we could steer if we were in real trouble. We had not seen a ship on the sea or a plane in the sky or even a piece of flotsam, since we left Guadalupe. The ocean was suddenly limitless and empty, and the *Aikane* very small and very frail.

Having nothing to do except worry, I tried to focus on what Jack and Benson were doing—which was to localize the leak and/or to figure out what was leaking, which would lead eventually to the same thing. I had once heard Jack call Paul Kettenburg on the ship-to-shore radio to ask for help in diagnosing a mysterious malady like this. But it was night now. No one would answer at the Kettenburg yard, even if we could get through to the marine operator in Oakland, which was almost impossible except in the early morning. By morning, we would be out of trouble or beyond help.

Jack and Benson were working in a curious way: partly with their hands, which I couldn't see, and partly with their brains, which I could hear. For each was working on a set of deductions, which he spoke aloud. Their minds worked very differently, and their competence was in different fields. Jack knew much more about sailing and navigating, but Benson knew more about engines, and Jack relied on his judgment here. On the other hand, Jack took the ultimate responsibility for everything on his ship, so he was doing his own diagnosing, making guess after guess (aloud), to most of which Benson replied with a "No, Jack, I don't think so," and went right on working out his own logic.

I couldn't follow either set of guesses, but I was fascinated by the way in which differences, which are sometimes irritating in close quarters, were being turned into real advantage in an emergency. Little by little, as I listened, I forgot to be afraid.

The "tomato juice" was finally identified as hydraulic fluid. The leak was located in the back pressure valve of the hydraulic clutch. By the time they had plugged it, they had figured out what caused it and how to avoid a repetition.

There was a sailing brake that held the propeller shaft rigid when the boat was under sail. When the boat was running under power, this had to be released. On our engine there was a safety device that kept the motor from starting as long as the brake was on.

Up till now we had been running the motor every twelve hours to charge the batteries and cool the refrigerator, but not to power the boat. We had got sloppy about putting the brake on after starting up. So long as it was not engaged, the shaft turned *backward!* We had been running long distances with this reverse motion going on, and forcing hydraulic fluid into places not designed to withstand pressure. Hence the leak!

Everyone was under orders to take the brake off every time the motor was started and put it back on at once, which was relatively simple for the men, but not for me. To reach the lever, I had not only to pull up a heavy section of the galley floor and lie flat on what was left, but reach in over my arm's length and push or pull a viciously uncooperative lever. There was only one operation I hated worse: opening or closing the engine's exhaust valve. (This had to be done to let out fumes when we were motoring, and to keep out the big following seas when we were under sail.) This valve lever was hidden deep in the lazarette. Anyone under five foot six had to crawl partway into this compartment, which was packed with an assortment of tackle boxes, bosun's chairs, and barbecues. If the boat lurched, one was apt to get one's teeth knocked out.

The problem of the wind that couldn't be found on Jack's chart continued to dog us. We were supposed to be in the trades, which blow from the northwest in this part of the ocean (except in July) and which would have put us on a lovely, comfortable, easy-to-steer beam reach. Instead we continued to draw a wind almost dead astern and a following sea, also almost dead astern. But the wind came from a little to starboard, and the seas from a little to port. The result was what Norris named "jibesville."

I was finally beginning to understand what happens on a jibe. A big sea would heave its shoulder under us, swinging the stern toward the starboard and bringing the trailing edge of the sail close to the line of the wind. If it actually crossed that line, the wind "got behind" the sail and slammed it violently to the other side. We had rigged a "preventer"—a nylon line passed through a system of chocks and blocks—which cushioned sudden swings of the boom and kept it from snapping one of the stays or the mast itself. But the preventer didn't really prevent jibes. One had to be constantly on the alert.

The problem was exacerbated by the ballooner, which was still wing-and-winging us along. Finally Jack decided we had too much wind for such a sail (with such a crew) and ordered the three of us to take it down and put up, not the Genoa, but the smaller working jib.

What followed should have been filmed with Laurel and Hardy in the leading roles. Being novices, we twisted the clew when we threaded the jib sheets through all the chocks on the way from bow to cockpit. We had made everything fast before we noticed our mistake, so we had to take it all out—lower the jib, untwist the clew, reverse the sheets, thread them through blocks, and so on, and make them fast on the cockpit cleats. Before we had finished, the wind had come up quite strong, and the rethreading was done with the heavy canvas of the jib flapping in our faces like a ghost with St. Vitus's dance.

Jack stood by and let us make our mistakes, find them, and correct them. When at last we were done, he watched the sails work for a minute or two and then said he thought he'd like to try to jib on the other side—not wing-and-wing. This change involved swinging the spinnaker pole from one side to the other, an awkward procedure under the best of circumstances. We (and the wind) turned it into a job for kamikazes. Finally Jack decided he would have to intervene, so he told me to take the wheel while he "supervised" actively.

For the first half hour I did pretty well, coming into the wind and falling off, over and over, keeping the pressure off the sails so the men could work them, but not losing "way" (that is, forward motion, without which one has no control over the rudder, as I was about to find out).

All at once, I had got us into "irons." The position is as ludicrous as that of a turtle on its back. You can't get a sail out in any direction to catch enough wind to get you moving in any direction.

On the whole Jack had been remarkably patient with his green hands. He had tried not to put down the tyro either by yelling at him in the moment of a fumble or by lecturing him after the fact. But this was his morning for behaving like a captain instead of a teacher. When I goofed, he turned on me as if I were the cause of the whole complex of error.

By the time he had finished telling me what I had done (and/ or failed to do), I was as indignant as any whipping boy, conscious for the first time of the difference between a whipping boy and a whipping girl, and furious with myself for "behaving like a woman." The engine had to be started to get us out of "my" irons, and that seemed the four-hundredth blow.

Then the wind shifted, and the sails had to be shifted again. There was another noisy little crisis belowdecks. We had been either on a starboard tack or running before the wind ever since we left Guadalupe. After ten days things had settled themselves on shelves and in cupboards and holds. When we heeled to starboard, they began to slide, fall, or roll, from the medicine chest in the head to the spice shelf in the galley. Books, duffels, flashlights, and a large can of scouring powder, which toppled over and sprayed green powder over the lobster salad that was secured in the double sink.

Everything but my ruffled feelings settled down on the new tack. The wind held steady, and we seemed to have sailed out of jibesville at last.

The calm and my sulks lasted till just after lunch. Benson was at the wheel, and called us to see our first albatross: a dark bird with a six-foot wingspread, who flew incredibly close to the tops of the jagged waves, dipping and rising, banking and turning, and never getting a feather wet.

The bird must have reminded Jack of the Ancient Mariner, for he announced that the time had come for our first overboard drill. The lecture that preceded this maneuver stressed the importance of combating one's natural instinct (if one is at the helm) to come about and go at once to the aid of the "man overboard." That, Jack assured us gravely, was the best way to lose the victim, especially in a confused sea, which is the type of sea in which a man is most likely to go overboard, and most especially at night.

Standard Operating Procedure is to:

A. Yell for help!

B. Note the compass bearing and time!

C. Throw over the life preserver and the flag float, both of which are within reach of the helmsman, and rigged so that one good tug on the cord will free them.

By the time one has done all this, the rest of the crew should be on deck. The boat is then made to come about and put on the reciprocal course—that is, the compass bearing you observed when the man went overboard, plus 180 degrees, or the same bearing subtracted from 360 degrees, if that's easier. By sailing the new course the same number of seconds or minutes, you will bring the boat to the approximate location of the swimming (you hope) man. Waves and currents will not have moved him very far from where he fell in.

The *Aikane*'s safety equipment was new and deluxe. The life preserver was a great horseshoe covered with brilliant yellow plastic. Attached to it by a one-hundred-foot nylon cord was a Minibuoy—a waterproof, battery-operated light that went on as soon as it hit the water, would burn for one hundred hours, and could be seen for nearly a mile. At night the swimmer is able to spot it when a wave tosses it, or him, up. He can swim to it and, having found the nylon line, follow it to the life preserver. The horseshoe shape of the latter expedites getting in, and makes it possible to rest your head and arms almost comfortably—even to sleep, without danger of going under.

The flag float performs the same service by day. It consists of a fluorescent red flag tied to an eight-foot bamboo pole, which is weighted with lead at the opposite end. About a foot up from the weight is a large barrel-shaped piece of some light material that keeps the pole floating right side up. The swimmer makes for it and looks for the life preserver in the vicinity. (They aren't attached, but if they are thrown in together, they stay pretty close.) For the searchers on the boat, the buoy (or the flag) acts as a direction finder in the same way. It's astonishing how, in a heaving sea, an object floating on the surface can stay hidden from an eye that is at approximately the same height above the water. Raising either eye or object a few feet enormously increases the chances of rescue.

Jack finished his lecture by telling us that he would be the man overboard, and would represent himself by a large carton of garbage. He suggested, since this was our first try, that we only pantomime the tossing of the life preserver and the flag.

Actually, we did quite well for beginners. The garbage was still afloat when we got back. The drill was pronounced a success.

But a few minutes later Norris lost one of our good plastic buckets overboard. (He was scooping up water to rinse the dishes, when a wave hit the bucket and yanked it right out of his hand.) This time we didn't do so well. We found the bucket, but it was already sinking. We could see it, but we couldn't reach it with the boathook, and it sank slowly out of sight.

It didn't occur to anyone to dive for it until too late, which seemed very strange in retrospect. Plastic buckets were valuable and irreplaceable in our circumstances. The water was about seventy-four degrees, and exquisitely clear. Benson had been nagging Jack to drop sail and let us all go for a swim. Why didn't he—or anyone else—dive in and retrieve the bucket?

The answer is that there is something awesome about the *idea* of diving into water three miles deep. It doesn't make logical sense. There's nothing that can happen to you in water that deep that can't happen in water just too deep to stand in, but it seems as if there were. As if something unimaginable might rise from the floor of the ocean and swallow one like Jonah.

Peace, uneasy but welcome, reigned between the four of us for the rest of that day and the next, but there were more minor disagreements than before.

First there was the debate about the refrigerator. As the temperature of the water outside the hull rose, it got more difficult to hold the temperature to the forty degrees we wanted. We could drive it down to thirty degrees by the usual half hour of motoring, but it would climb back to fifty degrees (as high as the gauge read) the first half hour after the motor cut off. We resorted to taping the cracks between the lids and the counter, making it a misdemeanor for anyone to open the box between breakfast and dinner, and piling all sorts of insulating material on the counter, but nothing made any significant difference.

Benson evolved a theory that the trouble was caused by too much unoccupied space. He argued that we ought to fill the entire cavity with cans, run the temperature down to thirty degrees, and hold it there till everything was chilled through. "The cans will act like canned ice," he said. Jack disagreed. He really didn't meet the argument; he advanced another: that Benson was endangering our reserves of diesel, which must be hoarded for the doldrums ahead. And he appealed to me for support! I was torn between thinking that Benson was probably right and the fear that I would have to remove a whole load of cans every time I wanted to get something from the bottom layer (which is where everything I wanted always turned out to be).

There was another argument that was beginning to get just slightly acrimonious: why the fishing was so bad. There were fish in these waters. We saw them jump now and then. Once we reeled in our line and found the hooks of the lure straightened out, as if a fish had taken it and later been pulled off. Jack said we were going too fast to troll, and was for giving up. Norris said we were getting strikes and losing the fish because no one (except him) was willing to sit there and hold the pole. (It had been lashed to a stanchion near the wheel, but no one really was tending it.) Benson said we needed a device that would signal us when there was a strike and that he would rig something up. I was turning into a nag in the classic "I-don't-care-how-you-do-it,-just-get-me-some-fish" mold.

And then there was the problem about cigarettes. The smokers (Norris and Jack) had run out. They had intended to. Or at least Jack had. He wanted to give up the habit, so he hadn't brought any. He was, he said, helping Norris to the same desirable end by smoking Norris's supply. Norris took it very well as long as there were still cigarettes to share. Benson and I had been impatiently waiting for the day when there would not be. He has a messianic urge to convert the heathen on this question, and I have an unfortunately sensitive nose. I get queasy when a trayful of stale butts is left under it, and this usually happened at the table where navigation lessons and practice went on—another reason why I was lagging behind all the others.

When Der Tag came at last, and the final butt was flipped overboard, Benson and I broke out a bottle of champagne (a bon voyage present that we had been hoarding) and proposed a toast. It was a mistake. We should have celebrated in private. The merriment was mother to a running gag that eventually gagged me. One form of it was a variant of the "I'll just run down to the corner for a pack" ploy: for example, "to the cigar store on the fantail," "to the vending machine in the head," etc., etc. Another ploy was built around the question of what there was aboard that might be dried and smoked: for example, used tea leaves, old shoelaces, shredded Manila line, oatmeal, etc., etc. It is one of the problems of living aboard as small a boat as the *Aikane* that custom not only can, but does, stale the infinite (?) variety of available jokes. Humor, which had been our best pressure-letting device, became the enemy of peaceful coexistence.

Ten days out of Guadalupe we began to get modestly stormy weather. Until then, as if in deference to our inexperience, things had been untypically pacific.

The new phase was ushered in by an accident that sounds funny as I write but that was really quite painful for the victim. We were tearing along at better than six knots on Norris's after-supper wheel watch. It was not quite dark, but I was about to turn in for the two-and-a-half-hour nap I took before my own turn at the wheel. Suddenly the boat lurched, and all sorts of objects hurtled through the cabin like guided (or unguided) missiles. Jack ducked to avoid being hit and yelled at Norris to put the wheel hard over. It was too late. We were already in irons.

Norris had been hit in the face by a flying fish, and momentarily lost control. Worse than the pain was not knowing what had happened. The man at the wheel is always under a certain tension—both physical and psychological—and to be assaulted without warning by an unknown enemy is a shock.

Norris pulled himself together pretty quickly, but not in time to forestall a jibe, and going into irons shook him up in still another way. I understood it very well, having gone through the same humiliating experience, but no one (not even Norris) understood all the ways it affected him until several days later.

Meanwhile we had to adjust to a quite different environment belowdecks. Whatever was not secured was becoming a potential "flying object." A jam jar could take off from the breakfast table and shatter against the quarter berth. Fielding was not so much a sport as self-defense. Bathing even on deck was now a dangerous sport. I shampooed my hair (in a soapless shampoo, which worked well in salt water), slipped in my own rinse water, and executed a classic pratfall. Other accidents included the loss of another plastic bucket over the side by someone who underestimated the force of the water he was trying to scoop up.

Another adjustment: the association of warmth, instead of cold, with a storm wind. We had by now shed all our woolen clothes, even on night watch. By day, clothes were used to keep the sun off, not to keep body warmth in.

By this time we had eaten up most of the perishables in the hopelessly inefficient refrigerator. The last of the marinated beef went into an improvised casserole that was successful enough to record:

BEEF STROGANOFF "AIKANE"

Thin slices of teriyaki beef (we had about 2 lbs.)
Sliced (raw) onions (about 1/3 as much as beef)
1 can condensed mushroom soup
½ can evaporated milk

Fry the onion slices in oil till clear. Add the beef and cook only till it changes color. (If you are using leftovers, just warm it through.) Season with salt, pepper, and anything else you like. Curry powder, for instance, changes the whole tone of this dish, but not for the worse. Add the condensed soup, and blend. Finally, add enough evaporated milk to get the consistency you want. Serve with:

INSTANT PILAF

> 1 (generous) cup of instant rice
> ½ pkg. of dried onion soup
> Water, half salt, half fresh

Fry the spices and dried onion of the soup mix in oil for a minute or two. Add rice and the amount of water needed to cook it. (Consult the directions on your package.) Cover and steam it till ready.

As the storm blew on behind us, we began to settle into the new routine. The noise of rushing water under the hull no longer kept me (or anyone else) awake. On the contrary, my worst nightmare in many years was caused by the sudden cessation of that sound.

I had been dreaming something about the express train on the Eighth Avenue Subway in New York and suddenly the train stopped at a station! I was awake. There was absolute silence—uncanny, unnatural, menacing.

It took what seemed a long time to fight my way to complete consciousness; I was still fighting when the noise began again. I fell asleep without having figured out what had really happened, and continued to dream alarming explanations.

When Benson came off his watch and woke me for mine, he explained. A big sea had caught us just right, and the *Aikane* had planed down the front of it like a surfboard. The noise stopped because we were being carried forward at the same speed as the water itself.

I kept hoping for another surf ride all through my own watch, turning to look over my shoulder and judge the size and direction of the oncoming waves. There was no moon, and the phosphoresence in the water made the sea brighter than the sky. We were dragging two drogues to steady us, and the wake looked like luminous blue soapsuds in a giant's washing machine.

Halfway to our destination (if the navigators were right) I tried to account for what we were doing with all the time we had expected to have and didn't. We had yet to open a single one of the various time-passing devices we had been given as parting gifts, even the seagoing Scrabble set with the nonslide board!

Each of us was standing six hours of wheel watch out of every twenty-four. (Jack and I made up some time during the day for the shorter watches we stood at night.) Each was getting at least eight hours of sleep in one five-or-six-hour stretch and the rest in naps at odd hours. That left ten hours for cooking, cleaning (dishes, clothes, berths, and selves), navigating, eating, and drinking. Granted that each of these occupations took more time than it would have ashore, it seemed incredible that the total could add up to ten hours!

This may be the place to explain that, except for a glass of wine with the evening meal, the only alcoholic drinking done aboard was at Happy Hour. Everyone showed up for this ritual, which took place in the cockpit at about 5:00 P.M. There was a Bloody Mary or a Scotch and soda—as long as the soda-making cartridges held out—as well as some sort of hors d'oeuvres and a half hour of the sort of irrelevant conversation that goes on at cocktail parties ashore. Sometimes it seemed to me that the real function was not so much "relaxation" as the imposition of a little man-made order on the enormousness of the encircling sea and limitless horizon, much as dressing for dinner in the jungle is supposed to do for British imperialists of the old school.

Each of us did something a little different with the portion of the ten "free" hours that was really his own. I was reviewing a chapter of French grammar a day and writing journal. Benson was constantly inventing or improving equipment: a snubber and a bell for the fishing line, an astrolabe for the life-raft survival packet, a self-cooling water jug, a rack to hold glasses and condiments on the dining table, or a pelorus—an instrument used for taking bearings on other ships or landmarks, neither of which we had seen since leaving Guadalupe. Jack spent a good deal of time consulting that clouded crystal ball the Chart of Prevailing Winds, and he too was keeping journal. Norris did navigation problems all day long and part of the night. The reason for this diligence (or obsession) was not clear, but at the time I assumed that it was rooted in ambition, a doomed hope of supplanting

Jack as Chief Navigator. In the wisdom of retrospect I wonder
if it was not the same subtle instinct of self-(serenity)-preserva-
tion that was working in all of us. For Norris was at that time
fighting a private war that had begun with the slap in the face
by the flying fish, and the decisive engagement was still to come.

Norris, incidentally, was the only one of us who had
yet done any reading, apart from Bowditch (*American Practical Navigator*). He was reading Melville's *Typee*, and
hallucinating aloud about the beautiful Marquesan girls who
were going to swim out and pelt us (or him, at any rate) with
gardenias and plumeria as we sailed into the harbor of Taiohae.

As for the rest of us, the library I had so carefully compiled
was a waste of space. We did play the tapes I had brought along,
and enjoyed the comedy routines as well as the music. It was
easier to listen while doing other things than to read. For that,
one needs time free of all other responsibility, and this we didn't
have on the first sea leg.

The reason, it seemed to me as I pondered it, was that no day
watches had been set. At night each of us knew exactly what was
expected of him: either to stand watch or to sleep in order to be
able to stand watch. But during the day things were not so clear.
At any time when one was not busy at a "necessary" chore, one
was under a certain obligation to volunteer for the wheel. I was
not the only one who kept busy at socially useful chores that
were no more necessary than reading for pleasure, just to get in
out of the sun.

The only book one didn't have to apologize for reading was
Bowditch, and what a book! I knew the story of the great
Yankee Nathaniel Bowditch who set out to break the monopoly
of the officer caste of his day in the secret art of navigation by
inventing a simple, practical system. What I didn't know was
that his book had been kept in print and up to date for 164 years
and had been expanded into a complete, concise compendium of
nautical knowledge. In it one can find every relevant fact and
the directions for performing every necessary operation in the
world of ships, and all so lucidly and sparsely written, without
a word too many or too few or not quite *juste!*

One of the plums I pulled out of this 1500-page Christmas pie
was a star chart that enabled me to find the Southern Cross in

the sky. It had been visible on my watch for several nights before I identified it, partly because it came up lying on one side and disappeared behind the mainsail before it had straightened up, and partly because it's not quite the shape of a Christian (or even an Iron) cross. One of the lateral arms is forked; there are two stars near, but none in, the exact spot where it ought to end. The Southern Cross is not a constellation you can steer by, I discovered by some practical navigation of my own, because it moves too fast. But despite all these shortcomings, it was certainly the most glamorous piece of sky scenery we encountered on the whole voyage.

Like both Dippers, it has the *feeling* of a constellation, a certain magical unity imposed on one segment of the infinite disunity of the night sky. One knows it is not real unity, but the length of time men have insisted on its "prehensile unification" gives it another order of reality. The legends and symbolism attached to it over centuries by men of different worlds are real in the sense that any fantasy mutually accepted by whole societies acts really upon the real world.

For instance, the navigators who steered the great double canoes that carried the first men to the Polynesian islands watched the movement of these five stars. They constructed stick charts to show their relation to other groups of stars and stick charts of the islands that punctuated the sea as the stars did the sky. They wove stories about stars and islands in their creation myths, and these myths gave them courage to embark across unimaginable distances and eventually to create a new race of men and a new culture.

One of the myths about the Southern Cross (which was not a cross to the Polynesians) explains the very black space in the sky to one side of it as being the place from which all the bright stars were plucked to form the group. American and British whalers who once sailed these same seas called it the Coal Sack.

Just before we hit the doldrums there was an upheaval aboard that solved some of our problems and temporarily relieved but did not resolve others.

It seemed to be Norris's show, though even from the start it was obvious that the rest of us were almost as strongly affected by the outcome. The pressure that caused the explosion had been building since the night of the flying fish. Going into irons had made a deep wound in Norris's self-confidence. He did his best to keep it covered up and to look busy and cheerful, but it was festering, not healing. Warning signals there were, but none of us, including Norris himself, knew how to read them.

Benson, who had the watch before Norris, noticed that he was getting slower and slower at showing up for duty. It was not only that Norris was hard to wake. Even after he was up and moving around, he seemed to find one reason after another to procrastinate: a cup of coffee, a trip to the head, a return to the cabin after he was actually on deck because he had forgotten to brush his teeth, a last-minute clothes change, and so on. Benson was the most patient of the four of us, but when a man has stood alone at the wheel from 1:00 to 4:00 A.M., that sort of stalling becomes an intolerable imposition. At last, one particularly dark hour before dawn, he lost his temper and told Norris to stop puttering and take over.

Norris apologized and took the wheel at once, leaving Benson so ashamed of himself that he came down and woke me up to explain and excuse his behavior. "What I don't understand is that he volunteers for wheel duty all day, especially when there's any sort of blow. But at night he acts as if he were fighting some sort of fear. What's the difference between day and night?"

I could have answered that rhetorical question, but it would have spoiled the last precious two hours' sleep. I too was fighting night fears. Perhaps I had caught them from Norris. Fear is highly contagious in close quarters. You don't even have to be aware that it is in the air, any more than you have to know you're catching cold in the incubation stages. Or, to put it another way, the only reason I wasn't "scareder" sooner was that Jack and Benson had absolute confidence in themselves, in each other, and in the *Aikane*. Confidence is also contagious.

But to return to Norris and his private ordeal, there was a sort of vicious circle operating. Fear gives one real cause for fear in circumstances like ours. It muddies your mind when you most need it clear; slows and distorts reflexes just when you must depend on them. I am guessing all this after the fact, but there is no question that Norris was under growing tension and that it reached the breaking point at precisely five thirty one morning.

At that instant water came pouring through the open hatch above our berth, and I woke with a mouth and nose full of it. Benson was already on his way aft, and Jack was choking and spluttering in the quarter berth.

The cause of the shower baths was a bad jibe. Norris must have gone to sleep and been too groggy to bring himself out of it in time. When Benson got to the cockpit, the jib was back-winding so that it perfectly balanced the main. Neither sail could be moved. Starting the engine would have solved the problem, of course, but the engine wouldn't start. (It turned out that someone had failed to push the governor button all the way in when we shut down the motor after its evening battery-and-refrigerator duty.) It took the best part of an hour to get us on our way again.

It was not really an unpleasant experience as far as I was concerned. Dawn came on like a blush, soft, pearl-colored iridescence in sky and sea. The breeze was gentle and body temperature; it felt like being fanned. Everyone was cheerful and relaxed, even Norris, who didn't seem unduly distressed by his goof.

But after breakfast, while we were all still at the table and the automatic pilot was holding us on course, Norris suddenly said, with a vehemence that was most unusual for him, that he didn't think anyone ought to stand more than two hours of night watch at a stretch. "You just can't keep sharp! I know because I've tried!"

It was unmistakably an ultimatum, although it was stated simply as a fact of life.

Jack capitulated without argument. It took less than five minutes to work out a new schedule that gave everyone two hours on and six off. Everyone immediately felt better. Benson admitted now that he had found three hours something of a strain. And I caught myself feeling as relieved as if my personal chore had been lightened, which was not the case.

I must have been more "put down" than I realized about standing an hour less than the others (without Jack's excuse), for now that everyone was on the same basis I felt equal to another try on the navigation front. I had all but given up on this, secretly more and more convinced that I was congenitally incapable of mastering not only the arithmetic but also the theory involved in "advancing the line of position." In my new euphoria, I summoned the courage to ask some questions that had seemed too embarrassingly elementary. I got answers I understood, and for the first time I actually managed to find where we were without peeking at anyone else's tracking sheet.

Norris was never again under perceptible strain, but my remission was only temporary.

The trouble seemed to be that there was only one sextant for three of us and that the noon shot (which determines latitude) had to be taken at noon. Taking turns was not really practical. Only one of us could take an accurate reading on any given day.

Benson removed himself from the competition by taking up "simulous," an oddball system for getting a fix in a single operation by taking a shot about fifteen minutes before high noon, and another, the same number of minutes and seconds afterward. Arthur Piver, the trimaran designer, worked this out and called it "simulous" because "it's so simple, it's ridiculous." Jack was irritated by Benson's fooling around with unorthodox procedures when he hadn't really mastered the s.o.p., but it had one good effect: it reduced the struggle for the bubble sextant at 11:58 A.M. to a contest between Norris and me.

Whichever way the round was played, I seemed to lose. If Norris got to the sextant first, he would tell me what my reading was going to be, or rather, what it would have been if I had taken it at noon and got it right. This infuriated me because I felt patronized and dependent. On the other hand, if I got the sextant first and managed to hang on to it through the moment of truth, with Norris being polite but very impatient indeed, I felt guilty of "playing" with equipment that others needed for "work." Norris reinforced this by making cracks of an apparently friendly sort, like "Well, well, well, are you still figuring your figures?" Or "Come any closer today, Jan?"

Jack's prediction that we would all be able to navigate without him at the end of the first week at sea was still a good deal short of fulfillment, as far as I was concerned, at the end of the third. By which time we were entering the temper-trying doldrums.

Anyone who has read accounts of voyages in the Pacific —or *The Ancient Mariner*—has some notion of these watery badlands, which have entered the language as a symbol of ennui stretched to the danger point. For the first day or two the reality seemed much less formidable than I had expected, in some ways really quite interesting.

For one thing, the sea was not flat although the wind had dropped so low that we had to motor to keep enough way to steer. It was curiously gray and wrinkled, and it kept heaving up a shoulder like Kipling's mysterious sea beast who ate in one gulp all the food Solomon had prepared for the animals of the world. It was hot, oppressively hot belowdecks, but not so bad above, as long as the sun was obscured. The sky was full of omens. At one point, I remember, there was a sample of almost every possible cloud formation in one or another segment of the dome. In one direction, an area of dark storm-blue with small gray-white, flame-shaped clouds superimposed like a textile pattern. In another direction, a big slate-colored slab of nimbus was letting down a column of rain. In another, the sky was light, and a fleet of chubby little cumuli sailed across it with their lower edges straight as if drawn on an imaginary line. Behind us the sea had lost all color, except when one looked straight down. Then it was the ultramarine of infinite depth.

We had all been told (or had read) about the possibility of getting a freshwater shower courtesy of one of the many rain squalls that hit in these latitudes. The hazards we knew: that if one got all soaped up in expectation that a promising squall would act as a rinse, the squall might veer off at the last minute. Rinsing with seawater is possible, of course, if one uses detergent for soap, but by this time our bodies craved the feel of fresh water.

We were taking salt in pill form because without it we felt even worse. But our exteriors were painfully crusted with the stuff. Our clothes and our towels were gritty with fine crystals, and there were mutinous murmurs about using some of our freshwater supply for washing. Jack had finally relented and said we could each have a basinful from the tank we had filled at the Kettenburg yard (which tasted bad anyway). But the pump in the basin in the head was so hard to work that no one had the energy to get a bowlful. (Investigation revealed that someone had dropped wood shavings into one of the water tanks, and they had worked their way into the pipe that led to the washbasin. Nothing could be done till we reached a port where we could apply air pressure to the line—which turned out to be not until we got to Honolulu.)

Finally we worked out a scheme for collecting bath water in buckets, either from the small canvas sunshade we had precariously rigged over the wheel or from the natural spigot formed by the tack of the main. Water that had rinsed the salty canvas was no good for drinking, but it did well enough for washing, and there was enough—eventually—to go around.

The egg crisis occurred in the doldrums, too. Probably by coincidence, but it would have been less horrendous at a higher latitude.

Norris had offered to dig out a half-dozen eggs for me, it being almost beyond my strength to get into the far corner under the "settee" where the egg carton was stowed. Suddenly he drew back. "There's a bad egg down here," he said, and gagged.

His gagging made my stomach cramp, and I fought nausea with asperity. "I'll get it out, if you can't," I said, hoping he wouldn't let me.

But he did. He held the lid of the compartment out of my way, while I dug down. The bad egg was one that had been slightly cracked in the packing process, and it had been slowly leaking and spoiling ever since. The shell was stuck fast to the paper divider, and the *Aikane* was wallowing awkwardly, but I was able to get my fingers around the evil thing at last. The crack was much larger by then, and the smell much worse. Even so, I think I could have beaten my rising gorge to the lee rail if I hadn't stumbled en route.

The egg flew out of my hand and splashed its muddy green contents right in the middle of the galley floor. Until that moment I had never really appreciated the figure of speech, "stinking like a rotten egg," but I shall never use it lightly again.

From that day on, we broke each egg into a separate bowl before adding it to the scrambling pan, the way my grandmother used to do in the days before electric refrigeration.

Other untoward things began happening as the days wore on frayed nerves, and time forgot to move forward. Norris woke Jack up one night to report that he had seen a torpedo heading for us. It had missed, but Norris thought it important enough to wake the captain. Jack assured him that he was hallucinating, and went back to sleep. Norris resumed his post at the wheel. A few minutes later he saw several luminous blue streaks heading at us from several directions, weaving wonderful patterns in the water, and knew that it was a school of dolphins playing games.

It was Jack who lost his grip on reality the following day.

Both he and Norris had taken the noon shot and got a reading of ninety degrees, which was, of course, the absolute maximum angle. It meant that the sun was directly over our heads, which can only happen at the equinox. We had been approaching this point rapidly, as the sun was traveling north as we traveled south. No one was particularly surprised at the reading, but after Norris went below to do his figuring, Jack took another shot, just for fun.

His sextant read $91° 40'$!

He began muttering to himself and trying again. I happened to be at the wheel, wrapped in the Olympian detachment that came over me there, but I was dimly aware that Benson was now taking a shot, at Jack's request. Soon Norris was on deck, too. All three of them were muttering. "One of the sextants could be off," Jack said, "but not both of them. Try again." There was a pause.

"Ninety-two," said Norris.

"The same," Jack said. "What do you make of it?"

The note of alarm in Jack's voice was serious. Something had gone wrong with the sun!

Then they caught on—all three of them, independently and almost simultaneously—popping off like three small firecrackers linked by a single fuse.

The sun had passed us. Instead of ninety-two degrees they should have read eighty-eight degrees. Shots would have to be taken from the other side of the boat from now on. We had sailed into summer.

But the navigators looked shaken, like men who have seen gravity suspended and chaos crouched to spring.

On one night much like any other we crossed the equator during Norris's watch. It was the first time over for all four of us, so no one could play King Neptune. Instead we broke out a bottle of lukewarm champagne.

Some time later that night a ship passed, the only one we were to encounter on the whole leg!

We were motoring. Jack had ruled that in these waters it was not necessary for anyone to stay on deck when the automatic pilot was on, but Benson was restless and went on deck to look around. The lights of a sizable ship were disappearing over the horizon. There was no way of knowing how close it had passed, and it was a sobering thought that we had been running without either our masthead or navigation lights on.

At least it was sobering for Benson. Jack was unperturbed, though he was quite willing to make a new rule: that someone must be awake and on deck at all times. He paid no attention to the argument for turning on the lights (more light meant more diesel consumed) and I could see that he was irritated by the phrase "our near-miss" which Benson insisted on using.

I kept out of argument, busying myself with such house-wifely chores as the trimming of the cabbages, which were all that was left of our produce department (except for a dozen lemons and a peck of onions). There were two dozen eggs left out of the 144. We had consumed 120 of these irreplaceables in twenty days. Six eggs a day, for four people. Not too bad. But when was our supply of protein to be replenished? It might be another two weeks before we sighted land. Were we going to have to make do with canned pork loins and cheese?

I knew perfectly well that nagging was not catching any fish but I had no workable alternative. Besides, I had nothing much else to do. I would have tried rigging a line myself if I had not been convinced by constant reiteration that there weren't any fish in this part of the ocean anyway.

And then we almost ran into a net!

It was about noon when I sighted three large glass balls, the kind that wash up on the Oregon coast after a nor'wester. Jack altered course so that we could make a stab at retrieving one. Benson was at the bow with a boathook in his hand, looking like a harpooner poised for a strike, when—at the same moment—we all saw the great circle of nylon gill net, half a mile across.

The glass balls I had seen were only a few of the dozens that held the upper edge of the net at the surface so that no fish could escape. Several of them had tiny flashing lights, and there were three that supported miniature Eiffel Towers—radio transmitters, Benson said.

The ship we had passed in the night had probably left this net. One of the floating Japanese canneries that operate in the Pacific can set out as many as six nets that size and make the rounds at intervals to harvest the catch. The flashing lights are to warn other ships away so they won't tear the mesh and/or foul their propellers in it. The radio signal is to guide the mother ship back.

It was a temptation, but we did not cut loose even one of the glass balls. It was also a temptation to point out that there must be fish in these waters after all. To this temptation, I succumbed. With just the sort of result I might have expected. Which, as I see it now, I deserved.

It is really discouraging to find oneself incapable of acting on reliable information, of taking advantage of advance warnings about "doldrum nerves," and avoiding the sort of seizure that caused the Ancient Mariner to shoot down the albatross. But I was right on the verge; I knew it and couldn't save myself.

I was not the only case aboard, but I may have been the worst—up to my nostrils in umbrage most of the time. Jack was unquestionably picking on me (as a change from picking on Norris). Every goof of which I was guilty became the subject of a long lecture or a short but nasty crack. I was getting so I expected to be chewed out every time I was given an order. As a result, I never failed to foul up and give Jack grounds.

I suppose that running out of cigarettes had something to do with the state of Jack's nerves. God knows he and Norris talked of nothing else those days. I was so weary of both ploys—the one about where they could buy a pack and the one about what they could use as a substitute, and even the new subploy about what they would do for a single drag—that I daydreamed of stuffing a carton down both of their throats.

For the first time privacy became a problem, and not at all in the way I had anticipated it might. The problem of modesty had never really presented itself. Clothes changes can be managed easily enough even in close quarters. At night, darkness acts as a curtain. By day, I could use the door to our cabin if I wanted to be screened. The men would ask me to turn my head at first, when I was in the main cabin and they wanted to strip. I usually turned without being asked, and they soon forgot to ask.

The real privacy problem had to do with ventilation and the position of the head. Benson and I had a hard enough time sleeping in the forward cabin on sultry nights and could make it only if the door to the main cabin was left open as well as the door that opened from our cabin into the head. That way we had cross ventilation, but we also had to put up with the ghastly, gagging-choking noise of the pump that cleared the toilet. Also, all subsequent airing took place across us. It was like sleeping in a sewer. And Jack and Norris had been beforehand about moving up to the benches in the cockpit. There was nothing to do but endure.

Then we caught a fish—a really fancy fish, about four feet long, shaped like a barracuda, but without the ugly undershot jaw.

We were all sitting in the cockpit having Bloody Marys and discussing the dinner menu, whether we should shoot the remaining eggs on an omelette or face another slice of canned ham, when suddenly there was a great clicking whir as the line ran out on the reel. Benson got to the pole first and began to fight the fish in. Considering that the line was only forty-pound test and that the fish weighed at least forty pounds, it was quite a feat.

While I supervised the butchering, Jack looked at the fish

book and decided that we had a "wahoo," called *ono* in Hawaii:
"Skin like a shark's; dark blue on back, silver belly, wavy
camouflage lines on the flanks; large oblique gill slits; a brilliant
two-inch dorsal fin running the length of body, and a tuna-
shaped tail."

We got steaks enough for three dinners, hacked about two
pounds of solid meat into chucks for canning, and made *sashimi*
out of the scraps.

SASHIMI (Japanese raw fish)

Very thin slices of very fresh, raw fish
Dip sauce made of soy sauce diluted with water and
slightly sweetened

There are various schools of thought about the proper
slicing of *sashimi*, the orthodox being on the bias and across
the grain. That is almost impossible if you are using belly
scraps or irregular-shaped pieces. What matters most is that
it must be uniformly thin.

Good Japanese or Hawaiian restaurants serve these delicate filets on a bed of shredded white radish (*daikon*) with
a gob of hot green mustard floating in the dip dish. We used
a paper plate, a common dipping bowl, and did without the
mustard. It was still delicious.

The wind picked up soon after the wahoo, but interpersonal
relations didn't improve as much as I had hoped. It was still hot.
Each day was brighter, hotter, and bluer than the last. Salt pills
were no longer effective. I began to have a persistent headache
and a vaguely queasy stomach. And there was all that fish!

THINGS TO DO WITH A FISH THAT'S TOO BIG

1. Sashimi (cf. above).
2. Steaks, pan-broiled, served with sauce made of melted
   margarine (or butter), garlic (or powder), tarragon,
   and capers.

3. Cold steaks (leftover) for breakfast or lunch, in the latter case with a sauce made of mayonnaise, doctored with the same medicines as above.

4. Chowder, a main dish for any meal when it's not too hot for soup. Flake up some of the canned fish (cf. below), sauté a cup of chopped onions (or steep some dehydrated onion bits in stock), add the fish and jellied fish juice, and heat. Add evaporated milk and cream-style canned corn. Add water and wine in equal parts to dilute to desired consistency.

5. Breaded steaks. Coat fish in beaten egg and corn-flake crumbs (or cracker crumbs or flour) and fry in oil till brown on both sides. Serve with either of the sauces above.

Even the above didn't use up the wahoo. Three nights of steaks was all I felt safe in planning, so I was driven to "can" the rest. It worked better than I could have hoped, and was useful more than two weeks later (for aspic). Once our refrigerator really cut out, I had to give up, but I believe we could have kept the canned fish as long as we could hold it at forty degrees.

CANNED (JARRED) FISH

Butcher the fish into thick chunks of light meat; discard the darker meat, which doesn't keep as well, and steam in a heavy pot with a good top, in a mixture of fresh water, dry white wine, onions, and herbs. Tarragon is best, but there are many alternatives.

When the chunks are cooked all the way through (test by peeking to see if the flesh is opaque), pack as tight as possible into jars with good screw lids. (We used peanut-butter jars. Any wide-mouth variety will do.) Fill the interstices with pot liquor, which will jell when cold. Tighten the tops by hand and store in the coolest part of the refrigerator.

I had given up navigating entirely by this point in the voyage, and I wasn't paying any attention to the comparing of plotting sheets that went on around the table whenever it wasn't being used for a meal. I knew there was some hope that we were within a few days (or hours) of land, but it seemed unlikely that anything good was going to come of that. Like a slave on the Middle Passage, I could hardly get up the energy to scan the horizon. Life stretched, not ahead, but around in a circle like a treadmill.

I was slightly seasick and deeply depressed.

One of the causes of this sudden slump in my spirits was that Jack and I had worked up a real Hatfield-McCoy feud. We were snapping at each other aloud and in public. Norris and Benson were appalled. So was I. The strangest part was that I really didn't know what we were bickering about. Once or twice Jack had called me by someone else's name, and since he had been doing a lot of self-analysis in the long night watches, I assumed that he was sticking pins into the wax image of someone else. But I was feeling the pricks, and jabbing back hard enough to pierce the armor of his introspection.

If I had had any choice in the matter of whereabouts, I would have got mine as far from his as possible. Across an ocean would have been about right. Forty-three feet, the maximum possible on the *Aikane*, was no good at all. It is said that no small boat enters and leaves the harbor of Papeete (Tahiti) with the same crew, and I was beginning to understand why. Every time landfall was mentioned, I found myself daydreaming about jumping ship.

In the middle of one such revery, I heard Jack call "Land ho!" There was a scurrying for binoculars, a flurry of minor controversy (the land was not precisely where it had been expected and had appeared a little in advance of even the most optimistic prediction), and a crescendo of self-congratulation. We had crossed over two thousand watery and empty miles and found the pinpoint of land we had been aiming for! It was, the men agreed, pretty damn good navigating!

Someone finally remembered to hand me the binoculars, which I accepted with cold (and bad) grace. All I could see in the direction they pointed was a faint blue shape several degrees to port (at least thirty degrees, as it turned out) of where the island of Nuku Hiva should have been. The shape could just as well have been the space between two shimmering clouds as an island. I was unelated, unimpressed.

"It's too late to make Taiohae before dark," Jack said. "We may as well heave to, have a swim and supper, and start sailing sometime around ten."

Taiohae! That was the port where Melville jumped ship in 1842, got away from his tyrannical captain, took refuge among the cannibals of Typee Valley, fell in love with the beautiful Fayaway, and nearly got himself eaten before he finally got free. I was ready to take my chances with the inhabitants of any valley on Nuku Hiva, but how would I ever get home? Melville, as an able-bodied seaman, had been in demand whenever a ship came in to port. Benson might follow his example if a tramp schooner came in shorthanded, but who would want a woman aboard?

The mainsail was dropped and the sail ties broken out for the first time in nineteen days (February 21–March 11), and Benson dove into the warm blue water. Even he had to admit it wasn't the treat he'd been lobbying for.

I followed him in, but I had to move fast before I had time to think about the depth. The water was tepid and full of some semitransparent life that looked like the shells of shrimp but wasn't as substantial. It was pleasant to turn my back on the boat and pretend I was swimming away, breasting the huge, slow swells, but after a minute or two it was scary. I swam back to the boarding ladder and climbed it. Norris, who was the best swimmer of the four of us, could hardly be persuaded to come in at all. Again, the terror of the idea of infinite depth . . .

Heaving to had always sounded restful, like pulling over to the side of a road, heaving a deep sigh, and curling up to sleep. But the *Aikane* became a haunted house the instant the main was dropped. Even with no perceptible wind and a calm sea, we slatted around so sickeningly that the men had to raise the main halfway while I cooked and we all ate supper.

Halfway through the meal, Jack suddenly excused himself, took his charts, and went up to the cockpit. I thought he was seasick. (No one was eating with much enthusiasm.) But when I looked out, he seemed to be taking a shot. It was long past the hour when accuracy was possible. Fifteen minutes later he came down to announce that the land we had sighted was not Nuku Hiva at all.

"I knew it couldn't be that far to port," he said defensively. "It was missing the noon shot that threw me. And I forgot about Ua Huka because we aren't going to touch there. But that's what we see. Nuku Hiva is right where it's supposed to be. We can't see it because of the cloud cover. But we were right on the beam!"

There was another round of self-congratulations, and we all looked at the chart, the three plotting sheets, and the dark shape on the port bow. This time even I felt a faint shiver of recognition. Land! My real element, no matter how exotic! Perhaps things were going to be enough better to be bearable.

The men raised sail to take advantage of the wind that had come up as the sun set, and I stood my six-to-eight wheel watch. Ua Huka was dark when we closed in and began to skirt her northern coast, but a great electrical storm fired a welcoming salute, peals of thunder and flashes of lightning, the first we had seen on the voyage. By 10:00 P.M. there was an even more spectacular storm off the starboard bow, and once I thought I could make out the ragged crest of a great mountain, silhouetted against the lightning-bright cloud.

That must be Nuku Hiva, where tomorrow we would not only see but actually touch land. Norris was hallucinating again, the old refrain about the girls who would swim out to greet us. The only new note was that his particular Fayaway was going to be carrying a waterproof plastic bag in her teeth, and, safe inside it, guess what? a full package of American cigarettes.

As I lay in my berth later, trying to sleep, I could see us hitting the shore and bursting apart like a piñata at a Mexican Christmas party, scattering into three or even four directions. I needed to be alone. Alone on a rock or under one.

Nuku Hiva

By the time I was awake and on deck in the morning, Nuku Hiva stood like a great rockslide athwart our course.

This was not what I had expected. Not at all. No amount of reading, from Melville to Willowdean Handy, had really erased the dream image of a low coral atoll, beaten upon by hot sun and bathed by brilliant blue-green waters piling up in lacy surf on blinding white sands. But the Marquesas are sheer black walls or tall gray towers, rising from a cold gray-green sea into gray-blue cloud. There are no white beaches, no protecting coral reef, only deep fjords and embattled headlands between them. Awesomely beautiful; or better, both awesome and beautiful; forbidding rather than beguiling.

It is curious how assiduously one attacks the unexpected with words. Not only a writer who has the habit. Everyone was busy describing what we were all looking at. I did it in silence (because I was still a little sulky); the men did it—in snatches—aloud. Four very different observers, trained to see quite different aspects of reality, trained to express or record observations in quite different media; with different "sets" toward the vocabulary of metaphor that is always in the process of becoming cliché.

And yet we were all striving with the same problem: to reduce the unexpected and unfamiliar to familiar terms. All of us kept saying (or thinking) "It's like——" something else.

As we came up to and passed the first great cape and began to coast along the southern face of Nuku Hiva, the island of Ua Pou became clearly visible to port. We all reached for the same cliché to defend ourselves against the incredibility of its conformation. "Straight out of Disney," Norris said, and all of us agreed.

Then we passed the mouth of Typee Valley (Taipivai). We could see only a little way up, but it looked as lush and serene as Melville said. The palm trees that clustered on both sides of the little river were not tossing their heads, although only a little above them were wild heights where the rags of storm cloud were torn on the rocks and wept into rain. And there was no sign of life.

Norris kept the binoculars trained on the river for as long as there was any hope of a canoe full of Fayaways putting out. All he could report was something that might be a thatched roof or might be a dead pandanus tree. Even the possibility of a hut, a human habitation, past or present, is something to make the heart beat faster after being for so long the only specimen of one's species on the watery face of the world.

At last the great bay of Taiohae opened in the rock wall, a

Melville's and Fayaway's stream at Taipivai (Typee).

sheltered harbor several miles deep, guarded by two sentinel rocks a few hundred yards apart. A school of dolphins appeared from nowhere to escort us through this gate, playing crisscross tag in front of our bow like Mardi Gras jesters embellishing the progress of a royal float.

The human greetings we got were less flattering. There was an outrigger canoe (with an outboard motor) heading out to sea. We assumed that it was coming to see us in, but the fishermen passed without altering course, waving so casually that we felt snubbed, until it occurred to us that we were not nearly so welcome a sight to them as they were to us.

I went below and got Mrs. Handy's *Forever the Land of Men** to compare her first sight of this place with ours:

> There before us lay the beautiful bay and valley which had always been the central arena of the great conflict of peoples and cultures in these islands. My eyes rose slowly from the gray waters of the long, narrow inlet and the thin rim of white that etched the meeting of water and sand, up the slopes of three or four branch valleys, whose descending streams were half-buried in lush vegetation, up to the circling vine-clad precipices three miles away, and up to the 3000 foot peak whose head was beginning to darken under an accumulation of cloud cap. . . . I could make out the ridges between the five fingers of the valley which sub-tribes of the Tei's had held for centuries until the French had "accepted" or confiscated or "bought" four of them. . . .

My own eyes caught the shimmer of bright red that told Mrs. Handy flamboyant trees were blooming near the government compound, whose dull red tile roof I could also make out now. Then I saw something for which she did not prepare me: a real building! Painted yellow-beige with the words KAOHA NUI spelled out in large brown letters! (*Kaoha nui* is Marquesan for *aloha nui*, which is Hawaiian for a large hello.)

---

* Willowdean C. Handy accompanied her husband on an expedition to the Marquesas in 1925. He was an ethnologist, working under the direction of the Bishop Museum of Honolulu; she went along to study tattoo designs and string figures. Her retrospective account, written in 1964, is the best written and most perceptive book on the Marquesas now in print.

We could see other buildings now, two of them with the steep thatched roofs of ancient Marquesan dwellings. There was a small pier, jutting a few yards into the water. To the right of it, a small cone-shaped hill with a lighthouse on top of it; to the left a black sand beach, behind which stood an impenetrable forest of palms and hardwood trees unfamiliar to us. In front of the beach was another sailboat, a ketch about the same size as the *Aikane*. As her stern swung coyly around to face us, we could make out the words, *Lizard*, Honolulu. The first human figure that moved in the land- and water-scape before us was a woman, unmistakably American, aboard an American boat.

She waved and shouted a greeting, unintelligible at that distance, but Norris could see that she was not Fayaway. "Maybe they weren't expecting us till tomorrow," he said, with a weak but gallant smile.

We all felt, I think, a little like people who have come a long way to pay a call only to find no one at home.

Great Bay of Taiohae.

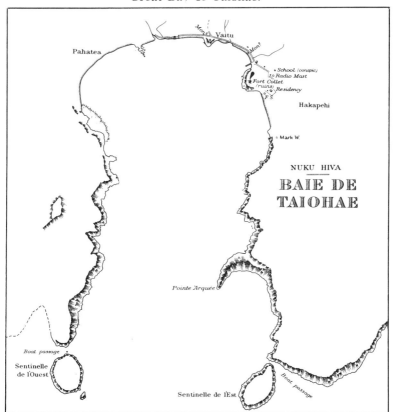

Jack and Benson dropped the anchor three times before they were both satisfied that it would hold. This involved using the electric anchor winch, a toy with which they had had no real opportunity to play till now. By the time they were done, two members of the *Lizard* crew had rowed over in their dinghy to present us with fresh fruit and bread, and to warn us that we could neither take on visitors nor go ashore till we had been cleared by quarantine.

One is supposed to summon the officials who can do this by flying a yellow flag, but we had none. The young men from the *Lizard* seemed to think we were in trouble. If we didn't fly the quarantine flag, no inspector might ever come aboard. But if we went ashore to look for one, we might be arrested for violating some international law. We were not as distressed as they, but we agreed to stay put while they rowed ashore and informed the Gendarmerie Nationale that we awaited their pleasure.

It took a couple of hours for the mission to accomplish itself (I was boning up for the coming encounter with non-English-speaking people and trying to think French), but we used the time enjoying the *kaoha* gifts—better than keys to the city!—making everything shipshape and getting into our shore clothes. Mine were too hot, and the first thing I planned to do ashore was to buy the material for a muumuu or sarong or whatever the local ladies wore.

The official party that boarded us turned out to be one Chinese-Tahitian *infirmier*, substituting for the *Médecin-Chef*, who was otherwise occupied; one Marquesan lieutenant, who looked Hawaiian and never said a word; and one authentically French representative of the Fifth Republic.* They looked at all our papers, and seemed relieved to find them all in order, after which they accepted *un petit coup du vin américain*. The authentic one confessed himself agreeably surprised to learn that American wines should have so much flavor. By this time the strain on my recently exhumed French was beginning to show. I stuttered apologies, but the Frenchman assured me that I did far better than either of his colleagues, which called for another *petit coup* all round.

---

* The full title is "Fifth Republic and French Community," of which latter the Marquesas are a part.

The conversation, all of which had to be channeled through me, turned to serious matters, like where to buy cigarettes, change traveler's checks, get some cold beer, shop for bed sheets (sleeping bags had become repulsive), meat, paper towels, and articles of clothing. All these things, our friend said, could be accomplished Chez Maurice, a combined bar and general store just a half mile up the road that led along the beach.

It was after the hour of noon by the time our official reception committee could tear itself away from the unexpectedly acceptable California Mountain White. By that time there were a few people visible along the waterfront—men, very dark, dressed in navy-blue shorts and T-shirts or faded cotton prints, all wearing straw hats as protection against the ever-threatening *coup de soleil*.

We were watched as we launched the *Lili Aikane*, which all but swamped with the four of us, rowed to the pier, and scrambled up its slippery ramp to *terra* which was supposed to be *firma* at last. The watchers gaped at us, unsmiling, as we staggered the length of the pier, giggling and reeling like drunks. (The wine may have accounted for the giggles, but not for the gait.) Even the solid rock of the roadway, when we reached it, heaved and rolled under our sea legs. It was not the dignified sort of arrival the American Republic and/or the Playa del Rey Yacht Club had a right to expect of its (their) representatives.

We all started out for Chez Maurice together, instead of making off in four directions. Once there, and assured that they could order cigarettes and beer in English, Jack and Norris settled down in the bar, to chain smoke, complain about French tobacco, and congratulate themselves on having discovered Tahitian beer. Benson and I took our beers into the general store.

But by the time I had selected a meter and a half of bright blue cotton for a *pareu* (Marquesan for sarong) and Benson had picked out a straw hat to keep the sun from stroking him, Jack joined us. Norris had struck up an acquaintance with two young Danes who were camping up the beach. (Norris is of Danish parentage and had spent a year in Copenhagen learning the language.) Jack found the conversation dull. Besides, he wanted to do a little shopping too, go by the post office to see whether there were letters or radiograms, and "have a look at the town." It seemed the most natural and pleasant thing in the world that the three of us should saunter off together, like the *anciens amis* that we were.

Taiohae had (in March, 1965) a population of about three hundred people, including the French administrative colony that rules the whole archipelago of Les Iles Marquises. The town occupies a quarter moon of flat land at the inner end of the long inlet.

The eastern horn of the moon is the closed world of the administrative colony: a few substantial stucco homes, a two-story administration building, which also houses the post office and radio station, and a small but very modern hospital. In the center of the crescent there is a little clutch of buildings: the pier; the warehouse (the Kaoha Nui building); the jail; the public school (attended by girls and Protestant boys); a public toilet and shower bath, constructed for the use of the prisoners in the barless prison, but used by the yachting colony as well; and the two thatched-roof, pseudo-Marquesan pavilions, put there for the convenience of Matson Line tourists, who arrive at long intervals but in large numbers, and are entertained by native dances and feasts. (Between Matson liners the pavilions serve as temporary shelters from sun or rain, but not for any greater pleasure.)

Halfway between this center and the western horn of the crescent is the commercial center which Norris called "downtown." The only road to the interior of the island takes off here, and there is a battered signpost that lists all the possible destinations one might reach if one turned away from the sea at this point. All the business establishments of Taiohae are within a coconut's throw of the signpost: Chez Maurice, the Chinois Bleu, and the Chinois Jaune (terms that refer to the color of the paint on the clapboards of the storefront, not of the proprietor's face), the bakery, the house of the wood-carver, and the tiny Protestant chapel. The volleyball court, which is the Sports Palatz of Nuku Hiva, lies between the signpost and the surf.

At the hour of the afternoon we first saw this center, there were only a few desultory shoppers exchanging gossip in the shade near the signpost—handsome, dark women in their thirties, dressed in boldly printed cotton pareus, wearing flowers in their lush black hair, and smiling unselfconsciously despite the appalling fact that none of them had all their upper front teeth.

Continuing on up the beach road, past Chez Maurice, one comes to the house of one of the two local celebrities: "Old Bob" McKittrick, of whom it is said that he is the father of the half-caste Maurice (who looks like a French sailor), but refuses to speak to him or his progeny. Old Bob's other claim to fame is that he is mentioned in one of O'Brien's books about life in the Marquesas in 1919.* Still farther along the road is the house of old Taniha (Stanislas) Taupotini, honorary *chef* of Nuku Hiva, whose picture appears in a more recent and more scholarly work on the islands,† over the heading "One of the few remaining full-blooded Marquesans."

At the western end of the beach is the Catholic colony: a crumbling, mold-splotched cathedral, a series of comfortable stucco bungalows for Monsignor, the Bishop of all the Marquesas, and teachers, both lay and clerical, and a complex of two-story gray concrete school buildings. There are actually three schools in one here: an *internat*, or boarding school, for boys that houses about two hundred youngsters under fourteen, brought together from all the six inhabited Marquesan islands; a new *lycée*, or secondary school, which was, when we visited it, inaugurating a program under which the brightest boys and girls of the Marquesas will be prepared for the *baccalauréat* and possibly for further study, either in Tahiti or in France, and finally a nursery school for forty local toddlers. The *lycée* is secular and was only temporarily housed in the parochial buildings. Benson determined to present his official letter to the faculty of the *lycée* as soon as possible. We made inquiries, and

---

* Frederick O'Brien visited the Marquesas in 1919 and wrote a very successful book about them, *White Shadows in the South Seas*. Although most Americans have forgotten this and other best sellers of yesteryear, dwellers in the Marquesas have not. They refer to O'Brien's book and its two less-distinguished sequels as educated Englishmen might refer to Shakespeare. One really has to have read them to keep up with a conversation.

† *The Island Civilizations of Polynesia*, by Robert C. Suggs.

learned that there were only three teachers: a bachelor school-master who lived alone, and a young French couple, who had two little daughters and lived on the hill near the Protestant church.

The first day ashore was drawing to a close by the time we had finished our inspection. Work had ceased. Men and women were strolling in pairs or larger groups along the beach-front road. There were no automobiles to be seen, but quite a number of noisy mobilettes (the French version of the motor scooter) were buzzing up and down the road, carrying the wives (and a few husbands) of the official colony. As often as not there was at least one child standing on the foot platform and a Marquesan domestic mounted behind. The drivers had the proud look of one who rides a fine horse—which was more than could be said for the single equestrian we met.

At the volleyball court a spirited game was going on, both teams being mixed as to sex, race, and social class, and all the participants barefoot on the stoniest of ground! The beach was full of children playing in the quiet surf. There were divers and fishers, coexisting peacefully on the little pier. On the steps of the nondescript clapboard bungalows placed here and there under the shade trees with no particular relation to the main or any other road, people sat chatting with other people, watching their dogs or children quarrel or play. One man was playing a guitar, not well. No one sang.

When dark came, the day was over. Oil lamps shone in one or two windows, but most of them were black. There were hard gleams of light from the vicinity of Chez Maurice, and one could hear the noise of the Delco generator that was producing them. But a few unshaded light bulbs did not create a festive atmosphere even in the bar. Norris had been hoping for something in the way of night life, perhaps a demonstration of the *tamure*, the Marquesan-Tahitian version of the Hawaiian hula, but there was nothing doing in that department. He gave up and accompanied the three sobersides back to the boat.

It was a fine night for sleeping on deck, and now that the *Aikane* was moored, Benson and I could rig a hammock on the deck of the main cabin and count stars as well as Norris and Jack.

The first few days ashore left me feeling that life was too rich and complex and exciting to be absorbed. My head felt stuffed with sights, sounds, smells, tastes, words, facts, and impressions—none of which I wanted to lose, and all of which were getting rubbed dull by new ones piled in on top of the old. I decided to keep journal on one category only: women— Marquesan, French, and American. Women who lived in Taiohae, and women who came ashore from visiting boats.

For example, there was Mary F., the American who had waved to us from the *Lizard* the morning we arrived. Like me, she was the lone woman in a crew of four, but she was not married to any of the men aboard. Neither was she living in seagoing sin. She was a good-hearted, hardworking, wholesome young woman in her thirties, the sort you might find heading up a P.T.A. chapter or high in the councils of the Camp Fire Girls. A good Catholic, she had herself rowed through the surf on Sunday mornings in the *Lizard*'s very unstable dinghy, dressed in her one wash skirt, a clean shirtwaist, and a straw hat. We watched her wade through the shallows and trudge up the beach, carrying her shoes. The irreverent men she left behind referred to her as the Virgin Mary, but they were fond of her, each in his own way. They relied on her, not only for such womanly contributions to the general welfare as cooking and sail mending (one chore I refused to perform) but also for three hours of watch at sea and a good deal of carpentry in port.

I don't know what Mary proved about the question of being a woman aboard, but at least she separated the love of the sea from the fleshly love of the men who go down to it.

It was Mary who introduced me to the most Marquesan (by traditional standards) of all the women we met: Théodora, the wife of the master of the public school, and her *cousine*, Marie Salomé, a sixteen-year-old tomboy who virtually adopted us during our stay. We came upon the two girls, struggling to converse with Mary, both sides suffering so acutely from the other's bad French that they were between tears and giggles. I offered to translate. At the first sentence of my particular brand of bad French, Marie Salomé clapped her hands, threw her arms around me and hugged me, and said that it was the delight of her life to find someone with whom she could "keep up" her French, that she would "do all things" for us and show us how it was possible to live on her island pleasantly and "without the necessity of money."

We were all a bit floored, even Norris, who was still looking for Fayaway. Marie Salomé was all wrong in that role—not that she was without charm. About the height and weight of the average American girl of her age, the color many Californians achieve by the end of a summer, with huge deer-brown eyes and a cloud of soft, wavy black hair, she was beautiful—in a Marquesan way. And formidable, which is very Marquesan too.

We eventually met two of Marie Salomé's sisters and innumerable *cousines* and aunts. They were all beautiful (except when they smiled) and all formidable. But the most beautiful and most formidable of all was Théodora, and she had all her front teeth. I remember how she stood—absolutely immobile, but utterly relaxed—during our opening interview with Marie Salomé, looking like the slightly-larger-than-life wood carving of a Polynesian Diana. Where Marie Salomé was exuberant, Théodora was sultry—tall, lithe, and feral.

Théodora's husband was said to be very jealous of her. He had forbidden her to dance the *tamure* with the Groupe Folklorique that performs for the Matson Line tourists. I don't doubt he had reason to be jealous. Théodora seemed to have very little to do during the hours when school kept her husband indoors. Most of her time was spent on the beach or walking along the main drag. Sauntering was a better word for what she did, and it took the eye of every male she passed, including the prisoners in the unbarred jail. Théodora would have stopped traffic if there had been any, and she was entirely aware of it.

She apparently came of a line of women of the same genre. One day we were chatting about her very pretty (and mischievous) two-year-old, whom Marie Salomé looked after in a casual sort of way five mornings a week, Théodora informed me that she had another child. "But she lives with my mother and her husbands. In Taipivai."

I thought at first she had made an error in French. I knew I had heard *ses maris* not *son mari*, but French was not her native tongue either. When I made a friend of whom I could ask such a question, I reported the conversation and got my answer. There was nothing at all out of the way about a woman having two husbands, or even three—though that was more unusual. Polyandry is an old Marquesan custom. It has been outlawed by the French administration and branded as sin by the church, but it flourishes all the same.

The same is true of drinking (hard liquor) and eating (other people). Both are frowned upon, but brandy is brewed from oranges and the liquor of coconut flowers in every settlement on the island except the capital city, which is police-ridden. There are said to be villages on the north coast where no adult draws a sober breath, and only the intervention of the government keeps the community from starving itself to death. As for the custom of eating "the long pig," I got the impression that it was talked about much more than it was done. It shocked the French, and shock was one of the few weapons the Marquesans had left. I was told that when a Marquesan gets drunk and quarrelsome, he is apt to bite off and eat the ear of whoever he is quarreling with, and I actually saw two men who were missing one ear.

But to return to Théodora, it seemed to me that she could manage two, if not more, husbands, and that she was suffering from the ennui that afflicts a large spirit in a confining environment. That may explain why the schoolmaster was willing to pay Marie Salomé a wage to act as mother's helper and companion to her cousin during the hours when duty kept him from her side.

Marie Salomé had paid us several visits on board the *Aikane*, although she got seasick every time she ventured belowdecks. Sometimes she brought a friend who wanted to inspect the boat; sometimes she brought gifts of fruit or flowers. Each time before she left she made a point of reminding us that we were to spend Sunday morning on an excursion she was planning. We were to meet her outside the cathedral after mass, stop at her home so she could change her clothes, and hike to her favorite *rocher*, which she kept trying to point out on the rock-strewn face of the mountain to the west. Also, we were to bring no food. She had some sort of gastronomic surprise planned. (Norris, who was not coming, said it would be "long pig.")

Sunday morning was beautiful, bright and breezy on the water. Ashore and out of the wind, it was muggy. I was wearing my one proper dress, and stifling, but I carried the meter and a half of cotton I had bought from Maurice. The raw edges were hemmed, and Marie Salomé had promised to teach me to wear it as a pareu. ("*Tout ce qu'il y a du plus simple,*" she said.) Jack and Benson wore shirts and shorts. They had tennis shoes; I had espadrilles. Not exactly the footgear for a mountain climb, but the best we could do.

Marie Salomé emerged from the morning service in a tight-waisted cotton dress under which she wore the stiff crinoline petticoats that were fashionable in the States a year or so ago. She was perspiring, and her petticoats scratched her bare legs, and she couldn't wait to get home and change, so she hurried us along the trail at the fastest clip I'd ever seen a Marquesan achieve.

Home, to the Tamarii family, was the side yard of what used to be the greatest temple or feast place of ancient Taiohae. The road to it was now only a footpath that led through disorderly plantations of coconut palms, mango, and breadfruit trees, past the houses of various *cousins* and *cousines* of Marie Salomé's. (Everybody in this valley seemed to be related to the Tamariis in one way or another, and this gave Marie Salomé the right to pick fruit or stop off for refreshment at every dwelling or plantation she passed. No wonder she didn't need money!) We made only one stop on this leg of the journey: at the home of a *cousin* who is a wood sculptor, specializing in suitcase-size miniatures of ancient Marquesan war clubs. Here we were offered a stickful of sweet roasted chestnuts, which tasted like marron glacés. The chestnuts grow wild, but the preparation was done by the Chinois Bleu, and cost someone some money. But not Marie Salomé.

Just before we reached the Tamarii home, we paused—but did not stop—at a second house, where the family of *cousins* was just sitting down to their Sunday dinner. Their sleeping quarters were constructed in the old Marquesan style, with walls of woven bamboo and a steep-pitched roof of pandanus thatch. The dining-room-kitchen was a separate shack, roofed but unwalled. Cooking was done here over a wood fire, and the table laid on the ground to the windward. (When the *no-no* flies are bad, one eats to the leeward, in the smoke.) The menu seemed to consist of fish, rice, and fruit. The fish was cut into chunks and soaked in a thick cream extracted from ripe coconut meat. (I couldn't tell whether it was raw or cooked; it's eaten both ways.) There was a pile of ripe bananas before each diner's place, and other fruit in the center, within easy reach.

There were no children visible, and as we walked on, I asked Marie Salomé why.

"Because it is Sunday. *Les copains* are gone early. Like my brothers. They won't be back till dark or after."

"Don't they eat on Sunday?"

"But yes. They are perhaps fishing. If they catch, they will eat. Or they will pick mangoes. Or eat *chez les cousins.*"

I tried to put myself into the place of a Marquesan house-keeper who had to plan Sunday dinner without being able to count mouths. "You mean nothing is *prepared* for them at home?"

"But yes, it is prepared." Marie Salomé was puzzled by my puzzlement. "You saw it just now."

"Well, what happens to it if the children eat somewhere else? Or what if other children drop in here to eat? More than there is enough for?"

Marie Salomé shook her head. "There is plenty. Not of rice. That is costly. But of breadfruit, which is my *préférable.*"

I began to see that I was dealing not only with an economy that was outside my ken but also with a culture. What would happen to America if no mother were to call her children to meals?

The Tamarii house was less attractive than the *cousins'*: a two-room shack of unpainted boards, raised on shaky pilings, roofed with corrugated iron. The cooking shack was also iron-roofed. The yard was hard and bare and littered with the droppings of pigs, dogs, and chickens. But there were many *tiare tahiti* bushes, hibiscus shrubs, and banana trees. And across the path by which we arrived, a tremendous stone terrace, the ruin of the great temple. From it the Tamariis, and neighbors, living and dead, have stolen shaped boulders to make outdoor hearths. The stones on which breadfruit was roasting had once been parts of an altar bloodied by the sacrificial victims of a cannibal feast.

Two of Marie Salomé's sisters were at home to welcome us. Anna was a dark pantherine beauty of eighteen, still unmarried (which is a wonder), employed as a part-time housemaid in some bureaucrat's home, and reputed to be the best *tamure* dancer in Taiohae (since Théodora had been taken out of the competition). Marguerite was twenty, married, the mother of two children, and quite pretty except that she has lost four or five of her front upper teeth. She was cooking the Sunday meal for the family, although she no longer lived at home. I was curious about what was in the pot, but she did not offer us a sample. Instead she pointed to the bunches of bananas that hung from the beams of the cooking-shack roof, and indicated that we were to eat as much as we liked.

Anna gathered *tiare tahitis* and came to put one over the ear of each guest. Benson and I had our left ears decorated—like Marguerite's. Jack was asked which ear he wanted. He pointed to Anna's, which was the right. Much giggling from all the girls! (The left ear signifies that one is married or otherwise accommodated; the right ear means "still seeking.")

Marie Salomé had taken a quick bath in the little river that runs through the yard, and now she led me to the house, so we could change into pareus. In the room we used, there was a very old woman asleep and snoring on a pallet. Marie Salomé paid no attention to her, not even lowering her voice to answer my whispered question about who she was.

"*Une grandmère à moi!*" she said casually.

Which does not mean that she is the mother of Marie Salomé's mother or father. Simply she is a relative of the generation of a grandmother, which gives her the privileges of grandmothership in the households of any of *les cousins*.

Marie Salomé opened her small wooden clothes chest and showed me a dozen carefully folded pareus. (I am convinced this is the perfect garment for this or any other warm, humid climate. The material is cheap, but not sleazy, cotton, printed in bold patterns of black on saturated blue, red, yellow, orange, and sometimes duller and more interesting brown, green, and purple. The motifs are taken from old tattoo or *tiki* designs, or from the leaf and flower of the hibiscus, the palm, the banana, or the pineapple plant. O'Brien says that when cloth was first introduced here by the Europeans, the prints were ugly. But William Morris convinced the British textile manufacturers that Polynesia was a market worth special treatment. A genre of pareu designs was developed that is perfectly suited to the bodies and the background of these beautiful people.)

Marie Salomé chose her loudest pareu, egg-yellow on black. All she wore under it was a pair of rayon panties and a black strapless brassiere, which she called a "*soutien-gorge.*" To dress, she simply wrapped the cloth around her body, took one corner and a piece along the top edge and tied the two of them together very tightly, the knot coming between her breasts. What was left—about half a meter—she folded into a deep pleat, which she tucked into the *soutien-gorge.* (If you don't wear one, you just roll the cloth in, the way French girls roll stockings.) Anna wore hers with a difference. She had a new *soutien-gorge* that was very handsome, so she tied her pareu around her hips. But Marie Salomé's drape was the classic model, and it really was a classic in grace of line and in practicality. She could run, swim, climb trees, and even play volleyball thus attired.

She could, but I couldn't.

Even after all three of the Tamarii girls had worked on me, using every possible variation of drape, I couldn't walk across the yard without having to clutch my *décolletage* to prevent an unscheduled striptease.

The sun was at the zenith by the time I was "dressed," and we were all hot and hungry. Marie Salomé said it would be cooler at the *rocher*, and started us off. We wondered when we were to be "surprised" by food. All she was carrying for our picnic was a basket woven of a palm frond, and a short, sharp knife. Perhaps we would drop in at some cousins' up the path. The men hoped so in English, which I did not translate.

We had gone only a few yards when the meal began. Marie Salomé disappeared into some bushes and reappeared halfway up a giant mango tree. Fruit began to rain down, beautiful pale yellow "lemon mangoes," some ripe, some not quite ripe. (Marie Salomé ate hers green.) When each of us had a couple, she filled her little basket, came down, showed us the best way to peel a mango, and led on.

For the next two hours we ate steadily: purple pistachio fruit (the nuts seem not to be eaten here), oranges—mandarin and ordinary thick-skinned ones—papayas, bananas—some Marie Salomé had brought in her basket, and others of different size, shape, and color that she picked as we went along. And coconuts: the hard, white-meated kind we have tasted at home, as well as unripe and overripe ones.

As we walked and munched, Marie Salomé kept up a per-

Marie Salomé.

fect Chamber of Commerce spiel about the joys of the life we could lead here if we should choose to settle down. Fish for the fishing, fruit for the picking, an infinite supply of *mayoreo* (breadfruit) in and out of season. I asked how it was kept between seasons. Very simple! It is made into poi, which is stored in pits in the ancient fashion. Or it is fed to pigs and chickens, which can be eaten any time.

Jack wanted to know if the trees we were stripping were wild or if they belonged to someone. Marie Salomé shrugged indifference. They had been planted and had once belonged to someone. But many plantations were deserted, and trees had seeded themselves; besides, there was plenty. She interrupted herself to reprove me for picking up a fallen mango. They have worms! I dropped my prize, and we walked along, treading gingerly on fruit that would be priced out of reach in markets at home.

Ever since we left the beach, we had been climbing. Now the trail was steep. The lush verdure was thinning out into lantana thickets and scrub acacia. Now and then our way led across small ravines, cut by one of the five streams that divide the cup-shaped surface of this valley. Along the watercourses there was mud underfoot and shade overhead, and no wind. We were all sweating. Jack thought he was being bitten by *no-nos*, the almost invisible flies about which Melville complained, and which are still the curse of Nuku Hiva a century later.

"The next time we cross a stream, I'm going to have a bath," Benson muttered to me. "And a drink. I'm dying of thirst, and there's a gnat trying to fly into my eyes."

This time I translated the complaints for Marie Salomé, who said yes to Benson's bath, but begged us not to drink. If we could preserve our thirst intact till we reached her family's coconut plantation, she would offer us the milk of the green coconut, which was *"très joli et très frais."* One must be parched to appreciate fully its restorative powers.

The water of the next little stream was dammed into two pools by the strange, wall-like roots of a great chestnut tree. The men took off their shorts and shirts, and bathed in their underwear, in one of the pools. I took off my pareu and bathed in my underwear, in the other. Marie Salomé and Anna (who had caught up with us by now) removed themselves a discreet distance and carefully averted their eyes. I believe we were more shocked at this sudden onset of prudery than they were at our bathing costumes. It was not thus in Melville's day!

Soon Marie Salomé called time on us. We must be getting on up the trail. Rain was threatening and would catch us unprotected. And the treat in store for us would be worth all our pains.

She was absolutely right. It would have been worth the long, hot, insect-plagued climb only to see Marie Salomé, knife in teeth, pareu caught tightly between her legs, walk up the smooth gray trunk of a palm tree at least one hundred feet tall. She was giggling so hard I was sure the knife would fall and stab one of her skinny dogs, who were sitting at the base of the tree, wagging their flea-bitten tails in anticipation of treats for them too. But all that fell was coconuts, dropping like great green basketballs, bouncing on the soft floor of the grove and rolling away in all directions.

They didn't crack open, which was too bad. Opening an unripe coconut is not easy. If you have a machete, you can whack the top off, slicing through the husk and the soft covering of the nut. But it's awkward to drink from a cup with a lip three inches thick. The approved technique is to husk the nut on a sharp stake, firmly planted in the ground. (Every Marquesan home is provided with such a convenience, and so was this grove.) Anna stabbed and ripped till each of us had a husked nut. Benson's hunting knife was used for the next step, which was to tap an airhole and a drinking hole in the sprouting end of the nut. When we had all been served, we lifted our goblets and drank to Marie Salomé. The nectar was all that she had promised: cool, very faintly flavored, and almost magically refreshing. After we had quenched our thirst, she and Anna showed us how to scrape the soft, jellylike coating of the husk with a fingernail.

It was beginning to rain, and Marie Salomé said the nearest shelter was her *rocher*, which was still a mile away, up a trailless slope. We were really too tired to make it with any pleasure. Marie Salomé read imminent refusal in our faces and turned on her hard sell. It was by far the best place to view the valley of Taiohae. Many tourists had made the climb and thanked her for bringing them. Tourists from the *Mariposa* had even taken moving pictures there!

"Also of Marie Salomé climbing palm trees," said Anna with a proud smile. "She will be seen in the moving pictures of the United States."

"If those octogenarians on the *Mariposa* can make it, so can we," Jack said, and started after Marie Salomé as if his honor were at stake.

The rain caught us halfway there and washed us clean of the dust and sweat we had accumulated since our river bath. Rain doesn't chill in this climate, and isn't really worth running from. We refused the banana-leaf umbrellas the girls cut and offered to us, and struggled onward and upward till we reached the *rocher*.

It is a hunk of close-grained, igneous rock that must have rolled down from the high cliffs. The size of a six- or seven-story

Marie Salomé opening a coconut.

apartment, with two dwellings per floor, it is poised on two points that are about the size of a large dining-room table. It slopes in on the seaward side and makes a sort of cave, in which we sat and looked out over the slope up which we had come,

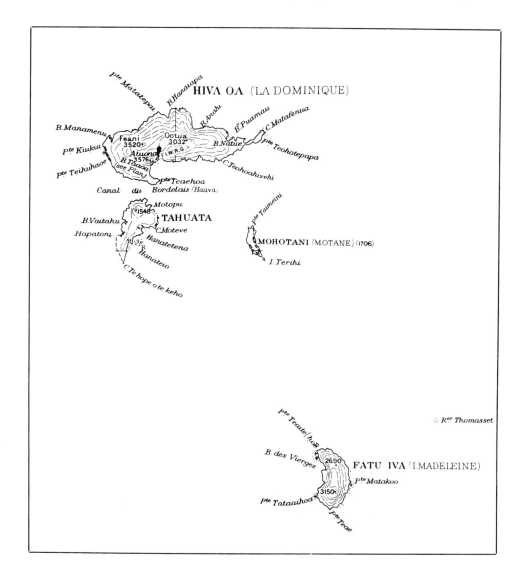

The Southern Marquesas.

down to the blue water where the *Aikane* bobbed at anchor like a baby's bathtub toy.

We saw why other tourists had thanked Marie Salomé for bringing them here. We thanked her, too. But now we had had enough. We would have liked to take wing and glide down to what we called home.

Instead, we walked and got caught in another rain. About an hour later, we arrived at the Tamarii house. Dinner was over, but that was all right with us. We were stuffed. We took showers in the unscreened bath behind a hibiscus bush. I got back into my dress, and we began our grateful good-byes.

Marie Salomé was desolated. She had expected us to accompany her to the evening *Salut à Marie* at the cathedral. Monsignor was expecting us. And after that there was to be entertainment in the annex—three film cartoons, one of them American, and a double feature about the miracles of Fatima and the shrine of Lourdes, both of which Monsignor said were *très jolis.*

We felt that to disappoint Marie Salomé was an act of crass ingratitude, but we were ready to drop. I made an excuse which implied, but did not actually say, that we had other denominational obligations of a Sunday evenings, and we dragged ourselves along the waterfront toward the pier.

Norris was *chez* Maurice, and he hailed us cheerfully. There was to be dancing later, he said, possibly the *tamure.* But we were too far gone even for vicarious exercise.

We split a bottle of Hinano among the three of us and went back to the *Aikane* to rest and recover from the Seventh Day.

We had a great pair of salads out of the fruit Marie Salomé had taught us to eat: the hard green meat of what she called a lemon mango. All the ingredients of the first were obtainable "without the necessity of money" if one had friends. For the second, one had to visit the garden of M. Gendron, a gnarled old Frenchman who might have modeled for Van Gogh.

FRUIT SALAD TAIOHAE

> **Chunks and/or slices of:**
> orange

> papaya
> red and yellow bananas
> pineapple
> mango
>
> Marinate for an hour or so in a dressing made with lemon juice instead of vinegar. Serve with chunks of coconut meat; or grate coconut meat over it.

VEGETABLE SALAD TAIOHAE

> Chips of crisp green mango meat
> Avocado (the Marquesan variety is yellow-skinned)
> Cucumbers (sliced or chunked)
> Radishes (sliced or whole, if small)
>
> Toss the above in a good French dressing and allow to stand for a half hour or so. Then serve on leaves of young lettuce. Not iceberg!
> Either of these salads, with a sliced (cold) pork loin and cold Tahitian beer, was a fine middle-of-the-day meal, when it was too hot to cook.

Benson's letter of introduction opened many doors to us in the islands where we used it, but none pleasanter than that of the *maison* Le Bouget. Hélène and Albert Le Bouget were the sort of dedicated and creative young intellectuals France ought to send out on educational missions to the "French Community," but apparently seldom does.

They were not only functioning as two-thirds of the faculty of the new *lycée*, with some sixty students, and all the problems of the first year of any enterprise, as well as the delicate diplomatic chore of getting on with the authorities of the Catholic schools whose "walls" they were obliged to use; they were also engaged in a program of rescuing as much of the dying Marquesan culture as possible: collecting and recording *récits* from ancient illiterates whose memories were already faltering, copying old *tiki* and tattoo motifs, and trying to involve their students in carrying on the same work.

Hélène was one of the most admirable European women I met ashore in any of the French islands, perhaps the only one, I felt, who had successfully blended the best of her own culture with the Polynesian. Having more than enough to do without housekeeping, she hired Marquesans to do the chores and look after her two daughters (about six and nine years old at the time), and accommodated herself to the resulting compromise between their ways and her own with a grace that made her more popular as an employer than anyone else in Taiohae, male or female, French or *indigène*.

Her dress was another graceful compromise: usually a comfortable cotton dress, well and simply made, of the same bold printed material as her housemaids' pareus. She wore her hair, which was lighter but just as lush as theirs, in a long, loose braid that could be twisted up into a chignon whenever comfort or convention required it. On her feet she wore sandals, which protected them from the rocks of the roadways, but did not cramp or overheat her toes. Her house was one of the substantial stucco bungalows in which all the Europeans in Taiohae lived, utterly undistinguished, but cool even in the heat of the day, and well protected from the storms that now and then swept down from the mountains. Hélène wasted no energy trying to make a silk purse out of this architectural sow's ear. She enjoyed its comfort, ignored its ugliness, and arranged the furniture so that attention was directed outward to the breathtaking panorama of the bay and Ua Pou beyond. On the tile-floored porch-sitting-room that provided the best view, the Le Bougets were at home in the late afternoon, reading to or talking with the children, sipping a drink and nibbling an hors d'oeuvre (while in the kitchen the Marquesans prepared whatever sort of supper seemed best to them). Here they welcomed any visitor—friend or stranger— who happened to drop in. There was always plenty of ice (courtesy of the Delco generator, which also provided the light by which both Albert and Hélène often worked till late at night). And there was a fine library of books and records on the music, the art, the history, and the physical geography of the Marquesas, plenty of good conversation, knowledge, and enthusiasm to be shared.

It took less than a full Scotch and soda for the Le Bougets and Benson to discover that they were pedagogical soulmates, rebels against the rigid educational system (here or anywhere) that attempted to make good little bourgeois out of the best students, and passive participants in the French Community (or Great Society) out of the rest. Albert Le Bouget arranged for Benson to interview a number of teen-agers of both sexes at the *lycée*, without the intimidating presence of any authority figure (even Albert himself), and Benson was able to repay the favor by doing some nonverbal testing of the students who were coming up for their *bacs*. (A crateful of *matériaux psychologiques* that Albert had ordered had gone astray somewhere between Marseille and the Marquesas. He was a little uneasy about making value judgments unsupported by any academic abracadabra, and was grateful for Benson's results—which confirmed all but one of his guesses, anyway.)

Another serendipitous result of Benson's letter of introduction was the friendship Jack struck up with another cocktail-hour guest of the Le Bougets: Dr. Jean Pierre Chastenet, the *Médecin-Chef* who had been too busy to come aboard and clear us from quarantine. He and Jack managed not only to communicate via a mutually agreed-upon combination of sign language and pidgin, but established a real rapport based upon a number of common interests, of which tuna fishing from a speedboat was not the least.

An ex-paratrooper, in his middle thirties as far as we could judge, Dr. Chastenet was as handsome as Adonis in the same classic style, a *bon vivant* and a sportsman, a totally unconvincing ironist who told horrendous black jokes ("*humeurs noires*"), gave no one a word of sympathy and who was worshiped like a miracle-working saint by the people of Nuku Hiva and other islands as far away as Hiva Oa.

We spent a morning with Dr. Chastenet in Taipivai, and walked with him several times around Taiohae, and talked about him with dwellers in Ua Pou and even in Atuona. It was always the same story. He had the healing touch! Women and children, and even men his own age, would collect in his wake, follow him humbly until they could summon the courage to reach out a hand and touch his arm, as if that alone would cure the toothache, the agony of infected *no-no* bites, or whatever else ailed them. I'm sure he was an excellent surgeon and a devoted general practitioner, but those skills and virtues were only incidental to these invalids. They adored him because it gave them comfort and because he seemed to them made to adore.

The *vahine* who had landed this greatest of matrimonial catches was the nearest thing to Fayaway (or Cio-Cio-San) that we were able to find. (*Vahine* means woman in Marquesan, but when the French use the word it is to distinguish an unmarried mistress from a wedded wife. The word *femme* means both woman and wife, and the distinction is sometimes important, especially for visitors.)

Judy was physically a perfect match for Jean Pierre: almost as tall as he, darker, and even more handsome, also radiantly healthy, vigorous, and as graceful as a (tamed) panther—Théodora, without claws or fangs. The first time we met her was on the threshold of her home. The doctor had asked us to drop by for a noon-hour apéritif, but he had been detained in surgery. Judy was dressed in a black strapless brassiere and a blue and black pareu, which was knotted at the waist so that it hung in a sweeping drape that suggested a train. She had *tiare tahitis* in her hair, and her bearing was that of a young queen, but her greeting to us had a humility that was almost obsequious. She invited us into the open-sided, tile-floored *salon*, offered us chairs, brought us cool beer, and tried to make conversation in French—looking apprehensive, as if she expected us to do her some injury. When Jean Pierre arrived at last, she flashed him a propitiatory smile, and vanished, not to appear again as long as we were there.

I saw her several times afterward, and talked to others about her, and it seemed to me that her sorrow was rooted in the fact that Jean Pierre did not love her. I'm not sure she loved him, but she was attached to him in *almost* the way an American woman in her position would be, not at all in the way of a Marquesan *vahine*. The difference has nothing to do with shame. The unmarried state was socially acceptable there, except perhaps to the hierarchy at the other end of town. Marie Salomé thought the doctor ought to marry Judy "because she has a baby to him." But Marie Salomé was under the influence of Monsignor, and that influence didn't extend very far or very deep in the community. From what I heard it was the same everywhere in Polynesia. Neither Catholic nor Protestant nor Mormon missionaries have made real headway against the Polynesian approach to sexual relations, in which marriage as we know it is irrelevant.

Judy suffered acutely from isolation, but not because she was ostracized as a fallen woman. On the contrary, one of her troubles was her sudden elevation. She had—or at least she lived in—the most attractive residence in Taiohae, and she was the only Marquesan woman with a full-time, sleep-in servant. Yet she couldn't invite any of her former friends to visit her. Jean Pierre Chastenet would not have welcomed them. He didn't like Marquesans (except Taro, the shark fisherman). But he didn't like Frenchmen either. He was not a misanthrope, just highly selective about his friends. Perhaps it was because he came into contact with so many people in his professional life under circumstances that drained him emotionally—however cool he pretended to play it. For his private life he needed only a very few of his peers. Judy did not qualify except, one must assume, in bed. She was ignorant and dumb, in both the true and the slang sense of that word.

The loneliness sometimes got too heavy for her to bear. When Jean Pierre had gone out of an evening, she began to drink. Judy had access to liquor (Jean Pierre's) that other Marquesans were forbidden. When she had drunk enough to be bold, she took her baby and wandered out into the darkness, looking for company along the road, or perhaps paying a visit to some house where she saw a light.

We met the doctor one night searching for her on his mobilette. As we stood and talked in the pitchy darkness at the foot of the pier, he held up his hand and quieted us. All I could hear was an odd little whimpering, which I took to be a baby. But it was Judy herself. The baby was asleep in her arms. Jean Pierre did not scold her, and I felt she was sorry that he didn't. He had been worried, that was clear, but whether on her account or the baby's, or on both, would be hard to guess.

The baby was a girl, named Jeanne after him, and she created a problem that was eating at his peace and his self-respect. He had less than a year of duty left there. Then he would go back to France, spend a few months, and accept another assignment on another outlying French possession or protectorate. He had no intention of taking his *vahine* with him, but he could not abandon her without abandoning his child. He was fighting a very complex battle with his feelings on this point, and projecting it in the form of biting sarcasm about the Marquesan attitude toward children.

"They have no feeling for children," he told us very belligerently one day. "They give them away like a bunch of bananas or a pig! They care nothing!"

But he was at least 50 percent wrong. The Marquesans are absolutely dotty about children, especially infants. They spoil them to death. I never heard a child cry any longer than it took the nearest adult to reach it and begin to comfort it. Babies are carried till they are able to walk, swim, and climb coconut trees, not only by their mothers and grandmothers and sisters and *cousines*, but by all the males in the family and the neighborhood. It is true that children are frequently loaned or even given away. But this is not because Marquesans don't care. They just have a poorly developed sense of property in children. They don't feel they *own* their offspring as we do. And they are racked with pity for anyone who hasn't at least one child under the age of five years in the house. They give to those in need. Or at least they did until very recently. M. Le Chevanton, the Administrator, told us that the population explosion, which was rescuing the race from the extinction that had seemed to threaten it (circa 1919), was putting a strain on the individual family's ability to feed their own brood. There were very few childless families now, and few in a position to adopt another mouth to feed. Marie Salomé to the contrary notwithstanding, there was not enough for all "without the necessity of money," it seemed.

At any rate Jean Pierre Chastenet was going to do just what he inveighed against: give his child away while she was at the most adorable and vulnerable stage of babyhood. I think he was ashamed, and that is what made him so angry. But really he hadn't much choice at that point. If he had picked a Théodora, or even a Marie Salomé, he would have been in a different position. There are Marquesan women who could be turned into superb Galateas by any reasonably talented Pygmalion. But Judy was hopeless. She hadn't the fortitude. She cowered and waited for the blow to fall, and probably crumpled under it when, at last, it came.

About a week after our arrival, the *Taporo* came to Taiohae, bringing letters from home (via Tahiti) and the possibility of sending answers to them. The name means "lemon" in Tahitian, with none of the pejorative connotations the word carries in English. She was really romantic-looking: the classic tramp schooner (*goelette*) of the post-sail era. The *Taporo* was a diesel-powered cargo carrier, with bridge and cabins aft of amidships, a long open hold forward for loading copra, a white hull, and a clipper bow with vivid rust streaks from the bow

The *Taporo* at Taiohae.

anchors that ride on it. Unfortunately (as she was moored to windward of us), she didn't smell as good as she looked.

Copra, the reason for the odor of rancid coconut that engulfed the *Aikane* whenever the wind came up, is the one product of these islands that is exchanged for cash, and exported. The labor involved in making it is not arduous, but neither is it child's play. Mature coconuts are collected as they fall and heaped up till there are enough to make it worthwhile cutting them. This cutting is a skilled occupation at which every male Marquesan is expert. Boys can swing a big knife to split the hard shells or twist a small one to scoop out the dry nutmeat just as well as their fathers and grandfathers, and they earn just as much for their labor. The copra is dried in the sun if the owner is poor, or in a protected shed if he is rich. The quality of the product is affected slightly by mildew, but not enough to bother the poor producer. The price it commands is set by an officer called the supercargo—a sort of seagoing business agent—and it depends on the condition of the meat, how much moisture is still to be extracted from it, the market condition locally, and other imponderables like what sort of public relations he (or his factor) want to maintain. The seller can either accept the price or store his copra against a possible change for the better. There is very little chance of another copra-buying boat coming along within several months, so to hold out implies a very long view of things, a rare quality in any part of Polynesia.

The copra is sold in Papeete to representatives of French cosmetic firms, shipped to Marseille to be pressed and made into soap and beauty oils, some of which are shipped back and sold to the mothers and sisters of the men who cut the copra.

The captain of the *Taporo*, a lean, lined, very dark Tahitian with the reputation of being the best sailor in all French Oceania, was at Dr. Chastenet's one day when we stopped for an apéritif. The doctor recommended Captain Amaru to Jack as the best of oracles on any question about whether to stop at the Tuamotus (Dangerous, or Pearl) Islands, and how to manage if we did. Ordinarily, we were told, Amaru was quite reserved, not to say haughty, but he made himself agreeable to us from the start. He was, he told us, a wind sailor at heart. He was interested in looking over the *Aikane*.

Jack invited him to come aboard the same afternoon, and

before that visit was over, it had turned into such a love feast that we decided to have a dinner party aboard, invite Captain Amaru, Dr. Chastenet, and the Le Bougets, and an elderly English pediatrician who was spending his holiday as a passenger on the *Taporo* and having rather a poor time of it because he was uncomfortable mixing socially with the "lesser breeds" who made up the rest of the cabin passenger list, not to mention the poor "devils" who slept on the deck over the copra hold.

It was a great party, thanks to the cocktail hour that preceded the dinner. There was no meat to be had in either of the Chinois's or Maurice's. Norris scared up a chicken from his laundress's flock, but it was undersized and tough. The one dish that had anything to recommend it was an aspic I made from the last of our canned wahoo.

ASPIC (OUT OF WHATEVER FISH YOU HAVE AROUND)

Canned (jarred) fish, flaked into small pieces
Canned vegetables, beans, peas, even carrots
Fresh onion, chopped fine
Unflavored gelatin, 1 tbs. for every pt. of liquid mayonnaise

Make a gelatin out of the liquid from the canned vegetables, the jellied liquor of the fish, a little salt water mixed in with the fresh you use to bring it to the desired amount, and perhaps some white wine. (You don't have to use the vegetables' liquor or the salt water if you don't want to. Please your own palate.)

Mix enough mayonnaise into the combination to flavor and color it. Chill it. Before it sets, pour into a mold—a mixing bowl will do if you have nothing else—into which the fish and drained vegetables are lightly packed.

Chill till it is hard. Unmold it if conditions permit and there is going to be any opportunity to observe the visual virtues of the dish. Otherwise, don't bother. Serve with a sauce of mayonnaise doctored with lemon juice and some delicate herb like basil or tarragon.

The night was beautiful and everyone seemed to have brought along a bottle of a different brand of Scotch. We all sat in the cockpit, except Hélène Le Bouget who developed a Marquesan case of *mal de mer* before she was well on board. (For her we rigged a bed on top of the cabin where she could hear the tape recorder playing Juliette Greco's *Saint-Germain-des-Prés* without smelling the food.) In no time at all the decibel level was up to New York indoor-cocktail-party standards.

Albert Le Bouget was explaining to me the possibilities, as he sees them, of rescuing the Marquesan language from extinction, and his vew of contemporary fashions in nonobjective poetry (he is, I discovered, a distinguished contemporary poet), while Jean Pierre Chastenet was analyzing the Marquesan character for Jack and expecting me to translate. ("They live entirely in the present . . . have short memories for sorrow or sin or anger. . . . We try to make our lives more simple and theirs more complex. . . .") The pediatrician was telling Benson about the time he was "victorious" in a campaign to prove that babies could eat meat at the age of five days. Captain Amaru was telling (in a combination of French with a Tahitian accent and English with a French accent) a derisive tale about an American tycoon for whom he had once captained. I was trying to translate the doctor's Oxford English, as well as Jean Pierre's French to Norris, who was speaking Marquesan, to no one in particular.

We disturbed the peace of the bay till well after midnight, but there were no guardians of it to send after us. Eventually, Madame Le Bouget summoned the strength to face the return trip. Jack ran her and her husband to the pier in the *Lili Aikane*, with its fine little British Seagull motor making a fine, refined British noise. That, unhappily, was its last flight.

Jack came back to the boat to pick up Captain Amaru and his passenger (and Dr. Chastenet) to run them over to the *Taporo*. The most credible account of what happened thereafter was that when the dinghy nosed up to the landing stage of the schooner, the pediatrician stood up, a little unsteady, but brave, and stepped on the gunwale of the *Lili Aikane*. He also reached for the handrail of the landing stage, but there wasn't any. Captain Amaru and Dr. Chastenet moved to save the old man

from falling, and the shift of that much weight was too much for
the dinghy.

She turned over, spilling all four men into the warm, calm
sea. The sailors who were on deck to see their captain aboard
fished everyone out in no time, and righted the boat.

Everyone dried out and warmed up with a few shots of
cognac, and no one was any the worse for the wetting. Except
the gallant little two-and-a-half-horse Seagull. A shot of cognac
in its carburetor might have been a good investment, but no one
thought of it. By next morning, it was too late. For the rest of
our stay at Taiohae the *Lili Aikane* was rowed to and from the
pier.

It was made clear to us from the start of our visit that ten
days was tolerable, and anything over that increasingly intolerable to the absentee landlords in Paris who made policy for the
French Community. None of the flesh-and-blood deputies of
those absentees was personally hostile or even uncordial, but they
were also, *hélas!* obligated to carry out the policy "except in the
case of a veritable emergency"—which, *hélas!* we came very near
to having our last Sunday in port.

Norris and the younger set (the Danes, two young men from
the *Lizard*, a young couple from another American sloop,
Breeze III, which had just arrived, and some girls from the *lycée*)
had gone on a hike to Anaho, on the northern coast of the island
—an excursion known aboard the *Aikane* as the March from
Bataan. Theoretically there was no conflict between the hike and
our announced time of departure at dawn Monday morning. The
hikers left Saturday very early and intended to be back late Sunday afternoon. But anyone who has read Melville on crossing the
interior of Nuku Hiva could predict that a fifteen-mile trek was
not the work of a single day. Besides, Anaho was reputed to be
one of the towns that kept itself in a perpetual orgy on orange
wine. I wondered a little that Jack didn't object aloud to Norris's
going, and I was more than a little curious to see how he would
solve the problem if Norris didn't show up on time.

Would he postpone our departure? Somehow I doubted it. It
was not in Jack's character to be "permissive" about matters like
that. And to go soft on discipline at the very start of a long set of

shore leaves would set a bad precedent. But to sail without one quarter of the crew was a pretty severe form of "natural consequences."

Jack never discussed the question. He went about his preparation for leaving as if nothing stood in their way. And in the process of the most important of these preparations, the *Aikane* was driven aground at the end of the pier.

I didn't actually see the accident happen; I was diving in the murky shallows for our cast-iron barbecue grill, which had got lost when we tried to use it as an anchor for the dinghy. The last time I looked at the *Aikane*, Jack was holding her in close to the pier while Benson attached our plastic hose (one hundred feet long) to the freshwater spigot there. The sails were down and the motor on, and the problem was to keep her nose just a little closer than a hundred feet and also keep off the jagged cement of the pier on one side and a nasty set of rocks on the other. The tide was on a fast ebb, which should have helped, but the wind was blowing fresh from the bay, which didn't.

I came up, spluttering, with the griddle in my hands in time to hear Benson shout something to Jack. His tone was alarmed. Jack apparently didn't hear, and Benson shouted again.

"You're on the bottom—back her off!"

This time Jack heard. He threw the motor into reverse, but the *Aikane* didn't handle well in that gear. Her stern swung to starboard and on to another sandbar. She was fast, and the tide was still running out.

I was sent for help, but having no clear idea of what sort of help was wanted, I rowed frantically in the direction of the *Lizard*, "catching crabs" in my excitement and spinning in most unseamanlike circles. Behind me I could hear Benson and Jack shouting to each other over a rising babble of other voices. The pier was full of children and Sunday fishermen, and they were all getting into the act.

The *Lizard*'s skipper had been watching for several minutes and needed only the first words of an invitation. He was in his dinghy rowing for the pier, yelling at me to row out to the government schooner (moored in the *Taporo*'s old spot) and ask the standby crew to come in with their power launch.

Meanwhile, back at the pier, Marie Salomé had arrived and

was organizing a group of *copains* who seemed to be trying to topple the *Aikane* over on her side! They were hauling away for dear life on a line fixed to the spreader. I could also see the motor launch (property of the Chinois Bleu), behind which Théodora and her husband had been water-skiing, making for the pier with its throttle wide open. Before I reached the government schooner, there was a roar and a cloud of exhaust smoke, and I knew that the launch had tried to pull us off, and failed. Time and tide were running out.

Jack's and Benson's descriptions of the next few minutes differed in some details but agreed on the fact that it was a miracle we didn't end up with a split hull. Neither could hear the other over the brouhaha of the children, the prisoners (who had emptied the jail), the *capitaine* of the *gendarmerie*, who was ordering them and everyone else about, and the roar of the Chinois Bleu's outboard. Neither could they hear the skipper of the *Lizard*, who was directing the children who were pulling on the line to the spreader. No one could hear anyone, and everyone was giving orders. Not even hand signals were getting through.

I saw all this from the *Lili Aikane* as the government schooner's power launch took off to the rescue. It looked like a bright, beautiful, but very bad dream.

It was all over before I had finished rowing in.

There was a tremendous cheer and a roaring of motors. I looked over my shoulder and saw the Chinois Bleu's launch taking off to starboard and the government launch taking off to port. The crew on the pier pulled and tipped the *Aikane* about thirty degrees from the perpendicular. And she slid! Slowly, but surely, as the two powerboats pulled at her stern, she slid free of the sand!

A second round of cheering echoed off the rocks like cannon, and ten dozen children dived from the pier and swam for the boat.

When we finally got anchored at the old mooring, rewarded the last rescuer with a cookie or a couple of dried prunes (the best items we could find for that purpose) Jack and I put on masks and snorkels and went under to see what damage, if any, had been done to the hull. There was nothing that showed. Jack was slow to accept the evidence: it was always possible that the strain would cause leaks to appear later on, but the chances were good that the worst strain was to our collective self-esteem. Nothing that couldn't be patched up once we got away from the scene of our *gaffe*.

Norris *et cie.* arrived just as dark fell.

They had been to Taipivai, not to Anaho, after all, following the trail, instead of Melville and Toby's route. They had had a wonderful time and were justifiably pleased with themselves. The *chef* of Taipivai had treated them like invited guests, housed them in a vacant school, and sent food for their supper. One of the girls from the *lycée* introduced them to the Marquesan widow of a famous American archaeologist, and she took them on a tour of the great stone ruins of the temple enclosure that Melville saw in use a little over a century ago. . . .

> . . . Here and there in the depths of these awful shades, half screened from sight by masses of overhanging foliage, rose the idolatrous altars of these savages, built of enormous blocks of black and polished stone, placed one upon another, without cement, to the height of twelve or fifteen feet, and surmounted by a rustic open temple, enclosed with a low picket of canes, within which might be seen, in various stages of decay . . . the putrefying relics of some recent sacrifice. . . .

The only price they paid for the adventure was a dreadful set of *no-no* bites. There seemed to be more of these almost invisible little gnats in Taipivai than in Taiohae. Melville also reported on them in *Typee*, and it would seem that in his time they didn't raise welts. They have learned a trick or two in the intervening century.

Our farewells to Taiohae were very emotional, considering that we had been there only ten days and had known most of our friends less than a week. The Le Bougets and the other teacher from the *lycée*, Dr. Chastenet, Norris's Danish friends, the crews of the *Lizard*, *Breeze III*, and the *Magnolia* (another sloop that had arrived from California only the night before)—they all came down to say good-bye, to give and sometimes to receive a *kaoha* gift, or to give us an errand to do at some port farther along. There was even a letter addressed to the daughter of an American family on the ketch *Tangaroa*, which might possibly be in Papeete when we got there.*

Marie Salomé brought as her gift neither fruit nor flowers nor shells but a piece of paper on which she had labored hard. She presented it as gravely as if it were a white magic that, properly used, might overcome the black magic of time and space: her name and complete address, carefully written out in French.

The last new friend we made was old Taniha Taupotini, the full-blooded Marquesan *chef*. As we chatted about the problem of the vicious *no-nos*, I remembered an article in the *Scientific American* about a new way to eliminate noxious insects without wrecking the ecology of an area. I promised to send a copy when I got back to the States. Taniha thanked me courteously, but he could not resist expressing some cynicism. A number of Americans had promised to send aids of different sorts—some writings, some chemicals, or other devices—but quite possibly the French had confiscated them at the post office in Papeete. How else was one to explain that none had ever arrived?

* It wasn't, but we eventually caught up with the *Tangaroa* in the harbor of Hawaii—proving that the Pacific is smaller than one might assume.

The Hop to Hiva Oa

We didn't sail at dawn after all.

We had to wait nearly an hour for the vegetable man to arrive (by outrigger) from Taipivai with our order of perishables. A fisherman in another outrigger came by and sold us some beautiful red fish that we had for breakfast, while we waited. Just as we finished the last filet, the vegetables arrived: lettuce, leeks, tomatoes, and mangoes in different stages of ripeness.

As we got the sail up and caught the morning breeze, Jack rigged a new and quite heavy nylon line with a steel leader and a big red feather lure—gifts from Jean Pierre Chastenet, who had assured Jack it was impossible to miss at least one tuna in the channel between Nuku Hiva and Ua Pou. We missed. But no one really minded, especially she who would have had to cook and can anything we caught.

It was a lovely morning's sail—what we would have called a day's sail in the old days of Sunday sailing at home. We crossed the channel between the two islands, and coasted down the western shore of Ua Pou, marveling at the gray stone sugar loafs along the water's edge, as dramatic as the obelisks of the interior.

The bay we had chosen (at the advice of Captain Amaru) was on the lee (western) shore, and was considered the safest anchorage (in this weather), though not the most interesting of the settlements on the island. But after the sheltered waters of Taiohae, Hakamaii looked appallingly exposed.

We anchored anyway, at what seemed to be a safe distance from the rocky beach, which was constantly washed by surges that would have smashed the fiber-glass hull of the *Lili Aikane*. Or so Jack thought. It was hot, and before long a swarm of flies had found us; not the sneaky, almost invisible *no-nos* that bit without your knowing and annoyed you only several hours after the fact. These were big, buzzing, black "house" flies, and they annoyed me so that I took my spear gun and went skin diving, breaking the rule about never going alone, in the expectation that Benson would be along in the *Lili Aikane* long before I had any catch to stow.

The water was warm and much clearer than at Taiohae, and the underwater scenery was magnificent. The big rock that gave what little shelter the harbor had dropped perpendicular and sharp edged as far down as I could see. It had obviously been fractured longitudinally in some volcanic upheaval, recent enough so that the action of the current on the break was negligible. And it was quite a current! Not even the silver envelope-shaped fish could swim against it. Shoals of them were swept around it, as I watched, first in one direction, then in another. A cluster of wine-colored sea urchins clung as close as possible to the edge, apparently enjoying the combing of their spiny coif-

View of the island of Ua Pou.

fures. But even they wobbled now and then when a big surge came.

I found a more propitious hunting ground and began to dive for dinner. There wasn't much to shoot at, and my aim was very bad indeed. For one thing, the water here seemed to be saltier than at home. I was too buoyant; it took a lot of finning to get down, and only one stupid perch failed to spook in time. Not enough for *sashimi*, let alone the main course! And when I came up and looked for Benson, I could see the *Lili Aikane* still bobbing alongside the big *Aikane*. The shark fisherman of Taiohae had warned us about swimming in these waters with a bleeding fish anywhere on one's person, and Dr. Chastenet had showed us the plastic surgery he had performed a year earlier on the shoulder of the supercargo of the *Taporo*, who had done just that.

So I swam all the way back to the boat, holding my ridiculous little fish high out of the water on the end of my spear. It was not only tiring, but embarrassing.

Back aboard, things were going from bad to worse in the fly department. There was no acceptable solution as yet to the problem of getting ashore: Jack refused to risk the dinghy (we had forgotten all about the inflatable rubber life raft we carried, which would have been great), and swimming was out if we wanted to shop and bring back the results. A man in an outrigger had come by and tried to make "some sort of a deal," but no one could understand him. There was something about him that suggested illicit enterprise, and Jack had a hunch he was offering to trade a ride in to shore for something. Ammunition? We had already been warned that this is more dangerous than trading hard liquor, if one is caught by the French.

The temptation is greater, even from a moral standpoint. The embargo on ammunition seems pointless and cruel. The only way the Marquesan can get the meat that runs free in his hills, and sometimes denudes them, is to shoot at it. Or to revert to the practice of his ancestors and run wild goats over the cliffs—which sometimes results in the mutual destruction of hunter and hunted. We had heard yachting parties of several nationalities defend their smuggling on the grounds that they were restoring the

Marquesans' "natural rights," but they always spoiled the effect by adding, in a casual parenthesis, that there is no item of trade goods that will get you better value for your investment. Not even American cigarettes!

Jack had made it clear at the start of the voyage that he was not going to smuggle anything, and now he was trying to make it clear to the outrigger man. It was rough going in sign language, and I was expected to do better in French. But the man either spoke none or didn't recognize mine. He was getting a little irritable, too. Norris suggested that if we wanted to use him as a taxi—and there was no alternative in sight—we had better go now, pay later. Surely there would be someone in the settlement back in the valley who could understand either English, my French, or Norris's new Marquesan, and help us work out an equitable arrangement.

We agreed—although it passed through my mind that we might very well get ashore and find ourselves blackmailed about the return trip.

It was possible to pantomime the request that he ferry us in, and the outrigger man acceded. His canoe was the first absolutely "authentic" one we had got close to, and the ride was worth it for that alone. There was not a nail or even a wooden peg in the whole structure: the hull was carved from a single tree trunk, beautifully shaped on the outside, but very crudely dug out inside, with simple thwarts for seats. The outrigger, which was supposed to keep it from tipping, was a pointed log, braced against the hull by two naturally curved branches, lashed with dried vines. It was a lot less stable than it looked, but the sulky owner was a marvelous paddler. He got us all ashore, one at a time, and only ground his hull against the barnacles of the beach boulders once.

The problem of making a date (and a price) for the return trip was postponed, and we started up the road with an uncomfortable feeling of kinship with many early invaders, including Captain Cook. (If the outrigger man and a party of his friends were convinced that there was ammo on the *Aikane*, what was to prevent them hijacking her? And/or putting us where we could tell no tales? There was no visible authority figure here. No French flag . . . no uniformed gendarme . . . no way of sending for the Marines.)

Our paranoia faded with time, but Hakamaii did not grow more attractive. The valley itself was lovely—a steep-sided ravine down which a clean stream rushed. But there was no wind to disperse the humidity or the flies, and both were oppressive. There was no one who spoke any language we could speak. The people looked drab, although healthier than at Taiohae. There were no bright pareus, only dull-colored, shapeless cotton shifts, possibly the influence of the Protestant mission, whose pastor is said to be Hawaiian, and very devout. (He was not there when we were, and the church was locked.) There were more front teeth in evidence, which may have been due to the lack of a Chinese merchant and therefore of candy and bubble gum.

The item we most wanted to buy on Ua Pou was carved *tou* wood, preferably in the shape of bowls. We tried asking, and gesturing, and got one nibble: a very eager seller who kept repeating a word that sounded like "plate." We followed him to his atelier, which was halfway up the side of the ravine, and discovered that he was the baker. "Plate" meant "bread." He was very proud of the product and the word. "Speek Meecan," he kept saying. We ordered six loaves from the gray mass that was rising in the trough, and started back toward the beach.

On the way we passed a building we had not seen before: a frame house, painted white, and looking so prosperous that it seemed it must either belong to some sort of official (in which case we ought to present our passports and papers) or to a merchant prince—perhaps the carver of bowls.

We mounted the steps and passed through the bead curtain that served as a door. The front room was small and full of sales items: most of them canned fish of Japanese origin. There were bolts of dark cloth, lamp chimneys, assorted fishing tackle, rope, but no carved wood. And no merchant. From somewhere farther within there were sounds of conversation—unintelligible—and another bead-curtained door led in that direction.

I stepped through—and backed out fast.

The room was small and lined with shelves on which there

were more cans, boxes, and jars (no carved wood). But in the very center of the floor, on a thin pallet, was a very, very old woman, so emaciated I thought for a moment she was dead. Her mouth was open, and as I stared, I heard her draw one short gasping breath.

(This was not the only instance we saw of the Polynesian indifference to old people which is the other side of the coin of the prevailing cult of baby worship. Hélène Le Bouget told us that the ties of affection seem to reach down only, that is, toward the new generation, never back toward the old. Dr. Chastenet's comment on that was: "Why not? Parents do nothing for their children. They wander where they like, live with whomever they like, grow up and take care of themselves. Why should they have feeling for their parents?" And yet, Marie Salomé and Anna had to fight back tears when they spoke of their dead mother. Perhaps it is no easier to fit personal affection into societal patterns here than in the West.)

We met the baker and the outrigger man on the beach, and haggled out some sort of bargain. The baker didn't want money! He wanted the T-shirt off Benson's back, and he got it. The outrigger man indicated that he would settle for the hunting knife (from Herter's of Minnesota) at Benson's waist. That being out of the question, he went back to his original demand. With the help of the baker's Meecan, we finally made out that he wanted whiskey or cartridges. Jack had been right.

What really tied it was that after he had accepted money (at a rate roughly equivalent to one loaf of bread per person per trip), he went back to town and fetched the gendarme, who spoke enough French to let us know that we had violated regulations by failing to report our arrival to him. He couldn't or wouldn't understand that we had tried to find him, and failed. Who knows how it would have ended if we hadn't remembered the arrival at Taiohae and the diplomatic power of California Mountain White.

The gendarme's and even the outrigger man's annoyance dissipated so speedily that they ended up giving us all lessons in Basic Marquesan. Norris, who had a real talent for languages, acquired enough of a vocabulary to keep us out of any serious trouble in the rest of the islands. But as far as we were concerned, Ua Pou had had its chance, and failed.

Not all Pacific islands are paradise to all comers.

Jack could hardly wait for eggs and coffee next morning in his haste to be away before the sun and the flies got up to full strength.

We coasted along another stretch of lee shore, heading for another point where Dr. Chastenet had assured Jack it was impossible to miss a tuna. As we hit the place he had marked on the chart, something hit our line, and it snapped. Another lure and leader gone!

The wind hit us at the same instant, and everything that wasn't double-pinned to the lifelines went, including Benson's straw hat and swimming trunks.

A few minutes later the shackle pin broke on the leech end of the main, and all hands were required to rig a temporary line to hold it in place. All the ties (that hold the main to the brass slides that hold it to the mast) were frayed, and several wore through during the next few hours. But there was nothing we could do about them for the time being.

The "day-sail" to Hiva Oa, which was supposed to be a rest after the all-but-sleepless night at Hakamaii, turned into a waking nightmare. For the first time on the voyage we were "beating" —and now I knew why it was called that! A stiff southeast wind was working itself into a storm. And our course lay almost straight into it.

Sailing close-hauled, we could get the *Aikane* up to three knots, on course. By falling off about thirty degrees, we could manage five and a half knots, but that was going to mean a long tack back to make port at Hanamenu, which was our destination on the north coast of Hiva Oa. There weren't quite enough daylight hours for us to make it at this speed. At least that's what Benson figured. But then he was seasick. Jack disagreed, and he was a bit disagreeable about it.

I was not seasick but I was afraid to go below and fix lunch. Even Norris was unwilling to make the effort to put peanut butter on a cracker. Besides, everyone was busy, either holding the wheel (which was such hard work that I had to use my feet as well as my hands) or hunting for a place that was level enough to sit on and out of both sun and wind. The former was lethally bright, and the latter chilling. We were all wet with spray and covered with goose bumps and conscious that we were getting sunburns that were going to be painful later on.

As the sun began to drop, we strained our eyes for some clue that would mark Hanamenu on the coastline ahead. (We had not been out of sight of land, but even now we weren't close enough to make out harbor mouths.) Jack and Norris had taken noon shots and were taking line-of-position shots and advancing themselves on paper all afternoon, but what we saw never seemed to match what they had on the plotting sheet.

Then, just about sunset, suddenly there was a channel in the center of what had looked to be a solid land mass! It was not one island, but two! Hiva Oa lay to port, and to starboard was its sister, Tahu Ata, separated from it by a strait that narrowed down to a couple of miles at one point. We were several miles off course to starboard!

It was easy to understand the error—Jack had forgotten to check with his wind and current chart, which showed a strong set to the west here (reinforced on this particular day by the oncoming southeast storm). The choice between alternatives that now faced us was not so easy.

We could come about and sail for Hanamenu on a starboard tack with the wind abeam, but we couldn't make port by daylight. There were two other ports, one on Tahu Ata and one on the channel side of Hiva Oa, both of which were closer, but neither of which could be reached before dark. Traitors' Bay (the Hiva Oa port) was the larger and more sheltered anchorage, and our chart showed that it had a harbor light (though we had learned at Taiohae not to count on such lights always being lit in these parts).

The other alternative was to stand offshore and wallow around all night in the trough of the seas, which were beginning to build up now. We would have to stand well offshore to be safe, and would doubtless be blown even farther off, if the wind persisted. We might even wake up tomorrow to find that there weren't enough hours of daylight to make it into any harbor in the teeth of an adverse wind.

Jack made his decision: to try for Traitors' Bay. He was grumpy and defensive, partly because he was breaking his rule about not making port in a strange place after dark, and partly because he had insisted until the moment the channel opened up that we were heading straight for Hanamenu. Benson was so delighted with the prospect of something "out of the ordinary" that he forgot about his *mal de mer*. Norris was very quiet, and so was I. But once the decision was made, all reservations about its wisdom were so completely suppressed that they might as well have never been. The efficiency level went up on a steep curve.

The men started on a cooperative calculation: measuring the distance from a bearing we would take as we actually entered the channel to the point at which we must make a sharp left turn into the narrow mouth of Traitors' Bay. The distance (on the chart) was then divided by our speed. The motor was going now, so the speed could be considered constant. Watches were synchronized, and as darkness closed in, Jack ordered every light aboard out—except for our red and green navigation lights. (By rights we should have had the masthead light on too, but we were all straining our eyes to see into the dark, and it would have blinded us.)

I had scrounged a cold supper during the calculating, and served it as we went along. One tray to Norris on bow watch for floating obstacles such as outriggers without lights. One to Jack at the wheel. One to Benson, who was matching the directions in the *Coast Pilot* and the chart to what we could see on the shore . . . until we could no longer see anything.

The water was very quiet in the channel—almost too quiet. The silence was getting oppressive. I would have played some music or the radio, but with the motor going they couldn't be heard. And the minutes were ticking away. An hour and ten minutes at six knots and we would make the turn! Then, if we were at the place we ought to be, and if we made the right number of degrees of turn and held our course true for half an hour, we should be safe in a small cove on one side of the Atuona light.

If we made a mistake, we'd be on the rocks.

It was dark enough now for stars to show at the zenith. But clouds masked the lower reaches of the sky. Land had disappeared on both sides of us. The darkness was pitchy. I took the wheel for a few minutes while Jack went to check some calculations with Benson. There was nothing to do but hold and stare at the floating numbers on the compass face, red now instead of white. . . . Time dragged so that I couldn't keep silent.

"Are you sure we haven't gone too far? What's the time now?"

It was just about right. Jack gave it an extra five minutes. Then he made the turn.

We watched the compass till it read what had been calculated as the final course, then looked ahead. Blackness. Silence. And then—from Norris on the bow came a shout:

"I think that's it! Dead ahead! The Atuona light!"

It was too good to be true, and I didn't really feel better for it. What if it were not *that* light, but some other? A house with an electric system? A car parked on a cliff? I kept my doubts to myself this time, but I went up on the bow and watched with Norris. We were close to a shore on the port side. We could hear water roaring against rocks. And once a light showed on that side.

"Someone's trying to signal us," Norris said. But we couldn't figure out why, and the light flashed only once more before we passed it.

The faint light still glowed in the right place ahead.

"Can you see anything?" Jack called, over the engine noise.

"Just the light."

"Keep looking. There's a big rock—a small island, really—plunk in the middle of this approach. We want to take it on our port. But we'll have to pass pretty close. If we give it too wide a berth, we'll run up on the rocks on that side."

Benson brought up a big portable lamp that we had been saving for this sort of emergency, and shone it in the direction of the expected rock island, but its beam died before reaching anything. We could hear surge breaking all around us, and knew that some of the sound must be echo. I understood now why people don't like to make new ports in the dark. If it had been up to me, I'd have dropped anchor right there, and sat it out till dawn.

Suddenly, the rock loomed up, right where it should have been, abeam of us, to port.

In another ten minutes we were dropping our bow anchor in a sheltered place right at the foot of the rock on which the harbor beacon gleamed. We put out a stern anchor, too, and went to bed and to sleep.

Atuona

When we woke in the morning, we found that we had anchored right in the mouth of the little bight of Tahauku, which lies to the south of the bay and settlement of Atuona. Tahauku has traditionally (at least since the time of O'Brien) been used for the disembarking of passengers, and there are two "landing stages" (slippery, wave-washed steps) cut into the face of the cliff that defines each end of the bight. (Cargo is run through the surf, on to the black beach of Atuona, because the road in from Tahauku is too long a haul.)

On the headland that separates the bay from the bight stood the beacon that had guided us in, a kerosene lantern in a wooden box, with a dirty four-inch lens. (Incidentally, it was never lighted again during the week or more that we stayed in port.) While we were inching closer to the headland, feeling for an anchorage, we were hailed by a voice that was unmistakably American. Its owner was standing on the road, just under the beacon, giving us advice that made good sense: that is, to get well inside the bight, anchor, and row in to the quiet little beach at the far end.

"You'll have a longer walk to town, but you won't get tossed around by the surge or bumped when the *Taporo* comes in and moors."

Our mentor, whom we eventually caught up with on the road to Atuona, turned out to be an ex-photographer for the *Chicago Tribune*, now a resident of a small valley on the island of Tahu Ata just across the way. His name was Tom Graham and he was married to what sounded like a "laborneck." While we were trying to make out whether this term referred to an

Temetiu Mountain at Atuona, Hiva Oa.

occupation or a bloodline, Tom led us along the road at a pace that left us all breathless and unable to interrupt his monologue even with pertinent questions.

There was a lot of useful information in that monologue, but it came so fast and in such disconnected snatches that we weren't able to absorb it all. There were several references to O'Brien that we were too ignorant to catch, but I got the impression that he was telling us that his wife (who was "a great girl") was related to a character known as Malicious Gossip. Next he was telling us that the road down which we were walking was Gauguin's favorite evening walk during his last days here. It was certainly a painter's view: the sweep of lacy surf fanning out on the black sand, the lush forest hiding the houses in the valley except for the white cathedral tower, and behind it the mist-shrouded column of Temetiu, mottled in dull grays, greens, and blues, with streaks of white—waterfalls threading down from the cloud and disappearing into the dark forests at the mountain's foot.

"How strange that Gauguin never painted the view," I said aloud.

"Maybe he did," said Tom. "They burned most of his canvases after he died. Same in Tahiti. You go look in the Gauguin Museum they just built there, and you won't find a single original. Auctioned them off for a couple of bucks or burned them up!"

And then we were passing the first of the houses of the town—capital of the southern group of the Marquesas, and perhaps the oldest French settlement in the whole archipelago. It seemed to have no more shape or cohesion than Taiohae.

"That's the house of the *chef*," Tom said without slowing his pace. "I'll introduce you to him later. After you've checked in with the gendarme. Very nice fellow. [It wasn't clear which he meant, but in view of what we later learned about his relations to French officialdom, it seems likely it was the *chef*.] The baker is a Chinese, but not bad, and his oven is built right over the place where Gauguin had his house. Nothing left of it, of course. But you can go up to the cemetery and see his grave, if you're interested."

In front of the stucco bungalow that housed the *gendarmerie* (two uniformed functionaries and one civilian aide who watered the flowers), Tom left us. He had some errands to do. If we wanted to do any food shopping, he commended us to the *chef*. An introduction was not really necessary. If our other errands could wait, he would be at our disposal later in the day and all day tomorrow.

"I just want to get off a radiogram to that damned *Taporo* and find out when Tei's sister and the little girl are due in. If Amaru is fooling around picking up copra in Hanamenu, Ye-Ye may just ride over the mountains and pick them up. Wonderful fellow, Ye-Ye. I'll introduce you to him later."

When we had signed the necessary forms and been officially stamped at the *gendarmerie*, we wandered for an hour or so up and down the roads of Atuona, which did not seem to follow any recognizable plan but which were all bordered by walls! Some of stone, others of blooming shrubs, and at least one by a wooden picket! It had been longer than we realized since we had seen such symbol of private ownership of the surface of the earth. It looked slightly obscene.

Otherwise it was a lovely "town," made up of larger stucco bungalows than we had yet seen, some of them with pleasant frame verandas, and all surrounded by magnificent trees—breadfruit, mango, golden flamboyant, avocado, strange hardwoods, and palm. The gardens were planted with *tiare tahiti* bushes, many showy varieties of hibiscus, plumeria, and canna lilies—the standard decoration of hospital grounds in the American Middle West in my childhood, which here grew lush and exotically beautiful.

We stopped in at the *chef*'s and transacted a most unusual piece of business. Eggs were expensive (sixty francs a dozen), small and of varied hues, but chickens were cheap: twenty-five francs apiece (in the feather)! We ordered a couple, and asked to have them plucked and dressed. When the *chef* got what we meant, and was finally convinced that none of us could (or would) do the job, he expressed his willingness to oblige. But he had no idea what to charge. He had never done such a thing —except for himself, for free. I offered twenty-five francs apiece. He refused to accept it. Finally we settled on twenty-five francs for the pair, but he was not comfortable about it, so we ended up with a gift of about twenty-five pounds of produce: breadfruit, mangoes, avocados, and bananas. Also the basket in which to carry away the loot.

The errands that we postponed till our second day were two: I wanted to buy, or acquire by any means possible, a dress or a muumuu with nice safe shoulders. (I had given up on pareus. They were just not practical for a woman of my age and shape,

Woman ironing at Atuona.

either to work aboard or to wear comfortably ashore.) And Benson wanted to consult with the local educational authorities about interviews with their teen-age students.

Tom Graham didn't put in an appearance in the morning, so we decided to try it on our own. I had been told that the *bonnes soeurs* of the convent school taught needlework to their charges, and I thought perhaps I might be able to hire the services of an apprentice dressmaker, or arrange to use a cutting table and sewing machine to remodel my pareu myself. The public school lay in the same direction as the convent, so Benson came along with me. So did Jack, who had never been inside a convent, and was curious.

The three of us were received by Madame, *la mère supérieure,* a stout Breton lady of such presence that she made me feel quite sheepish about the trivial nature of my errand. Somehow in my stammering introduction of my two companions and my attempt to explain what we were all doing in her domain, I conveyed the impression that Benson wanted to interview some of her students in connection with his *études psychologiques.* Mme. la Mère asked what it was that monsieur was interested in learning about her charges.

Benson said later that if he had understood the question, he would have backed off then and there. He could have guessed the sort of answers he would get from the *jeunes filles* of this *internat,* and was no more interested in them than he had been in the boys of the *internat* at Taiohae. But he didn't understand Mme. la Mère, and I was in too deep to get out unaided.

I explained that in the United States there was a group of educators who view the middle teens as "the troublesome age," and believe that its turbulence, rebellion, and anxiety are functions of normal human growth, whereas another group blames the troubles of our teen-agers on the society in which they are trying to grow up. Mme. la Mère interrupted to hazard a polite guess that monsieur belonged to the latter group of *psychologues.* I admitted it, and she signed to me to go on. It was hard to tell where she placed herself in this dichotomy.

Monsieur had brought with him a statistical study of the problems that a very large sampling of American youth *said* were concerns of theirs. Monsieur was hoping to compare this list with a list compiled from interviews with Marquesan young people, who—after all—came from an environment as different from urban America as it would be possible to find. He had already tried out the American list on the *lycée* students, who found most of them incomprehensible. And they had reported some concerns that might be hard to explain to American teen-agers. It had been *très intéressant*.

Mme. la Mère nodded slowly and was silent a moment. Then she asked if we would be so good as to discuss the matter in more detail with her cousin, a M. Plantec, who spoke English and would be better able to communicate with monsieur. M. Plantec was at this very moment conducting a class in English for the girls of the upper form. Would we be kind enough to follow her to his room?

We crossed a large close shaded by a huge old tree whose branches were hung with a strange fruit. On closer inspection it turned out to be baskets, plaited out of palm fronds. They were hung in all sorts of inaccessible places, including the far ends of the horizontal limbs. Mme. la Mère explained that each of the younger girls had her own basket, for carrying her clothes to and from the outdoor faucet that served as a laundry, or for gathering fruit or flowers or shells. The big tree was the equivalent of a locker room. Each child had her own special, inviolable twig.

The building in which the English class was going on was new. Its plywood walls were still unpainted, and bore the stamp of a lumber company in Coos Bay, Oregon! The coincidence seemed fantastic, but what didn't bear thinking of was cost—in money and energy—of bringing such coals to this well-wooded Newcastle.

M. Plantec suffered the interruption of his class with good grace. When all his pupils had risen, bowed, and said something like *"Bonjour, 'dame, 'sieurs, bonjour ma mère,"* he permitted them to sit again while he listened to Mme. la Mère's explanation of our request in French, and my explanation of Benson's work in English, and finally to Benson's further explanation in peda-guese. He looked grave. Finally, he suggested that Mme. la Mère conduct us to his home where Mme. Plantec would offer us some refreshment. He would join us within the hour.

We did as he suggested. It was very pleasant *chez* Plantec. Madame P. was a quietly pretty Parisian in her sixties, so well adapted to her role as the wife of a naval commander that it apparently mattered little where she performed it. An apartment in a faubourg of Paris or Marseille or Brest, government quarters in Algeria or Indo-China, or a termite-weakened bungalow in Hiva Oa—in any case she must make the interior comfortable, put up the colored photographs of children and grandchildren, and do something with the garden outside. She made us welcome, served us grapefruit juice, freshly squeezed by the girls on KP in the convent and noisy with ice, and told us a little about how she and her husband had come to this place. It was purely as a favor to Mme. la Mère, who needed someone to initiate a program for the study of English, for which as yet the order of teaching nuns was not ready to pay.

She was offering me a dress of her own, to use as the pattern of a muumuu, when M. Plantec arrived. He was still polite, but he knew what was up now. He explained with firmness (in English that was sagging as badly as my French) that his cousin was responsible for the spiritual welfare of her charges and that it was therefore necessary to be informed of the specific questions monsieur wished to ask. Would it be possible to submit a list?

Benson said it would not, because he had no idea what he was going to ask. It depended on what the girls said concerned or troubled them.

Ah! If that was all, it would not be necessary to speak with the girls at all. M. Plantec could himself assure us that they were not troubled. Their pure spirits were like flowers, and would remain so as long as they were in his cousin's charge.

At this point I tried backing off, but it was too late. M. Plantec asked if Benson had a letter of introduction that explained his mission. Benson said yes and fished it out. M. Plantec read it, frowning. His verdict was that it was bona fide. (That was good.) But it was from a secular authority. (That was not good.) However, the church, as represented by his cousin, had no objection to cooperation with secular authorities in any legitimate effort. And if our questions were legitimate, there should be no reason for not submitting them.

"I don't ask questions," Benson explained again. "I try to get the children to talk."

"About what?"

M. Plantec's nostrils were flaring as he sniffed for heresy. Surely monsieur understood that no letter from a secular official gave him the right to assume the role of a confessor and probe the consciences of these innocents!

It looked as if Benson would have to prove himself innocent or stand trial. We finally promised to make up a list of sample questions from the American study, which we offered for his inspection, but which he refused to read. We were asked to present ourselves at an hour in the morning which would give M. Plantec time to study the questions, translate them for his cousin, and come to a decision before his first class. It was going to mean starting from the *Aikane* with the dawn.

We did.

With a list which had nothing more provocative on it than a reference to "dating," we presented ourselves at the Plantecs' door in the very early morning. (I had been for removing even that question, but Benson had balked. If he was going to take the time to talk to the *internat* girls, it was going to have to be about something, and that was the only American "concern" the girls at Taiohae had understood.)

M. Plantec had neither shaved nor breakfasted, and he scowled as if he considered our promptness a discourtesy. He found and put on his glasses, ignored our explanation of how the questions were to be used, and sat down to read.

He didn't even get halfway down the list. "Totally unacceptable!" And he would tell us why. There were two objections: one was religious; the other, national. On the first question he began a condescendingly simplistic explanation of Catholic dogma on the confessional, drawing a parallel with the role of the Freudian analyst, and not omitting a reference to the couch that was obviously supposed to bring Benson to his knees. Benson protested that he was not a Freudian, but M. Plantec dismissed the disclaimer with scorn. Monsieur would have to take his word that the relationship between a *jeune fille* and her confessor was sacred. If it were profaned by one without spiritual training, indescribable harm might be done.

Now for Objection Number Two: the national question.

M. Plantec had all this time been controlling an anger too big for his valve system. Suddenly it blew. He lost his English and went for our national jugular veins in French.

I missed some of what followed, but I got plenty. I got, for instance, the line about "You Americans come with *les petits tests psychologiques* and zut! One has lost a country to you!" M. Plantec had seen it happen. He had been in Indo-China and in Algiers. "You have lost us both these countries," he shouted. "And Syria, too!" The Americans did their dirty work in these places under a banner of so revolting a hypocrisy that it was not to be endured! We criticized the French for exploitation and imperialism, while we had hands more dirtied by the treatment of our blacks! "I know these people [his browns, not our blacks]! I love them! I understand them! I have given my best years to them! I am here now with no thought to myself! You wish to tell me you will do more for them? I tell you it is a lie!"

We tried agreeing our way out. I managed to second his angry prophecy that the United States would learn a bitter lesson in Vietnam. Benson got in a word of agreement on the accusation that there was discrimination in the American South. But M. Plantec heard only the beating of rage in his own arteries. At last Mme. Plantec came in and sat down.

She said nothing, but her presence either calmed or embarrassed her husband. He finally ran out of accusations. Benson and I stood up. With as much dignity as I could scrape together after my scolding, I said we were sorry to have bothered him, that we were not C.I.A. agents, but precisely what our letter of introduction said we were, and that we hoped he would convey our regrets to his cousin.

On the way back to the boat, we met some boys who were obviously going to school, and Benson decided to go with them. The public school was where he had intended to do his work in the first place, and he was sure he could manage without an interpreter, or at least without one who involved him in the conflict between Church and State.

I walked on up the road that led around the headland toward Tahauku, and got there just in time to see the *Taporo* drop anchor and send her longboat in with a load of passengers.

Among those who waited on the rocky landing stage to embrace the new arrivals was the American, Tom Graham. He apologized for not having been able to assist us yesterday. "But Ye-Ye decided to ride over the mountain, and the whole family was upset. They were afraid he was going to beat up Amaru—start a feud that would take God knows how long to die out! That's the way these natives are, you know! But it's turned out all right. There he is—just getting into the longboat. That's his wife he's helping in now. My wife's sister. Wonderful girl! I'll introduce you to the whole family, once things get settled down again."

By this time I had reread enough of *White Shadows in the South Seas* to follow Tom better than I had the first time. Laborneck I now knew was Le Brunnec, a Breton trader who had befriended O'Brien during his stay in Atuona and who had subsequently married a Marquesan lady named Tahiapii (At Peace), sister to Tavahi (Malicious Gossip) who was a leading character in *White Shadows* as well as *Atolls of the Sun*. Tom was married to the oldest of the Le Brunnec daughters, Tei, who had mothered the rest of the brood when At Peace died. The youngest of the girls was married to Ye-Ye, son of the *ex-chef* and *fils adoptif* of the present one—an incredibly handsome brown giant who could have been type-cast for Tarzan. The other Le Brunnec girls were living dramatically unhappy lives in such places as Tahiti and Ua Huka (the island we sighted first). One of the two sons was dead, and the other lived with Old Dad, at a house up the valley from the little beach where Tom had told us to park the *Lili Aikane*.

We were invited to pay a call there any afternoon. "You want to talk to Dad while he's still sharp," Tom said. "His mind is clear as a bell, you know, but he's failing. Has to take a nap every day and can't ride a horse into town."

Tom and Tei did not live *chez* Le Brunnec; they were only visiting. Their home was on the island of Tahu Ata, across the channel. They had been to Tahiti (to get Tom a medical checkup and new glasses, while Tei visited one of her sisters). They were on their way home, but had not yet been able to arrange for a boat to take them on the last lap. "I'm going to work on Amaru," Tom said. "There's no copra crop to pick up over there, but it wouldn't put him out very much. And the way he's been zigzagging around this neighborhood—as far as the Tuamotus and back, just to pick up a dozen sacks!—that's what made Ye-Ye so mad, you know! He's been expecting Jeanette and the little girl every day for three weeks! One day Amaru radios that he's coming in day after tomorrow! Next thing you know, it's off because he's got wind of some cargo in Taiohae!

"Well, it wouldn't hurt him to do us a favor. Not that I cut any ice around here, but the Labornecks are very powerful. In with the natives as well as the French! And the Church, too!"

It bothered me a little that Tom used the word "native" as he did. I had been trying to discourage it in our own ménage on the grounds that it had a condescending connotation. (For some reason *indigène* never sounded so bad, but perhaps it was.) Norris now argued that it couldn't be a "put down" because Tom was not only married to "one," but obviously liked "them" a lot. It did seem that twelve years of living in a predominantly Marquesan milieu should have taught even an ex-news photographer acceptable manners. It was a puzzle, but only one of many about Tom Graham that closer acquaintance eventually resolved.

It took us longer than we intended to get around to the visit to the Le Brunnecs because Benson really lucked into something at the public school. The schoolmaster, Guy Rauzi, was a man after Benson's own heart: the son of an Alsatian father and a Tahitian mother, he was nevertheless a "native" Hiva Oan. He had been born in a house we could see from the boat, and although he had been sent away for his education, he had come home to put it to use. Full of energy and practical sense, he ran the school like an athletic coach whipping a team into shape for a big game—and ran the soccer team that was competing for the interisland cup as if he were preparing a home guard for national defense.

He understood Benson's project well enough to set up precisely the sort of conditions needed to get the maximum information in the minimum time. The graduating class of four-teen-year-old boys was given *congé* for an entire afternoon and sent to meet us on the Tahauku beach, where they swam for almost an hour and rough-housed with Benson until they had no shyness left. Guy's brother, Maxim (a radio operator in the French navy, home on furlough, with a magnificent New Caledonian *vahine* in tow) joined us to facilitate communication, for it turned out that the boys did not really understand or speak French very well. (I translated Benson's English into French that Maxim translated into Marquesan. It was slow, but it worked better than the more direct approach.)

We learned many things that afternoon, but the most important for Benson's purpose came as a result of a question of his which began something like this: "Suppose you were to find yourself an orphan tomorrow—no parents, no family of any kind to look after you—do you think you could make it on your own?" Maxim had to do more than translate this because the lack of living parents doesn't "orphan" a Marquesan teen-ager as it would an American. But when the boys got the central idea—absolute independence, economic as well as emotional, tomorrow!—they all nodded. One spoke. Then another. More nodding.

"They say yes," Maxim reported. "They could live well enough."

"Ask them how they would go about it—as specifically as they can put it."

Maxim translated. There was a silence. He prodded with a short question. One boy said a single word, and shrugged. Maxim must have told a joke, for they all laughed. Then the whole group seemed to catch fire. They talked louder, interrupted each other, made clearly boastful gestures, and in short gave every evidence of complete, joyful self-confidence.

Maxim waited till the excitement died down. "They say they can make a house if they can get a knife and a hatchet. One of them has both. Many have only one or the other. They argue about who will lend!

"The rest is not hard. For wood they can cut down coconut trees that no longer bear. Make pillars for the roof. There is plenty of bamboo for the taking. Weave walls. Get pandanus for thatch."

"Can they do all those things?" Benson asked.

Maxim shrugged. "If not, they can learn. One boy has already made such a house on the beach."

"How about food?"

"One says he can make a canoe for fishing in the channel. Also, they can hunt goat."

"Without a gun?"

"We do that for sport here," Maxim said. "Chase them off the cliffs, while someone waits in a canoe below."

"They don't need any money at all?" I asked, remembering Marie Salomé.

"They can cut copra and earn what they need."

"Do you believe what they are saying?" Benson asked Maxim.

The young man thought a while. "Maybe they talk big," he said at last. "But I believe they can, if they must."

Benson had one more question. "You know what we mean by juvenile delinquency? Is there any of it here?"

Maxim knew the term because he had often heard it used in Papeete (in English, since the French choose to regard it as an American phenomenon). He did not think there was any of it in Atuona. "Maybe sometimes a boy is in trouble with the gendarmes—one who likes the girls too much, or one who plays tricks and makes some man angry. You know? But not all the time, and not together, in *bandes*. That I have seen in Papeete, and in Marseille."

"These boys are going to graduate in a week or so. Not many of them will go on to school, as I understand it." Benson paused for Maxim's confirming nod. "What will they do when they get out of school?"

"They say they will do just what they have been telling you."

"They will leave home?"

Maxim nodded. "That is the big trouble here. When the boy finishes school, the father thinks: 'Now I will get him to work —cut copra, mend the house, do other hard jobs.' But the boy says: 'No. I have been in school too long. Now it is time to rest.' He goes away—maybe to Hanamenu, maybe to some other island; maybe he lives in the mountains with his *copains*. His father is angry, but what can he do?"

"When do the boys settle down, or do they?"

Maxim smiled. "When they get married. Or have baby."

All this checked out with Benson's conviction that much of the conflict between adolescents and adults in our society is rooted in the youngsters' feelings of dependence and of uselessness. As our schools and colleges act more and more as a way of delaying the entrance of youth into a labor market where they would compete with their fathers for a declining number of jobs, the youth feel more and more unessential, unwanted, overlooked. Their delinquency—especially in its violent forms —is a way of establishing an identity, a negative one being better than no identity at all.

Atuona and all the other Marquesan communities we visited offered another prospect to boys on the threshold of manhood: the challenge of taking the giant step unaided and uninhibited as soon as one is ready, to be self-supporting and self-reliant, beholden to no one at the age when formal education stops.

We spent another wonderful afternoon with the Rauzi brothers at a fête Guy and his wife arranged in honor of Maxim and his *vahine*—a sort of farewell, as the furlough was drawing to a close.

The *pièce de résistance* was a whole calf, barbecued on a spit made of the limb of a tree stuck into the ground at one end, and braced against a forked limb at the other. We arrived after most of the other guests, but Guy was still carving. He waved to us with his weapon—an extremely long, thin knife, with which he could work without burning his hands, although the fire was still bright under the carcass. We approached, picked out the portion we preferred, and were served; the meat was not done by our standards, but it was tender; the sauce was good, and we liked the baked plantains that substituted for potatoes or breadfruit.

The real treat of the repast was Mme. Rauzi's version of *poisson cru*. Every island (and perhaps every good cook on every island) has a different version of this Polynesian delicacy, but this was as good as any we ever tasted:

POISSON CRU (RAW FISH) RAUZI

> **Bite-size tidbits of a tender white-meated fish**
> **Raw scallions**
> **Tomatoes**
> **Tiny raw shrimp, shelled**

The tomatoes and scallions were chopped a little finer than

---

the fish, and the shrimp were shelled. Everything was marinated in lemon juice for a couple of hours. An hour before serving, coconut "cream" * was poured over the mixture, which was then chilled.

There were about fifty guests in all at the fête, but the religious contingent (M. the priest, Mme. *la mère supérieure*, and the two Plantecs) left soon after eating, and Guy himself had to be excused to supervise soccer practice. Many of the older guests drifted off to watch from the sidelines. Soon all that were left, besides the clean-up crew in the kitchen, were the playboy and bunny set—and the four of us.

There was Maxim and his *vahine*, who looked like a dark mahogany mannequin, dressed for photographers from *Vogue*. (Maxim apparently had no intention of marrying this regal beauty, but he was taking her to Paris with him when he reported for duty. We wondered how long it would take her to "better herself" there.) There was a French doctor, who looked like a young Maurice Chevalier, and was something of a *farceur*. His companion was a sophisticated Tahitian beauty, dressed in tight pink pants and a hand-painted silk blouse. There were a couple of unattached belles, also well but flashily dressed and coiffed, and a very good-looking young geologist-surveyor. And Norris, who was still looking forward to his first view of the *tamure*.

He must have asked if anyone could perform the dance, for

---

* Coconut cream is the one staple of the Polynesian diet that it is all but impossible to match at home. It is obtained by grating the meat of a fresh, ripe coconut in a certain fashion on a certain type of grater. In Melville's day it was a rowel cut out of mother-of-pearl; today most households use a steel one. An American food grater will *not* do the trick.

There is nothing to it if you know how to do it, and have a grating bench that will put your body in just the right position for the tearing motion that rips the meat the right way. Fifteen minutes of labor will get you a bowl of shreds that are already oozing juice. You can hurry the process by putting the shreds into a loosely woven cloth and twisting it till the cream runs.

But only if you have done it right! You can squeeze till your hands ache, and get not a spoonful if you haven't. The closest American equivalent of the real thing can be extracted from commercial shredded coconut by a food blender, after the meat has been soaked or simmered for an hour in cow's milk. But most commercial coconut is sweetened, and this spoils the cream for many purposes.

all at once Maxim began strumming the music on his guitar, and the doctor was staggering through a slightly comic version of the male role—a sort of Frenchified rumba, performed with knees deeply bent and pointed out. He invited each of the *vahines* to join him, and got gales of laughter but no takers. Finally he called for Philomène, the teen-age Cinderella who was helping Madame with the punch glasses in the kitchen.

It took a lot of coaxing, but eventually Philomène let herself be pushed into the salon. She was small, slender, darkskinned, with heavy dark hair, which she wore in a long braid, and she was dressed for kitchen duty in a plain blue skirt and a loose yellow blouse. She seemed to be protesting that this was no costume for the *tamure*, and at last someone gave her a large man's handkerchief, which she tied around her hips so that any movement they made would be clearly revealed. Then, with perfect gravity, she got two flowers from a vase and put them behind her right ear, slipped out of her thongs, and stood facing the doctor.

He was still clowning, but Philomène's dignity sobered him. He straightened his back in imitation of hers. Maxim tapped a commanding tattoo on the wood of his guitar, and began to play. Everyone clapped softly in time with the beat and sang the word *tamure* over and over again. No one was laughing by the time Philomène actually moved.

It began very quietly. Her torso was still erect and immobile, but her hands were beckoning in a graceful, inviting gesture. The doctor began his bent-knee approach. Her hips moved. It was unbelievable even when you saw it happen. They undulated in an arc that I can't describe. The movement was too fast for my eyes to follow. Fast, but not furious. Philomène's head and shoulders never moved.

As the intensity of the music increased, so did the speed of her convolutions. The doctor was doing his best, but it was not good enough. She smiled at him kindly, a little condescendingly. She was really not seeing him any longer. She was not even hearing Maxim. She was in another world of experience, perhaps the forgotten one in which the tatooed princesses danced before all the people in the firelight in the sacred groves.

It was so completely sexual a performance that it was quite

impersonal. And it was religious in a subtle, but unmistakable, way.

The next day we walked to Calvary in the rain.

Calvary is the cemetery where Gauguin is buried. We trudged up the muddy red clay road that winds around the hill behind the *gendarmerie*. It was sunny when we started, but twice on the way up we had to take shelter under the old mango trees, heavy with fruit, that mark the way like Stations of the Cross. Even so, we were drenched by the time we reached the cemetery gates.

Calvary is a dismal half-acre, fenced with worn white pickets. Graves are crowded so close together that it is hard to search for a particular one without walking on others. Most of the stones were cracked and overgrown by weeds, and the wooden markers, pitifully dilapidated. On one recent grave there were bouquets of withered flowers. Everywhere an air of weariness and neglect.

Near the entrance was a large excavation—too big for a single grave—with a temporary canopy of corrugated iron. A real downpour hit, and there was no other place to take shelter, so we jumped in. As we waited, silenced by the drumming of the rain on the iron over our heads, I thought about what I had read about the Marquesan penchant for preparing a funeral while the leading character is still around to enjoy the proceedings. Both O'Brien and Mrs. Handy have written of people who ordered their caskets well ahead of time and slept in them, not to mention the more common practice of superintending the digging of one's own grave. . . .

Marquesans fear the dead, but not death. It has always puzzled people of other cultures, including missionaries who are sometimes appalled by the literalness with which their converts take the promise of a better life hereafter. Some can hardly wait, and help things along! But it sometimes seemed to me that it was not so much the hope of heaven as the intolerable ennui of the present that moves them. All the Marquesans we met, except Marie Salomé, seemed to be suffering from a fatal anemia. A Navajo would have said of them that they were not in "good heart." And why should they be? Their culture is

dead: their art, their music, their sport, their vices and virtues,
their joys—their reasons for living have all been outlawed, by
Church or by State. They are responding to the new regime of
public health. There is no longer any danger of the physical
extinction of the race, which seemed a real possibility when
O'Brien was there. But so far no one seems to have found a
medicine that will keep their spirit alive.

Was the oversize grave in which we were sheltered a symbol
of this will to die? Had a whole family planned to expire
together, or in such rapid succession that a mass grave was the
most efficient way of dealing with the problem?

The rain and my revery came to a sudden end, and we went
back to our search for Gauguin's sepulcher, which we had been
told in Taiohae was the work of a leading contemporary French
architect-sculptor, and very fine.

Eventually we stumbled on it: a bulky stone blanket of dark
red rock, with the name PAUL GAUGUIN cut in simple letters at
the head—deep cut and filled with a curious pink plaster. It was
a disappointment, but it was certainly an improvement on the
bare cement oblong and poorly proportioned white marble slab
we had seen in a biography of Gauguin. In retrospect I like it
better than I did, for it seems a sort of Gauguinesque comment
on the bad taste of the other monuments. It is different from
every other in that solid mosaic of graves, and it is more in
harmony with the environment—the earth, the mountains, the sky
and sea, and the living people of the island—than anything built
since the ancient temples and *tikis* now dismantled and overgrown.

It was the beginning of the rainy season in Hiva Oa, and
we were always being drenched. One shower caught us on the
half-mile hike up the valley from the Tahauku beach. We
arrived for the much-postponed call on the Le Brunnecs, dripping and disheveled.

Tom was not at home, but would be very soon. Tei was in
the shower bath in the side yard, and called to the children (her
nieces and nephews) playing at the foot of the steps to take us
up to Papa. They led us to the steps, which were so termite-

eaten and so steep that I hesitated to trust myself to them.

"They will hold! Perhaps not for long, but at least for this season!" The voice spoke in accented but clear English.

I looked up and saw the ghost of Guillaume Le Brunnec, still more alive and vital than most of his peers in these parts would ever be. What a man he must have been in the fullness of his powers!

Probably he was never very big, physically, but he had shrunk so with age that the clothes he was wearing hung on him like hand-me-downs. His eyes were as blue as his baggy cotton pants; his hair was as white as his unironed but spotless shirt, and his neck and hands were red from the sun. His manner was cordial, but not effusive, and wryly humorous. His poise was profound, but not sophisticated. All that he was or knew was discoverable in short order, if one was interested enough to listen and observe. But it was not because he opened himself to strangers in the hope of gaining approval, friendship, or anything else. He was simply too old and too frail to shutter the windows of his self.

What he knew was considerable on almost any subject one could name. He subscribed to two newspapers, one Breton and one French, and although they arrived months late, he was at least as well informed as we on contemporary politics, European and Polynesian. Of America he knew little, since his friend O'Brien had stopped writing him. (One felt that this was one portion of the infinite variety of the world that he could afford to ignore, and did.) He was also well read on the geology of Hiva Oa, archaeology, anthropology, oceanography, meteorology, and ancient art. He had copies of the original reports of the Bishop Museum expedition—a collector's item in Honolulu or New York—and he left them on the porch table because he referred to them frequently.

We had covered all this ground—thanks to his excellent English—by the time Tei arrived on the porch. She was as great a girl as Tom had said, and somehow much better than what those words had conveyed: a combination of the best of both racial strains that were crossed in her, a superbly robust body, blue eyes like her father's, golden skin a bit lighter than the usual Marquesan color, and lots of soft, wavy black hair. Tei didn't speak English, and her French was like Marie Salomé's. She and I were soon chattering in what had become my pidgin, beaming mutual approval and pleasure.

She made me take off my damp muumuu and wrapped me in a clean, dry pareu of her own. Her way of tying it stayed up better than the Tamarii girls'; the only trouble was, I couldn't breathe.

"You must be careful not to walk alone at night here," she told me as she tucked in the last pleat. "Marquesans like women with big feet and big hips. One will grab you and carry you away!"

Next she was serving us coffee—Marquesan coffee, grown here in the valley and roasted in the house. Superb, but lethally strong, it was made in a fashion that reminded me of the extracting of "essence" in Mexico: boiling water dripped through a very long, narrow cloth bag. One demitasse set me on my ear.*

With the coffee, we were served dried bananas, also homemade and sweet enough to satisfy all the cravings the men had suffered since we ran out of chocolate bars. And pompelmous, a fruit that resembles but is not the same as grapefruit. Its English name is "shaddock," but I never heard that till we got home. A large, greenish, slightly pear-shaped citrus fruit, it has irregularly shaped sections and very large "cells," a tremendous quantity of juice, and a slight tinge of lime flavor. (We were all converts from the first bite, and for the rest of the time we sailed below the equator, we made sure to have enough pompelmous on hand for a half per person, per day. They kept better than any other fruit, even oranges.)

After an hour or so of pleasant talk and refreshment, we began to make polite excuses for leaving. (Tom had warned us that company tired Dad.)

"You will not wait for Tommy?" said Tei, distressed.

"When do you expect him?" I asked.

Le Brunnec laughed. "He has gone to try to persuade Amaru to take them to Tahu Ata, but it will do no good. He is hoping you will take them, if Amaru says no." (This was in English,

---

*I had all but given up drinking coffee on board. We had made the mistake of buying large jars of instant coffee, which lost its flavor long before it was used up. Many small ones would have been better.

so Tei did not understand. Also it was addressed to me, but the old man was watching Jack for a reaction. Jack made no sign of having heard.)

It was a slightly sticky situation. On the one hand, so far as I knew, Jack planned no stop at Tahu Ata. He had not said when he wanted to get away, but there were still things to do and places to visit on Hiva Oa. If we left Atuona, it might well be to circle the island and stop at Puaman, on the northeast coast. Also, Tei was not in as great a hurry as Tom to be away. She enjoyed the company in Atuona better than he did. And, finally, she was not going to be enthusiastic about travel in the *Aikane*. It was her exaggerated fear of deep water that made the problem in the first place. An outrigger could have taken them across the channel and dropped them on their doorstep any time they wanted to go. But Tei had told me that even a vessel the size of the *Taporo* made her seasick before the fact.

I couldn't figure out how M. Le Brunnec felt. He seemed slyly amused, but impartial. Did he want to get rid of the guests that crowded his house or to keep his oldest and favorite daughter with him? His intervention seemed less an attempt to help Tom out than the sort of playful gesture one might make to a beetle or a turtle, caught on the dead center of its own back.

Tom came panting up the stairs a few moments later, more agitated than we had yet seen him. Amaru had turned him down and given as an excuse "some sort of poppycock about orders from Papeete."

"Someone there has it in for me. I've got an idea who it is, too, but I can't prove it so I won't say. I got a hint of it from that Plantec fellow who teaches at the nuns' school. 'You ought to think about taking out French citizenship,' he said to me the other day, 'that is, if you're thinking about staying on.' How do you like that? After twelve years! And they can't pin any-thing on me about talking politics, either, and stirring things up, because they know I don't speak the language. Good thing I never learned!"

(It was beginning to get through to me that he had never learned Marquesan, either, so he and Tei did not have any lan-guage in common! And they had lived together for twelve years —apparently in peace and content.)

Jack cut into the monologue with a casual question. "Did you tell us there are petroglyphs on your place at Tahu Ata?"

Tom said yes, and held his breath.

"Well, if you and Tei could be ready to sail tomorrow, we could drop you off and have a look at them. That is, if it won't cut your visit here too short."

Tom jumped as if his knee reflex had been tapped, swallowed, and looked as if he were trying not to weep. Old Le Brunnec chuckled and explained the offer to Tei, who smiled and squeezed my hand.

"I don't know how to thank you," Tom said. "I didn't want to come right out and ask you—but I'll tell you the truth, I'm ready to take to drink or anything else you can get here! When a man gets to my age—I'm sixty-four, you know—he needs his home. I've been away about twice as long as I can stand it. I've just got to get back."

Tom put his arm around his wife and squeezed her. He came of New England stock, not given to demonstrations of affection, but for the moment his defenses were down. The odd part was that Tei was as embarrassed as a New England wife would have been. It occurred to me that we had never seen Marquesans of different sexes touch each other—even in the more passionate passages of the *tamure!*

We made arrangements to take the Grahams aboard in the early morning and said our farewells to Le Brunnec. He asked if we were planning to stop at Fatu Hiva, the southernmost of the Marquesan Islands. We said yes.

"Go to Omoa and call on Grelet. He is the last of those who knew the painter Gauguin. He does not remember much, but he will talk to you of him, if you ask.

"Tell him Le Brunnec is alive and well in Tahauku. I will not visit him again, but if he comes here, there is enough food and wine to keep him from starvation, and talk for as long as he can stay awake."

Tahu Ata

The Grahams were on the beach with their bundles at an hour which could reasonably be interpreted as early, and we were away only an hour and a half later than Jack had planned.

There was enough wind but not much of a sea, and it was really a perfectly comfortable sail. But Tei was seasick. (I wondered if Marquesan women were still influenced by the ancient taboo that forbids them to enter canoes. We never met one who was not a lousy woman aboard, no matter how fearless ashore.)

Tom talked the whole way across the channel.

He was really a desperately lonely man. "While we were in Papeete this last time, I used to go down to the quay where the yachts tie up, and just make the rounds. Talk to one American after another! It's funny how you get hungry for it."

(Not at all funny, I thought, since he couldn't talk to anyone in his "home" environment, thanks to his incredible resistance to languages other than his own.)

He had other problems, too. Many of them were medical, and even he was not sure whether they were somatic or psychological. He was "beginning to feel not quite up to par" in a situation where nothing but perfect health would do. There is no doctor at all on Tahu Ata, and no way to get across the channel to Atuona in an emergency. If he broke his glasses, there was no place they could be mended or replaced closer than Papeete, which was almost a thousand miles away. Tom thought perhaps a vacation in a cold climate might "tune him up," but he would not have the money to take Tei with him—even to Hawaii—and he would not go without her. And besides, he was afraid that if he ever left Les Etablissements Françaises de l'Océanie, the French might not let him back in.* His sense of insecurity was exacerbated by the fact that until he began to collect his social security (he was still only sixty-four), he was actually a pauper. Under French law, the house he built for Tei and all the planting he had done on her lands were hers, not his. If she were to tire of him tomorrow, he would have had to beg his way to the nearest American consulate.

"It's the same thing with Dad Laborneck," he explained to us. "He doesn't own a square yard of that land. His children could throw him off tomorrow. Of course they won't. But he's given up trying to make any sort of a crop. His son won't work, and you can't hire labor, so what's the use of beating yourself to death? I wish I'd listened to him ten years ago when he tried to tell me that."

We began to recognize the obverse side of a coin we already knew from our reading. One of the unique things about the Polynesian character, and especially the Marquesan variety of it, is its resistance to exploitation as labor for a foreign entrepreneur. Neither threats nor blandishments—nothing except addiction to opium, which is now outlawed—has ever persuaded these people to cooperate in the making of fortunes for their conquerors. They prefer death—slow or speedy, individual or collective—to slavery. Or, as Mrs. Handy put it, "They are adamant in their indolence."

Like many a "white" man before him, Tom had surveyed the land that was (practically) his and discovered that it was magnificently fertile. It would, he told us, grow the best coffee in the world without any investment of labor except that of gathering the beans. So he planted enough acres to make himself—and Tei—a fortune, and watched the price of coffee on the world market while he waited for the bushes to grow large enough to bear. He also strained his back, moving the stones to make a *pae-pae* (terrace and foundation) for a lovely little house, set high on a cliff overlooking a bay. No one warned him, not even Tei, that coffee is not like copra, that the berries must

---

* This sounded mildly paranoid to us at the time, but we met other Americans, married to Marquesan wives and the fathers of children by them, who felt constantly threatened by the specter of deportation and separation.

be picked when they are ripe, which is often in a season of uncomfortable heat. No one on the island of Tahu Ata could be persuaded to pick the Graham coffee crop. Not at any price that made economic sense, and not regularly at any price!

The fertile acres turned out to have a built-in catch as fatal as the three wishes of an old fairy tale.

"But I'm not complaining," Tom said, as we rounded the last point of land that sheltered the harbor of Vaitahu. "I've got my home and Tei. We cut enough copra to buy what we need. Next year I'll get my social security, and we'll live like millionaires here. If those damn bureaucrats in Papeete don't pull something dirty."

The harbor of Vaitahu was the scene of the first successful military invasion of the Marquesas, and the land seems to brood revengefully above it. The *Coast Pilot* warned of sudden gusts that sweep down from the overhanging cliffs and sometimes run vessels on the rocks, no matter how well they are anchored. Jack decided not to leave the *Aikane* untended overnight.

The Grahams were as deflated as children who have been promised a party and then denied. "You were to spend the night with us," Tei said. "I have planned to cook you a real Marquesan feast. And there are the old stones in the ravine to be visited. And my shells! I have expected to show you my collection of shells!" Tom was equally pressing and frankly selfish about it. "I don't know when I'll get to talk to Americans again, and I'm not talked out."

A compromise was arrived at. We would all go over to the little bay where the Grahams lived (if Tom could get our sick Seagull motor going) and hike up to the petroglyphs, while Tei prepared a supper. Then Jack and Norris would go back to the *Aikane* for the night. They would return in the morning, enjoy Tei's feast, and take Benson and me back to the boat. We would stay with the Grahams, inspect Tei's treasures, and let Tom talk.

The trip from Vaitahu to Anapoo (the Grahams' private bay) was made in a large outrigger that belonged to Paki, the only gendarme on the island. He had some official business (the investigation of a murder) to do at a bay farther up the coast, and his outboard was not working. So Tom got the Seagull going and more or less attached to the well of the outrigger, and we all squeezed in. It was the biggest outrigger I ever saw, but even so, when all the Grahams' baggage was stowed, and seven people perched on top of it, there was less than a foot of freeboard.

The distance was short, but it involved crossing a fair-size stretch of open water where surges that had crossed the Pacific unchecked rolled up against the most ominous land imaginable. The cliffs were a mass of coils, holes, and faults, and seemed to writhe in anguish. Along the tide line—uncovered at the hour we passed—there was a gruesome frill of coral, pink! like a lace garter on some obscene giantess's leg, and sharp enough to lacerate anyone who tried to climb it. It passed through my mind that without fins one could hardly hope to swim for shore if we should capsize or swamp.

But Tei was not seasick! She was too worried about the quilts in which her boxes were wrapped. Were they being splashed? And if so, would salt water shrink the woolen patches and make the colors run? Anxiety of one sort is remarkably effective as a countermeasure against another.

Leaving Tei to find the keys to one or the other of her houses

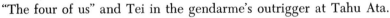

"The four of us" and Tei in the gendarme's outrigger at Tahu Ata.

(there was an old shack on the beach, as well as the new house on the cliff), and get ready some refreshments, we set out single-file after Tom.

The trail to the petroglyphs was steep, and the air was hot and steamy and full of mosquitoes. Under other circumstances we might all have enjoyed the hike and the lushness of the jungle into which we were being led, but all three of my companions were obviously bugged by something. Benson claimed later that it was nothing more mysterious than the combination of heat fatigue, mosquito bites, hunger, and thirst. But I had the impression there was more to it—that Tom's nattering monologue was undermining something more important than their somas, something that had to do with their confidence in themselves as men. As for me, he was beating the life out of any dream I might have cherished about retiring from the rat race to some Pacific island Eden. When and if I retire, it will be to a place where I can spend my old-age pension without exchanging dollars into any other currency, where medicine (if not Medicare) is available, and the bureaucracy speaks my language.

The petroglyphs were really very impressive—impossible to photograph without flash equipment because the foliage overhead was as dense as the walls of a house. Most of them were carved on the side of a single enormous boulder that must have been part of some ancient altar or feasting place. The most striking of them was a *tiki* face with very large, round eyes. Moss had grown in these circles. The effect was eerie and somewhat unsettling.

By the time we got back to Anapoo, even Tom was too thirsty to talk. Tei was in despair. She had not found the keys. They were doubtless in the pocket of the girl who had been looking after the places, the granddaughter of the copra cutter (Tom's only employee). She would return when the old man had done his day's work, which would be too late for Norris and Jack.

They settled for a freshwater shower, a couple of oranges from Tei's trees, and a sniff of a night-blooming cereus that had opened the night before but was overpowering even in decay. By that time, Paki was waiting for them on his return trip. They left, promising to come back in the *Lili Aikane* early enough to help with the preparations for Tei's feast.

The most dramatic of those preparations took place that night after supper. The girl helper had returned with the keys, and Tei had found canned *pâté* and butter and a jar of dark honey. That and some baker's bread she purchased from Paki made a meal.

"You will eat better tomorrow," she promised. "But now we must hurry. The tide is low. Tommy! Light me the lantern!" (That was in French; Tom understood the imperious finger that pointed toward the Coleman, if not the words.) "Tepi!" She called the girl helper and gave an order in Marquesan.

A minute or so later Tepi was back with two palm-frond baskets. Tei took one, Tepi the other, and the two of them led the way down to the boulder-strewn beach.

The surge was still formidable, but it did not intimidate either of the huntresses. Their bare feet seemed to curl around holds on the slippery rocks so that they could stand erect and balanced, no matter how the surf swirled. Fred was holding the Coleman so that it all but blinded us who stood behind it, but illumined the shoreline as Tei wanted it illumined.

She and Tepi began to make quick dashes for the seaward face of the rocks that were completely covered every time the surge came in. From these dashes they came back with booty— three- or four-inch dark-brown cowries, and now and then a chiton of the same size. The cowries could be picked off the rock face, but the chitons had to be beaten loose with another rock. And every second counted. Several times Tei delayed too long and was soaked by the next wave.

She was awesomely beautiful. Her yellow and white pareu clung to her body like transparent drapery. Her hair was wet, but it still fell in waves and curls, and she tossed it like a mane when she turned her head to shout a direction to Tom.

He never once understood what she wanted of him.

"Hold the light higher," she would say, and he would answer: "Yes, yes, I am coming. Don't be anxious." Or she would say: "Get farther back. You are too close. The light is no good."

And he would say: "I told you I am coming. Be patient. You are upsetting yourself over nothing."

I tried interpreting, but my voice was lost in the wind and the sound of the waves. Besides, what good was an hour's clarification after twelve years of misunderstanding?

I tried again, when we were sitting on the floor of the new house, looking at Tom's photographs and Tei's shells. "He doesn't understand what you say," I told Tei.

"He will not listen!" She insisted irritably. "I tell him something, but he gets so excited he pays no attention." Tom was saying at the same time, "She gets so excited she doesn't understand."

"I think she gets excited because you don't understand," I began.

But neither of them was listening.

Yet they settled down to sleep together, when the time came, like Baucis and Philemon. I am sure they loved each other no less devotedly, but the communication gap robbed them of many of the rewards of devotion—especially Tom. They communicated with reasonable efficiency on matters of the present: day-to-day agendas, menus, repairs, building, planting, fishing, and even about Tom's wood carvings, which Tei seemed really to enjoy and appreciate. But a man (or a woman) needs to "think aloud" with someone else about past and future, about concepts that can't be conveyed by pointing, or by the abominable pidgin that the Grahams resorted to when pantomime broke down. Without the radar screen of other human beings to bounce one's self off, one begins to lose track of that self.

Breakfast was served in the ramshackle little house near the beach, and it wasn't much more than supper's leftovers. Again we ate out of cans, which had been kept overnight in saucers of water, to prevent the ants from getting to them. The treat was some more of Tei's specially brewed coffee, served with canned milk, and drunk from a bowl.

But breakfast was only a prelude to the first course of the feast, which began as soon as we got down to the beach. First Tei sorted through the cowries and chitons she had gathered on her night hunt. The cowries were even more spectacular than I had thought: not only large, but of a brilliance that seemed artificial. The French call the animal *porcelaine* in tribute to that surface. Tei selected about fifteen of the best shells, and then —to our horror—began smashing the others between two rocks.

The foot on which the cowrie crawls is a meat not unlike abalone. She cleaned a couple, beat them tender, squeezed the juice from a fresh lime over them, and handed them to Benson and me to taste. It was good, and we said so. Tei looked as much relieved as pleased. (She had, she told me later, never had American guests who would eat seafood raw. If we had failed the test, she was planning on opening more cans.)

Instead, she took us on an excursion that was the marine counterpart of Marie Salomé's walk through the woods. Like her, Tei carried only a basket, a knife, and a few large limes. We left Tom on the rocks that were his dooryard, casting with a fly rod for small, bright-colored parrot fish. Tei called to him (in French) that she was taking us along the reef and would be back in time to make luncheon. He answered (in English) that he didn't think so right now, but there would be bigger ones when the tide started to come in.

Tei began to gather the fruits of the sea and offer them to us. First there were chitons—bigger than the California variety, but otherwise very similar. Scraped or pried from the rocks and scooped from their shells, marinated in the lime juice for a few minutes, they were much like the cowries. Then Tei found a sea urchin, one with short, stubby purple spines (not as dangerous to handle as the longer, sharper ones). She turned it "on its toes" and hammered at it delicately until she had broken loose its five converging jaws. The shell was mainly empty, but clinging to its sides was a yellowish paste that Tei called "*foie.*" She squirted lime into the cavity and set the urchin down. The involuntary movements of the spines continued, and the living cup walked slowly away as Tei dipped her finger in, scooped out some of the liver, and offered it.

I had to brace myself to get this down, but it was not as bad as I expected. It tasted something like the coral of lobster, which I often use in sauces. Benson liked it less than I did, but he put on a good face. Tei was delighted.

"It is a pleasure to do for you," she said, "because you like. You do not say no to everything. Most of the Americans Tommy brings here say no to eat this, no to drink that, no to smell of this. Afraid to climb here, walk there. . . . But you are different. Almost like Marquesan." After that we would have eaten devil-fish if she had offered it to us.

As it was, the fare got better as we went along. Some courses were served in the fingers of the hostess; others in shells that were collector's items by my standard. Benson and I hunted shells while Tei hunted food, learning from her to spot the prey hidden in the chaos of pink coral and to pry it off between surges. I had no idea how long we had been at it when we spied Jack and Norris rowing the *Lili Aikane*. (The Seagull was sick again.)

We all pitched in on the final preparation for lunch, like students in a domestic-science course, with Tei as teacher. Norris and Jack helped grate and squeeze coconut for the cream. (See page 117.) Benson helped clean the fish Tom had caught. I squeezed lime juice for marinating. Tei arranged everything in shell bowls: the tidbits of *poisson cru* soaked first in lime juice, with coconut cream added later; the shellfish marinated only in coconut cream. While these tenderizers were doing their work, we all had rum punches, with Tei's limes and a dark rum, made in the Pacific, but reminiscent of Jamaica.

Just as we finished, Tepi brought two big breadfruit that had been roasted over an open fire. Tei peeled them like baked potatoes and broke them into her largest bowl. Now the meal began in earnest. Each guest had a small bowl of his own into which he ladled some cream, after which he served himself what he chose from the various delicacies on the board. Hunks of baked breadfruit, held in the fingers, were used to sop up what-ever cream was left after the fish and shellfish had been picked out and eaten.

Everything was marvelously good. The breadfruit had a faintly smoky taste that kept it from being dull. The fish Tom had caught was tender and very delicately flavored. But the cowries and chitons were the best of all, and even more flavor-some than when eaten raw.

Dessert was a mélange of fruits, including an exotic and un-familiar one that reminded me of a guava. And there was another pot of potent Marquesan coffee—black, this time, and sweet.

Stuffed, and satisfied in other, more spiritual ways, we said our good-byes. We knew enough by now to prepare ourselves for the gift-giving *kaoha*. Norris and Jack had brought aspirin, salt tablets, and oatmeal from the *Aikane*'s stores. Tom almost burst into tears of gratitude, and Tei kissed me to show her appreciation of his greater need. For her there was nothing but a small shell (from Cuba) which I hoped she did not have in her chest. For us there were the fifteen perfect cowries, a supply of pompelmous, and for me a lei of tiny, sharply pointed brown shells, which felt like a crown of thorns, but was much more becoming.

Our last view of the Grahams was standing together on the *pae-pae* of the cliff house, waving to us. The quirks and crochets of their relationship faded at this distance. All that came through was its solidity.

Despite the difference in language and culture and age (she was sixteen years younger than he), they were more married—I realized then—than any couple I have ever known anywhere. Because all that each has is the other, and, on the whole, it is enough. They make a life together out of the enduring core of love—companionship—and the daily fulfillment of the simplest and most basic of human needs.

Fatu Hiva

We sailed around the southwest end of Tahu Ata and headed south and east for Fatu Hiva, the last of the Marquesas that we planned to visit. After that, we would head west for Tahiti, unless Jack decided to stop en route at the Tuamotus, the Dangerous Islands, where men still dive for pearls.

Fatu Hiva was visible on the horizon as soon as we rounded the point, and as we closed in on it, its face began to show an abstract design of great A-shapes. These turned out to be bare rock headlands, between which were indentations so deep and shaded that they looked blue-black from any distance. One such indentation in this coastline was our destination—a bay called Hanavave. According to the *Coast Pilot*, there were no man-made landmarks or navigational aids to mark it, but the mariner could recognize it from a distance of two or three miles by comparing the profile of the mountains with a sketch in the book.

This sketch was highly dramatic: a gap between vertical cliffs, at the far end of which, above a small beach, was another gap—like a fortress wall cracked open in some ancient upheaval. In the sketch one could look through this gate into an interior valley, which showed light against the dark shading of the cliffs. Obviously, one could see into this inlet only when one was directly abeam of it. The trick was to match the notching of the mountain crest against the sky, and so bring the boat in abeam of the opening.

We all strained our eyes for what seemed hours, with the bulky *Coast Pilot* open before us. We knew our position within a mile or two because the navigators had been taking shots every half hour, but a mile off in one direction or the other might lose us the glimpse of the "gate."

Suddenly we saw it! Exactly as the sketch showed it, even to the relative degree of light and dark indicated by the shading. And in color, which made it breathtakingly beautiful!

As we made our way in the mouth of the bay, we saw flimsy-looking platforms of bamboo, attached to the face of the cliff on the seaward side, inaccessible except by boat. That was on the starboard; on the port side, the cliff was not as steep. There were splotches of green here and there on its face, and white goats nibbling at them. We could see no trails by which they could make their way back to the mainland, but goats can do almost as well as flies at climbing walls.

It was still the middle of the afternoon, when we dropped anchor, but already the shadows were dark at the beach end of the bay. The settlement of Hanavave was hidden by them and by the palms, but there was golden light in the valley of the interior, which we could just see through the gap.

We ate the last of a kid we had bought from the *chef* at Atuona, and rowed to shore. Benson found the school, a one-room bamboo and thatch structure close to the water, but the teacher—we were told—was leaving.

"Tomorrow the *Taporo* will come and take her away," one of the older children explained. He did not know when, if ever, another teacher would come.

In the long twilight we explored the settlement. It was much reduced in size from O'Brien's description of it, but Hanavave is still the center of tapamaking in the Marquesas. The old art of making tapa fine enough for garments has died out. What is made now is used for wall hangings and table covers. It is made, as of old, from the inner bark of the breadfruit tree, beaten paper-thin and bleached to a skin color. The designs, which are painted on in black ink, are bold *tiki* and tattoo motifs.

We bought all we could find. Everywhere else we had been, we had been told that the *Taporo's* supercargo had either bought up or contracted for the entire local output of carvings, necklaces, embroideries, or whatever, along with the copra crop. This time we were there first, and we made the most of it.

Hanavave is also a banana-drying center. That explained the platforms on the cliff face. There is not enough sun in the settlement to reduce the bananas to the preserved state before they mildew. The ripe fruit are taken out there and left for a day, turned once, left another day, and then packaged in dried coconut fronds. The finished product looks like an extra fat Mexican tamale; it is bound with a fine braid of palm fiber, looped at one end for easy carrying. The men bought a number of these packets, and hoarded them like candy.

By the time we had finished our shopping, it was night. We rowed back to the *Aikane* and were spreading out our mattresses on deck, when an outrigger pulled alongside. Expecting a gendarme on official business, we made hearty welcoming noises and rummaged for our visas, but the boarding party consisted of four stony-faced young Marquesans, none of whom spoke French.

Norris did his best with his Basic Marquesan, but what saved the situation was the international language of gesture and pantomime. It took a while for us to get over the notion that, like the outrigger man at Ua Pou, they were looking for contraband trade goods. But finally someone remembered that we had been playing a tape when they approached. Jack had an idea: he broke out his guitar (which he had yet to play in the two months we had been at sea), and offered it to our visitors.

They almost smiled.

One took the instrument and began tuning it. Benson got a clean tape from the locker and set up the tape recorder to be ready for some native Marquesan music. What they played instead was either the way they remembered the programs beamed out from Tahiti every evening or American pop music that had suffered a sea change. It was certainly "something new and strange."

The guitar was handled—everywhere we visited in Polynesia —as if it were an oversize ukulele. The object seemed to be to set up and keep going as long as possible an insistent fast beat. Our visitors did that all right. They also sang one fast, insistent line, which they repeated over and over, with no variation in melodic line and only slight variation in the words. And just when I was going to sleep sitting up, under this treatment (it had been a long day!), they stopped. Right in the middle of the phrase!

We played back what we had taped, and they listened intently, but gave no sign of either approval or disapproval. Then we tried some of our own tapes on them: Ray Charles, a few Beatles' selections, and so on. One of our friends had told us that rock-and-roll was very big in Polynesia. Maybe it was. The four boys listened with the same intent impassivity as before, which may have been the perfect tribute.

We passed around cookies*—slightly stale chocolate chips—which delighted our guests so much that they pantomimed fishing. We finally got it: they wanted to reciprocate. Jack let them go through his tackle box. (It was once so full that we had a hard time opening the drawers, but we had by this time lost most of the big lures on fish we never saw.) The boys picked out a couple of rather flashy small plugs, attached them to drop lines, and let them down over the side.

Before they said good night, they had provided us with enough small (and very beautiful) perch for a fine breakfast.

The *Taporo* slid in and anchored next morning while we were frying the fish. Before we had finished eating them, her whaleboat had made a trip in to shore and was on its way back. The supercargo waved and shouted something as he passed us. (Had he discovered our victory on the tapa front?)

The next thing we knew, the *Taporo*'s engines were throbbing in reverse and she was on her way out. Jack had intended to row over and consult Captain Amaru on the still unsettled question of a stop in the Tuamotus, and we were all a little dashed at the apparent snub.

To console ourselves, we went skin diving.

The water was quieter, clearer, and warmer than at Ua Pou, and the fish more plentiful and much more spectacular. There were schools of small silver-blue fry (herring, perhaps) that

---

* In our experience, cookies were just as popular trade goods as whiskey or cartridges. Perhaps, in view of the dental situation, they are almost as lethal for the recipients. But there is no secular or ecclesiastical law against swapping Nabiscos for mandarin oranges or art objects, and the exchange rate is high.

swam just below the surface and jumped clear if frightened. There were also schools of larger fish: angels with broad diagonal stripes of yellow and silver, or the more usual black and silver; more of the envelope-shaped fish with postage-stamp eyes, with a long quill-shaped fin curving down from the corner opposite the eye. There were at least a dozen varieties of trigger-fish, all flat and almost circular in outline, and black, but each with a different decoration—spots of pink, orange, indigo, or white, differently shaped and placed on their sooty flanks. There were prisoner fish, wearing their black and white stripes verti-cally, and the bluest fish I have ever seen anywhere, with black velvet patches and yellow accents! And parrot fish, bigger and brighter than those we ate on Tahu Ata, and very tame. One followed me as I shelled along the reef, and moved in to clean up almost before I had my hand out of the way.

Shelling was not outstandingly good, but there were lots of handsome small cowries that looked like a garden snake's head, and are sometimes called just that. Norris and I got about two dozen of them; added to Tei's giant brown cowries it made quite a collection—and a problem. How to clean them before they started to rot and smell? Ashore in these latitudes people usually simply bury shells whose apertures are too narrow for easy extraction of the animal inside. Time and voracious ants do the work. We had neither.

Tei had suggested that we let the shells lie in the sun till the animal was dead, and then hang them over the side in netting which would admit small fish and crabs, which are almost as voracious as ants. The only netting we had was my nylon rinsing bag, which I sacrificed to the cause. But it didn't begin to hold our cowries, and there were going to be more and better shells in the waters ahead. Already the fantail looked and smelled like a biology lab when the formaldehyde has run low.

The problem was never satisfactorily solved. It was worse when we were in port without a wind to blow the smell away. At sea, however, there was always the risk of losing what we were dragging in the net.* The ideal way to collect shells on a cruise is, I think, to trade live ones for well-cleaned dead ones,

---

* On the very last lap of the journey, we lost the bag and its contents—including our only miter shells—because someone got careless about securing the line.

and since shell collecting is a Polynesian, as well as an American, sport, it is possible to make such deals in more out-of-the-way places than one might expect.

The *Taporo* came back and dropped anchor again while we were spreading out our cowries in the sun. This time Jack lost no time getting the *Lili Aikane* under way. He came back from his conference with Captain Amaru with a smile of satisfaction. He had been assured that it was safe enough to stop at Takaroa, one of the Tuamotus that lay practically on our course, and where, one of the mates said, the pearl dive was presently under way. As the dive is an event for which all the Paumotuans* gather from the whole far-flung archipelago, this was really serendipitous timing.

Also, Captain Amaru had invited us all to lunch aboard, and to watch the loading of the copra while we waited for the gong to sound.

The *Taporo*'s launch came by to pick us up, and carried us in to the rocky little beach where the copra sacks were piled. Actually, it was not the launch, but one of the two longboats it had in tow, into which we climbed. Each of the whaleboats had but a single crewman, seated at a large sweep oar at the stern. The launch started for the landing place with its powerful outboard's throttle open. A dozen yards short of a crash, it would veer off, letting go the painters of the two boats. The man at the sweep oar did some tricky maneuvering over underwater obstacles, and the hulls ground to a stop on the rocks.

The loading was as messy as the piloting was expert. Local stevedores tossed in whatever piece of cargo their hands happened to touch: a sack of copra, a stem of bananas, a hobbled pig or goat, a living and very noisy bouquet of chickens, miscellaneous boxes and bundles, until the boats were full. Then, at a command from the *Taporo*'s supercargo (the one the shark attacked when he was careless about keeping his catch on his belt), passengers and their babies would wade out and clamber aboard. Another order from the supercargo, and the stevedores would push the boats out until they floated free and turn them

---

* Paumotuan is also the adjective that goes with the noun Tuamotus. No one ever explained the variation, except to say that neither is a good rendering of the local name.

so the bows pointed out. Someone would toss the painter to the pilot of the motor launch, who had been hovering around at a safe distance. The return trip was made via the same double tow.

The most difficult moment of the second half of the maneuver came when the launch approached the mother ship. The boats had to be cast loose at exactly the right distance and exactly the right speed so that the steersman could bring his craft to the foot of the loading platform and stop, without brakes. The slightest error brought a scornful hoot from the crew members on the *Taporo*'s cargo deck, and a tirade from the first mate, known as the Angry Man.

There was one piece of strange cargo in the operation we witnessed: a very young girl who sat on a pile of her belongings, dressed in a clean, frilly white blouse and plain black skirt, receiving garlands and good-byes from children and adults during the entire hour we watched the loading. She looked too young to be the teacher who was being sent back to Tahiti, but that was who she turned out to be. And she looked so miserable that she wrung our hearts.

No one at the luncheon table on the *Taporo* knew why she was going home, but we eventually heard from a teacher in the community of Omoa that she had been unable to handle the language problem and the discipline problem that resulted from it. She was just eighteen when she was sent here, to her first teaching job. She spoke French and Tahitian. Her pupils spoke neither. Marquesan and Tahitian are as similar as Italian and Spanish or Portuguese, but no more so. The pedagogues in Papeete did not consider the problem important because the school was to be conducted in French. No one in Hanavave had complained about the young teacher. (We had seen from the farewells that they were really very fond of her.) But M. l'Inspecteur de l'Académie de l'Archipel came by on his regular rounds, and was appalled. Mlle. Rosalie was to be replaced— eventually—by a woman of more experience. The trouble with that solution, our informant said, was that the older teachers were even worse prepared in all aspects of education, except the maintenance of order in the classroom. It was very discouraging, and progress did not "achieve itself" very much.

Luncheon aboard the *Taporo* was the most elaborate meal

we had had in months. Unfortunately, it was preceded by so many whiskey-and-sodas that none of us had a very clear idea afterward of what we had been served. The conversation veered from English to French to some Polynesian speech, whatever the supercargo and the mates spoke. Sometimes Captain Amaru seemed to be talking all three at once. He was very proud of himself because he had outwitted the members of his crew who had tried to perpetrate an April Fools' joke upon him. I was asked to translate the details of his victory for my companions and the British pediatrician, who was still aboard.

Knowing that the morrow was the first of April, the day of the *Poisson d'Avril*, the captain had taken the precaution of going to bed with a fish. Whether this sort of bedmate is insurance against practical joking in France, or only in les Etablissements Français de l'Océanie, we did not know. But it was Marquis of Queensberry aboard the *Taporo*. So when someone rapped on the door of the captain's cabin in the dawn, with a phony radiogram from Papeete, Amaru opened one eye, pointed to his fish, and went back to sleep. There was general laughter, except from the supercargo, who looked as if the radiogram had been his *poisson*.

When the laughter died down, I heard the throb of engines. The captain excused himself, and a half minute later it was clear that we were under way. The crew of the *Aikane* looked to their captain, who smiled back, unperturbed.

"We're getting a lift to Omoa. I told you."

If he had, none of us had heard him. And how were we going to get back to Hanavave?

"Walk," said Jack. "It's a great hike. Captain Amaru says no one ought to miss it. Magnificent view!"

Benson had been spoiling for a hike ever since he missed out on the one to Taipivai, and Norris considered himself a pro at this sort of thing. I seemed to be the only unenthusiastic one.

"How long a walk is it?" I asked.

Jack wasn't sure. About two hours, he thought. There would be plenty of time, since darkness didn't set in till six o'clock, and it was not much past noon now.

Half an hour later, as we finished our coffee and canned peaches, the *Taporo*'s engines shut off. We were in the open roadstead in front of Omoa, the domain of M. Le Brunnec's friend Grelet. A real town, with a school on the waterfront, a cement pier (at least as good as Taiohae's), a church with a steeple, and the best-stocked general store in all the Marquesas!

Captain Amaru had space saved for us in the first launchful that went ashore. As we started away, I caught sight of the young schoolteacher, Rosalie, making herself as comfortable as she could in a nest of suitcases and bundles under the awning that covered the forward hold. She was going home as a deck passenger, which meant that she would live there on the copra for nearly a thousand miles, which might take as many as ten days, at the rate the *Taporo* covered distance. There would be no privacy. It was stifling under the awning when the ship wasn't under way, and one could hardly walk about on the deck, which was a floating stockyard, loaded with tethered goats, sheep, pigs, and chickens, and untethered dogs. Mlle. Rosalie had a little transistor radio, but nothing else, to amuse her. She had been given enough fat little packets of dried bananas to keep her from starving, but deck passengers are not fed by the *Taporo's* *chef*. I couldn't help worrying about the poor young woman. . . .

But I was worrying about the wrong female. A young Tahitian facing a ten-day voyage home was less to be pitied than a middle-aged American facing a day's hike to Hanavave.

We said good-bye to Captain Amaru at the pier. He was going up to call on M. Grelet. We sent M. Le Brunnec's greeting by this emissary, planning to pay our own call and make all our provision purchases at a later date, when we brought the *Aikane* over.

"The road to Hanavave?" I asked the first adult we passed as we strolled along the beach, past the school building, in the general direction a crow would have taken to get there.

We expected a confirming nod, but instead we got a rather long, excited explanation not much of which sounded like French. The man seemed to be recommending that we turn inland and strike out for the hidden valley of the interior. It was unsettling. We did turn in that direction when we found a cobblestoned road. It led us past the church, which had a handsome stained-glass window and a giant furbelowed clamshell font at the door. A few yards past it we met another likely-looking informant.

"The road to Hanavave?" we asked, pointing inland, the way he had come.

He shook his head emphatically and pointed back toward the beach. He did speak French, but not my kind. I got only bits of his advice. We were to go up the beach (in the original direction) to the hill at the end of it, ascend, take the right fork the first time, the left fork the time after that . . . or maybe the two times after that . . . And then no more turns.

The beach was full of squealing, naked children, playing in the surf. Other children were coming down the winding road that ascended the hill, carrying palm baskets full of ripe mangoes, which they were eating as they came. The moment their feet touched the sand of the beach, the basket was dropped, their clothes were torn off, and into the surf they went. I wished I could follow their example. I was already hot and tired, and my espadrilles were full of sand.

"The road to Hanavave?" we asked one group of what looked to be ten-year-olds.

They nodded, giggled, and dashed for the beach.

The road was very steep. I was out of breath when we made it to the summit. The view was dizzying. We could see nearly to Hanavave in one direction, even farther in the other, ridge after sharp blue ridge, slanting steeply to the sea, like great strokes of ultramarine. The sea looked pale, wrinkled near the shore by what we knew to be combers. The air was full of fine dust made luminous by the sun.

It was cool on the point, but hot on the trail that continued inland from it, except when we walked in the shade of the great mango trees. We were crushing windfalls at almost every step, and I was dying to quench my thirst, but Marie Salomé had warned us that all windfalls were infested with parasites.

I had rubbed the first blisters by now. My muumuu protected my knees, which was some comfort. The men's were exposed, and the undergrowth was beginning to tear at us. The trail had grown so narrow that we had to string out single file. And now we came to a fork for which we had no directions.

Either that or we had lost count. By my calculations we had got to the part where there were "no turns," but some choice had to be made.

At last we chose the left, the fork that kept us closer to the coast. "It may mean a lot of going down and coming up again," we reasoned, "but at least we know we're heading the right way."

The going got much tougher almost immediately. I was too tired to care very much. It had been going on so long. "Pick up one foot, put down the other," I told myself. "No! That's wrong! Put down the same one you picked up, you idiot!" Fortunately, my feet had done the right thing while I had been telling them wrong. "Keep it up and you'll get a second wind . . . someday." But what about night? How were we to follow a trail like this at night? Or how were we to camp in this wilderness without matches, food, water, covering, or insect repellent? . . . Well, mine not to question how or why; mine but to pick up one foot and then the other.

The trail had begun to slant very steeply down. It was comparatively restful, but I knew it meant climbing up just as steeply on the other side of the ravine. And now it was turning into a cliff! My rope soles slid from under me, and I would have gone all the way to the bottom if Benson hadn't blocked my way.

A dozen or so yards later, the trail exhausted itself in the backyard of a small homestead, where a young Marquesan and his wife were pushing back the jungle a little at a time. They and an indignant dog came forward to meet us.

Neither of them spoke French, but with the aid of Norris's Marquesan we got the bad news. This was not the road to Hanavave or, for that matter, to anywhere. We had missed some turn. The young man couldn't make us understand which one, but it really didn't matter now.

"It sounds as if he thinks we should go back to Omoa and start over," Norris said.

I couldn't accept it. A sinister alternative presented itself: he was taking advantage of our ignorance, weariness, and wealth. "He wants us to hire him as a guide," I said. "Or as a taxi. He's got an outrigger there on the beach."

"Great," said Jack. "Norris, see if you can make a deal. He can take us to Hanavave, two at a time."

But the young man refused. He explained why in detail, but not detail that Norris could get.

"Ask him how long it takes to walk to Hanavave from here," I asked.

The answer Norris got was: Four hours if one walked fast.

"But it was supposed to be less than that from Omoa!" I was beginning to have to dam back tears.

Jack took over. "I tell you what we'll do," he said with slightly hollow cheerfulness. "We'll go back to wherever it was we missed the turn. You and Benson go back to Omoa and ask Grelet to put you up. Norris and I will make it to Hanavave. I don't like leaving the boat alone all night anyway. And we'll bring her over in the morning."

That was all very well, but how were we to recognize the turn we had missed before?

The young man was offering to conduct us to it. His manner was urgently apologetic, as if he understood that I suspected him of wrongdoing and he wanted a chance to prove himself innocent. We started back up the cliff, which was harder to climb than to slide down. The trail was worse than before, and the setting sun shone directly in our eyes. The young man trotted ahead at a pace that not even Norris could match. I lagged way behind, struggling with the problem of whether to put down the foot I had just picked up or some other not so painful member, like perhaps a knee. Or both of them.

I was beginning to understand that I was angry, not at the agreeable young man, but at myself. All this was my fault. I was supposed to be the interpreter. It was I who had listened to the directions; I who had got them fouled up. No one was blaming me, but I was too tired to forgive myself.

Perhaps the whole thing was a *Poisson d'Avril*.

But who had played it on us? Jack had suggested the hike to us. Captain Amaru had suggested it to him. Did he know we would go astray like this? Was it one—or both of the men who had given us directions? Or our present guide? What if he got us all the way back to Omoa and then said, "*Poisson d'Avril*"? I carried no fish.

Jack and Norris and the guide were out of sight now, and Benson was muttering encouragement in a tone that indicated he expected me to collapse at any moment. I couldn't get the breath to reassure him. I was beat. I was not going to make it. The woman had got by aboard, only to fail ashore. The men could have got themselves out of the predicament I had got them into, if they hadn't had me to consider. I was a drag. . . . If only I could drag myself into the tall grass and curl up and hide . . .

We caught up with the vanguard at the very first bend in the road that led up from the beach. We hadn't counted that as one of the forks because the road we should have taken was nothing but a rut, leading straight into the interior.

We thanked the young man. He seemed relieved to be vindicated of whatever he had been accused of, and with an elegant hand gesture that refused recompense, he bade us farewell and started trotting back home. At this point, even Jack and Norris abandoned the idea of hiking to Hanavave.

"The *Taporo* is still loading," Jack said, after peering into the sun shimmer for a minute. "Maybe Amaru will give us a lift."

Under this spur of hope, I got myself down the hill and up the beach to the pier, only a few yards behind the front-runners. Our friend was not enthusiastic about the rescue mission, but he hadn't the heart to refuse a beggar as pitiful as I. The launch was ordered to run us back.

The return trip was incredibly beautiful. The sun was putting on one of those wide-ray productions that seem designed for the announcing of miracles. The launch hugged the coast so closely that we could see into each of the little bays that the Marquesans call "teeth." We saw the hut and the outrigger of our guide, and understood why he didn't want to put to sea at this time and tide. If one were caught in the surge that sucked in and out of those rocky teeth, one would be ground up like garbage.

It was dark when we rounded the banana-drying platforms and entered the inlet of Hanavave. The *Aikane* rocked peacefully at her moorage. All was well. We rummaged in the "goodies locker" and found a box of cookies for our seagoing chauffeur, and a large Edam cheese for Captain Amaru. It had been the *pièce de résistance* of a bon voyage basket, and we had been saving it. Now it would pay for saving us.

I eventually found O'Brien's description of the hike from Hanavave to Omoa, the route we had meant to take, but in reverse:

Up and up we went. The way was steeper than any mountain I have ever climbed, except the sheer sides of chasms where ropes are necessary. . . . I fell again and again; the horse floundered among the stones in the trough and fell too. . . . Rocks as large as hundred-ton vessels were on the mountain side above, held from falling only by small rocks interposed, feeble obstacles to an avalanche. . . . Orivie pointed out the tracks of such slides, and immense masses of rock in the far depths below. . . .

I climbed around the edge of a precipice and stood above the sea. . . . It was a thousand feet straight down; my standing place was but three feet wide, wet and slippery. The mighty trade wind swept around the crags and threatened to dislodge me. . . . On hands and knees I crept around the edge, for the wind was a gale and a slip of the foot might mean a drop of a fifth of a mile. . . . Higher we went and . . . could look through the pierced mountain, Laputa, through the hole, *tehavaiinenao*, that is like a round window in the sky, framed in black. . . . We came then to the veriest pitch of the journey, like the roof of the world, and it was necessary to crawl about another ledge that permitted a perpendicular view of 2500 feet. This was the apex, once safely past it, the trail went downward to a plateau. . . .

Mosses and ferns by the billion covered every foot [of it]. There were no trees. The trail was a foot deep in water, like an irrigation ditch. One still might easily break one's neck. . . . The rain began to fall again, and the wind came stronger. We passed under trees hung with marvelous orchids. . . . The trail became very dangerous at this point, a rocky slide with steps a foot or two apart like uneven stairs, and all a foot, sometimes two, under running water. I jumped, and slid and slipped, following the unhappy, plunging horse. Darkness came on quickly with blinding rain, and the descent was often at an angle of 45 degrees, over rocks, eroded hills, along the edge of a precipice. I fell here, and saved myself by catching a root in the trail and pulling myself up again. I would have dropped upon the roof of the gendarme's house a thousand feet below. . . .

I decided after reading that, that it must have been Captain Amaru's April Fool's joke, after all. Perhaps that is why he delayed his sailing to get his victims home. A good joker pays up when his joke misfires.

We brought the *Aikane* over to Omoa to stock up for the sail to the Tuamotus and Tahiti at the Grelet establishment. It was like a feudal barony: a large property enclosed by a fence, planted in lawn grass and shaded by great hardwood trees that M. Grelet planted fifty years ago. There were fruit orchards and gardens, a windmill to grind the grain grown on other Grelet land, corrals for horses, pens for pigs, sheep grazing—and thereby mowing—the lawns, and herds of white goats on the hillside beyond the pale. The comic touch in all this bucolic peacefulness was supplied by a brood of very military ducks, which marched here and there in single file with an air of intense and totally inappropriate purpose.

We wandered around, unmolested, apparently unnoticed, until at last we located the famous general store. It was not nearly as large as we had expected, and it was practically unmanned. There was a very pretty, indolent, and slightly arrogant young woman behind the counter, but she was conducting a flirtation with a young French-Tahitian surveyor who was leaning on the counter the better to hold her hand. She had no time for us.

"Could we pay our respects to M. Grelet?" I asked. "We bring greetings from his friend M. Le Brunnec."

"I am Suzanne," the young woman said. "Suzanne Grelet."

The young man explained in better French than Suzanne's that the father of Suzanne was the son of the lady who was now the wife of M. Grelet. (Said father was dead, and Suzanne was his only surviving child. She was, therefore, the heiress apparent. All this we discovered a little later in the day, but we should have been able to guess it from Suzanne's manner, which would have been hard to take from a Rose Queen, and was intolerable in the keeper of a store.)

If Norris had not been with us, I doubt that Suzanne would have troubled herself to send a messenger into the main house to arrange for an appointment with the seigneur of this fief. She gave Norris a look that took inventory and filed for future reference. To our questions about the price of this or that item we wanted to buy, she had but one answer

"*Sais pas.*"

Did anyone else know?

Suzanne shrugged. Her suitor explained that Suzanne's father had known all these things, but now that he was gone, there was really no one. Later in the day a trusted employee, who was now absent on business, might stop in for a few moments. If we would leave a list of the purchases we had in mind, perhaps he would be able to answer some of our questions.

Could we speak with this trusted employee ourselves?

The lovers consulted. It would be difficult, but not impossible to catch him. If we cared to come back and wait . . .

At this point the messenger to the manor house returned. We were in luck. M. Grelet would receive us upon waking from his nap. The exact hour of that waking could not be predicted. Perhaps the best thing was for us to return when we had eaten the meal of midday, and wait for whichever inter-view became possible first.

There was no public eating place in Omoa, and the row out to the *Aikane* was more than we wanted to spend on lunch, so we decided to split up and forage. Benson and I called on the head teacher, M. Armand Bertrand, a Tahitian, who lived in a charming little bungalow only a few yards from the back gate of the Grelet compound.

Over a cold beer (from his electric refrigerator) and some fresh bread (baked by the husband of the other member of his faculty), M. Bertrand told us a good deal about the problems of Polynesian adolescents, and none of it was encouraging. The best students, those who manage to pass the matriculation exams, are sent to the Lycée Paul Gauguin in Tahiti (or its counterpart in Raiatea).* There the girls are prepared to be teachers—like poor Mlle. Rosalie—and unfit for life in places like Hanavave, which is where they are needed. A few boys elect to become teachers, and for those who do not there is really no opening. Once in a very long time one of rare ability is sent to the university in Paris, from which bourne, in M. Bertrand's experience, no traveler has ever returned.

Those students, boys and occasionally a girl or two, who do not pass the exams and so would be through with school at fourteen, and who elect to continue their education, are sent to *centres d'apprentissage*, trade schools in Papeete that train electricians, carpenters, hotel workers, and so on. Fare is paid by the government, and tuition is free, but there is no allowance for living expenses.

"If the families cannot pay—or do not wish to—the children must steal. You will find many who join *les bandes* in Papeete. And others who join after the course is completed."

"Doesn't the government pay their way home again?"

"If they wish to come. But why should they? What they have learned is of no use to them here. There is no electricity—no work for a carpenter—no hotel or café. They stay on in Papeete because life is more exciting, but there is no work there either. They run in packs like the wild dogs of the hills." M. Bertrand smiled apologetically as he added, "It is the same in America, one hears."

The conversation drifted into other channels, and Benson remembered a concern that had touched us all as we watched the children playing in the surf on the beach or diving from the rocks at the landing pier.

"I've seen children who don't look more than four or five playing at all hours, with no adult anywhere in sight. Are there ever any accidents? Has a child ever drowned?"

M. Bertrand looked almost sheepish. "Not in the time I have been here. I must confess to you, my esteemed friends, the only child here who has accidents is my own.

---

* The *lycée* at Taiohae will eventually absorb all the Marquesan students, but at the time of our visit it was just getting under way.

"My wife and I are French as well as Tahitian, and we bring up our little one in the French way. She goes nowhere without the mother or the father following behind. 'Don't fall, Marianne!' . . . 'Don't climb there or you will fall!' . . . 'Don't go in the water! You will be made to fall by a wave!' . . . 'Don't go on the pier. It is slippery. You will fall!'" He sighed and spread his hands. "Marianne falls. The others do not."

"Why do you think that is?" Benson asked.

"I will tell you," said M. Bertrand with no trace of resentment. "We will speak of the climbing of trees, by example. It was forbidden to Marianne until she was five. Now I am trying to teach her to climb the big avocado tree in front of the house here. She has hurt herself so many times that my wife now says, No more! It is too late!

"The children of the Marquesans have been climbing such trees since they began to walk. That is the age at which balance must be learned. And it is the same with swimming. For Marianne it is too late."

We tried to reassure M. Bertrand that all was not yet lost. If he and his wife could grit their teeth and live through a few vicarious bruises and skinned knees, Marianne might still catch up. He was unconvinced.

"There is something else. We have made her afraid. We have said a thousand times, 'Be careful, you'll fall!' When she begins to climb, she hears those words and believes them. I will fall, she thinks, and it disturbs her balance. The idea of falling does not come into the minds of the other children because they have not been warned."

When we excused ourselves to keep our appointment next door, M. Bertrand offered to come along and smooth the way. "That Suzanne becomes difficult," he said, "now that she sees herself the owner of most of Fatu Hiva. When her grandfather is dead, not even her grandmother will be able to control her, and Madame is a woman of formidable strength! One hopes that Suzanne will take it into her head to travel. Here she will turn into an eater of men."

Thanks to M. Bertrand's diplomacy, we were able to order everything we needed, including some 180-pound-test monofilament that he recommended for fishing in these parts. The only problem was meat. We could buy a whole lamb on the hoof and in the fleece, but again the men of my crew balked at the butchering. In the end it was arranged to trade the hide for the killing, disemboweling, and skinning of the animal. The hacking up was really not difficult, M. Bertrand assured us. He would come out to the *Aikane* after school tomorrow and personally assist.

Just as the last of the arrangements was concluded, word was brought that the hour of our audience had come. M. Bertrand wished us well. We were led into the lower floor of the solid two-story house, through a sort of foyer in which were priceless objects of Marquesan art, both antique and modern: huge carved bowls and platters, full-size canoe paddles, war clubs, poi pounders, ancient ceremonial tapas, shell leis, and specimens of rare and beautiful conch and cone shells. It was the first and only museum of Marquesan art we saw in the archipelago, and more impressive than the collection in the museum at Papeete. We looked around for a Gauguin, but saw no paintings at all.

On a sunny porch above the foyer, Mr. Grelet was waiting for us in a carved *tou* chair that served very well as a throne. He was very old—about eighty-five, M. Bertrand had told us—very pale, thin, and erect, dressed in immaculate white knitted underwear, buttoned to the neck but cut off at the elbows (and not hemmed), a pair of white duck trousers, and leather sandals. Somehow he managed an almost papal presence despite the costume, and he spoke in a French as slow and sonorous as a church dignitary's. If I had not known something of his picaresque history from my reading of O'Brien, I would have been awed.

We repeated M. Le Brunnec's message (which he had already heard from Captain Amaru). M. Grelet nodded.

"He will not come to Omoa because the last time he got drunk and slipped as he boarded the boat to return, and suffered injury. He would have me risk the same danger," he said, and having disposed of the amenities, inquired our business.

I explained that we had made some purchases of provisions from his entrepôt.

"And now you are looking to purchase some paintings or carvings of Paul Gauguin if I have them and do not know the value. Unfortunately, neither is the case."

I suppose we deserved it, for we really had no errand that required his attention. We were simply curious tourists. But it was the only time we were ever rebuked for it. There was nothing to say but good-bye. M. Grelet did not deign to reply. He waved one pale, splotched hand, and the young Marquesan who had brought us led us away.

Our last day in the Marquesas was a fine and fruitful one. We started by taking our dirty clothes and bed linen to wash in the river that met the sea at the beach where the children played. We polluted its cool, fresh water with detergent, while everything, including salty bath towels, was washed, rinsed, and wrung out. When everything was hanging to dry on trees or bushes, we washed ourselves, lathering up like Lifebuoy advertisements. I even shampooed and set my hair.

Leaving the laundry and the *Lili Aikane* to the mercies of the surf riders, we made the rounds of Omoa: bought bread from the baker, were gifted with a whole stem of green bananas (which Jack and Norris tied to a pole and carried on their shoulders, mountain fashion); passed the Bernard home and were gifted with a basket full of avocados from the tree Marianne couldn't climb; and stopped at the Grelet entrepôt to let them know that we were ready to take delivery at the dock. As Jack signed traveler's checks, I did some arithmetic. We had bought a hundred very large oranges for 250 francs—at 2½ cents apiece, which was cheap enough. The lamb cost another 250 francs. If it weighed 25 pounds, which was likely, we were getting it at something like 10 cents a pound.

We bought mangoes and breadfruit, a good deal more than we were likely to use, unless we dug a poi pit in the bilge. It took a wheelbarrow to convey all the loot to the pier, and two trips in the dinghy to transship it to the boat. But at last it was done; the laundry was all retrieved, despite the wind and the curious children; M. Bertrand and Benson hacked their way through the lamb carcass, which I wrapped in foil, and stowed.

We all settled down in the cockpit to eat bread and cheese, drink Algerian wine, and listen to M. Bertrand talk about Papeete. It was his home, and he obviously loved it, but he was bitter about the fate that was overtaking it.

"Papeete is ruined. Soon all of Tahiti will be ruined. The Tahitian family is ruined. La Légion Étrangère and the bomb tests will finish what your M-G-M began."

According to M. Bertrand, the company that shot *Mutiny on the Bounty* spent nearly a year around Papeete. The combination of easily earned American dollars and short, sweet careers as bit players upset the economic and social stability of the Tahitian bourgeoisie. It never got a chance to recover. Foreign Légionnaires swarmed in on the heels of the departing Americans. Germans, Swedes, Africans, and Frenchmen with pasts they would like to live down had been brought in to build the test site on the atoll of Mururoa, several hundred miles to the southeast. Papeete was the supply depot as well as the place all personnel spent their leaves. The Légionnaires had plenty of money, and little interest in saving it.

Washday at Omoa.

"Tahitian men cannot hold their wives against such competition," Mr. Bertrand said. "Families are broken, children left to run the streets. And there are many crimes! Last year a Tahitian woman was murdered in the café she owned. It was resented by the Tahitians, so the police ordered that no more Légionnaires were to come. It was the only way to keep from more murders —a little war!"

"Doesn't that sort of thing put a café out of business?"

"No. The Légion is not everything. There is still the French Army, the Navy, and the Americans who come on the planes."

M. Bertrand also threw some light on the problem of coffee picking. It was true, he said, that the crop was spoiling, both here in the Marquesas and in Tahiti.

"It is *beaucoup de travail le plus pénible*, you understand. In the hot sun and many hours' ride from their homes. The wage to the picker is one half the price of the crop. That has been always. But no one can say in advance what the price will be.

Jack and Norris carrying bananas.

It is set by Donald in Tahiti—after the crop is picked, not before!

"Last year they gave 35 francs a kilo. [That meant 18 cents a pound to be divided between picker and grower.] It was not enough. But when one has finished the picking, it is too late to bargain."

"They can't afford to hold the crop off the market till the price goes up?" Jack asked.

"The crop does not belong to the picker."

We saw the dilemma, but not the solution. Remembering Tom Graham, I asked, "Is it possible to set the price before the whole crop is in? Or does that make it too big a gamble for the owner?"

M. Bertrand did not know. But, like a Marquesan, he does not consider it his obligation to solve the economic problems of foreign entrepreneurs.

As we talked, a bright satellite climbed the sky from southwest to northeast.

"It is one of yours," said our guest. "The others' go in the opposite direction."

Venus and a new moon burned at the edge of the sunset, and as the gold light faded, Venus made a star track on the calm sea. A lighted pirogue passed us, heading for Hanavave; then another, and another.

"They are going home. They came for the practice of the Eastern hymns," said M. Bertrand.

"They paddled all the way over from Hanavave, for choir practice? And after a day's work?"

M. Bertrand nodded. "They are not lazy, the Marquesans. No matter what the *popaa** says."

---

* *Popaa* means "foreigner" in Tahitian, and is usually applied to white Europeans or Americans.

The Dangerous Islands

Jack had been advised in California not to sail anywhere near the Tuamotus, and under no circumstances try to make a landing on one. Charts of the area are unreliable: islands are sometimes as much as five miles off their charted position; underwater obstacles are sometimes not charted at all; there are no reliable aids to navigation such as lights; "passes" into the sheltered lagoons of the larger atolls are very tricky to navigate because of strong currents that sometimes make whirlpools (*opape*) in which small craft are actually sucked down and submerged. During the twelve months before we sailed, two boats that were well known in California yachting circles went on reefs in the Tuamotus, including the famous *Wanderer*, which was still standing on the reef at Rangiroa.*

Captain Amaru and another young Tahitian captain whom we met briefly in Taiohae convinced Jack that by exercising reasonable caution he could manage a landing at Takaroa, the island where the dive was on, and perhaps at Rangiroa as well. It was simply a matter of staying well out to sea of any land mass when wind or darkness made it hard to see where one was going or to go where one intended to. Also, since it was important not to attempt the "pass" on either Takaroa or Rangiroa on the dangerous ebb, it was important to know the rhythm of the tides. There are no tide tables worked out for the Tuamotus, but Captain Hann gave us a sort of rough "do-it-yourself" scheme, based on the phase and position of the moon.

* Eight months after we left the area, a magnificent schooner, the *Valrosa*, which had moored almost next to us in Papeete during our stay there, went aground on an atoll near Rangiroa, and was broken to bits in three hours.

We were in the season of light winds and the week of an almost full moon. We had our engine to fall back on if the wind or tide opposed us. We all wanted very much to see the Tuamotus. And we all had confidence in Jack's seamanship. But even so, we were all tensed for what we considered the most challenging stretch of water in the whole projected voyage.

We got away from Fatu Hiva early, and sailed on something close to that "beautiful beam reach" one hears sailors talk about like the hope of heaven. The course was 225 degrees, so we were not beating into the trades as we had on our way through the Marquesas. But before noon, the wind had dropped and we had to motor.

There was not a cloud in the sky, except those that clustered over the mountain towers of Fatu Hiva, slipping slowly under the horizon astern. We caught a fine bonito on our new heavy tackle, but a bigger fish bit it in half while the men were pulling it aboard.

The problem of food was what to do with all the Grelet lamb. It seemed a crime to cook all the fresh meat we were going to have till we got to Tahiti (at least two weeks away), but the refrigerator hardly held its forty degrees while we were motoring. The moment we shut the engine off, the temperature needle rose to "Danger" and went out of sight.

I roasted one of the legs, and it was tender and tasty. No better than young kid, but much meatier. But running the oven made the cabin uncomfortably hot. I asked for a mandate to do the whole job and get it over. The men agreed. All the small, odd-shaped packets that M. Bertrand and Benson had wrapped in foil were simply moved from the refrigerator to the oven, and baked. When they were cool, they went back into the refrigerator. We had cold cuts every other noon, and lamb stew or curry every other night until the last of it was gone.

SEAGOING LAMB CURRY

Chunks of roast lamb (or beef, if that's what you have)
1 pkg. dried vegetable soup
Roux

Curry powder
White (or red) wine

We no longer had any fresh vegetables, but a package of a good brand of dehydrated vegetable soup gave both flavor and "garnish." I added less liquid than the recipe of the package called for, and mixed seawater, fresh water, and wine. (I went on the assumption that seawater was full of all sorts of health-promoting minerals, and used it whenever I could. But if we had been sailing near any bomb-test site, I would have fallen back on the saltshaker.)

Heat the bite-size chunks of meat in the soup until they are warmed through. Then thicken the mixture with roux and curry powder, blended. (I brought some homemade browned flour for roux in a moisture-proof jar, but when it eventually ran out I found that a can of some condensed cream soup, chicken, mushroom, or even celery, did very well.)

The trick is not to boil the flavor out of the curry powder. If one is using condensed soup instead of roux, a very good strong curry flavor can be obtained by sprinkling the powder over the meat before it is put in to warm.

We grated coconut over it just before serving, and combined it with mashed potatoes (instant). Possible alternatives in the starch department include bean thread (a clear, stringy, spaghetti-like product made of soybeans), rice, or baked breadfruit.

On the second night out, the wind picked up and we sailed, making between four and five knots. The navigators calculated that if the same wind held, and no current interposed, we would make Takaroa on the fourth day out of Fatu Hiva, and at 1:00 P.M., which was ideal as far as the tide was concerned.

Captain Hann's tide chart consisted of a clockface that referred to the position of the moon. At twelve o'clock (that is, when the moon is straight overhead) the water was presumed to be slack. The same held for three, six, and nine o'clock (moon time). Fast ebb was halfway between three and six—or about five thirty; and between nine and twelve—about ten thirty. Fast flow would thus be at about two thirty and seven thirty. The object of the game was, of course, to avoid fast ebb, at all costs, and make the pass by daylight.

By consulting the almanac and studying the information about the moon for this day, week, month, and year, our navigators established the fact (*sic*) that there was only one time when all the auguries would be right: Thursday, April 8, at Local Noon. On Friday, April 9, there was a pretty good hour at 1:00 P.M. But since we couldn't (or didn't want to) hang around offshore for a full twenty-four hours, Jack decided that if we missed the first target date, noon on Thursday, we would give up Takaroa, and try for the next island, Manihi, on Friday.

Under this pressure of suspense, navigation became frenetic. The three men were taking shots or making calculations from civil twilight before sunrise to civil twilight after sunset, and Benson was reading up on moon shots. I made an occasional feeble effort to participate, but I was definitely low man (woman) on this totem pole, hopelessly outclassed in the struggle for the second-class sextant, more and more prone to make simple mathematical errors as I hurried my figuring to get an answer before Norris or someone else told me what it ought to be. For the most part, I retired from the battle and studied French—particularly the sort of technical terms I would have to use in Tahiti when I translated for Benson in conference with the *grosses têtes* in the Ministry of Education. Also, I began reading Michener's *Hawaii*, parts of which ought to be required reading for everyone cruising the volcanic islands of the Pacific.

It was somewhere between Fatu Hiva and the Tuamotus that our ship-to-shore radio suddenly began to work again. We had spoken to Los Angeles a few hours before we sailed into the electrical storm off the Marquesas, and that was the last time we had made contact. But now we were out of whatever baleful influence disrupted communication, and when we could get through the bottleneck of the marine operator at Oakland, we could talk to Jack's sister's home in the San Fernando Valley and get news and complaints. Our cables from Taiohae had arrived, but no letters! (The letters we had written were still in the hold of the *Taporo*, which might or might not beat us in to Papeete and the post office.)

On the third day, the wind shifted. It was still pushing us along at five knots, and we still had hopes of making Takaroa by noon Thursday. But we were no longer on a beam reach. We were running again, sailing wing and wing, with the main to port and our big-bellied Genoa to starboard.

Late in the afternoon Jack set a problem that even a retired navigator like me could work on. Given our presumed position (which was not absolutely reliable because we had missed the noon latitude shot, owing to overcast), and knowing that we wanted to sight Takaroa at dawn in order to come abeam of the pass at noon, at what hour should we heave to? Part of the problem was an estimation of the distance we would drift when the sails were dropped. But the critical factor was the value judgment: What constituted a margin of safety?

Everyone worked the problem alone and came up with an answer of something close to 11:00 P.M. Just to give ourselves an extra margin on the margin, we dropped the sails at ten thirty, the Genoa completely, the main only partway, in an effort to steady us so we didn't slat around all night.

It didn't do much good. The noise was like the sound track of "The Haunting." All sorts and shapes of objects rolled back and forth in lockers, cupboards, and even on deck. The worst sound of all was the snap of the reefed main, which we knew was tearing and sawing the already worn sail ties.

"Running on a reef would be a real relief," I muttered to Benson, who was not sleeping either. And that set me off on an unsettling memory train.

My great-grandfather did run on a reef in these waters, long before Melville put Tahiti on the literary map. We had his journal aboard, and I had recently reread the section entitled

The Wreck

. . . when we left Nookaheeva [he meant Hiva Oa], we spread all our canvas to the breeze. . . . On a clear night, when we were about 830 miles south-east of Otaheite, we were running close-hauled of the larboard tack with a fresh topgallant breeze, some of the watch were pacing the deck, others were seated on the windlass, listening to a song, whilst the ship was making merry music as she plowed the salt foam. Suddenly the whole crew was thrown into consternation by loud cries from the look-out—breakers! breakers!

"Where away?" shouted the officer of the deck.

"Right ahead, sir," shouted several voices almost simultaneously.

"Call all hands! Starboard the helm! Stand by to tack ship!" These orders were given in quick succession and as quickly obeyed. The helm was put to leeward immediately, and the ship came to the wind, but the maneuver was performed so quickly, and there was so much confusion that the ship lost her head-way before the sheets were started and consequently she missed stays.

Having failed in the attempt to tack, the captain gave orders to fill away the sails and wear the ship to starboard. Those who are acquainted with nautical evolutions are aware that a ship in wearing makes a considerable circuit, and being so near the breakers, before we could bring the ship out on the other tack, she struck on a coral reef. The first breakers that boarded us, tore away the hurricane house and swept away all our boats but the larboard bow boat and the starboard quarter boat. In attempting to lower the bow boat, it was filled by a breaker and our cooper, Mr. Churchill, was precipitated into the sea, and being an able swimmer, he reached a small rock from which he was taken next morning. By the vigilance of our mate—Mr. Norton—we succeeded in lowering the quarter-boat safely with which the Captain and seven men made their escape from the breakers.

Mr. Norton took immediate measures to get the remainder of the crew from the ship. There was no time to be lost, for every breaker that struck the ship, lifted her from the reef and then let her fall with such violence that her timbers broke and spars fell at every collision.

We saw the rocks apparently not more than 60 yards from the bow of our ship, and as they seemed to be tolerably level and only a few feet above the surface of the water, we concluded that we might land safely upon a raft.

This was soon formed by lashing together the hatches, loose spars and such boards as we could knock off from the waist of the ship, for the concussion was so violent that the ship bilged and filled with water in a few moments after she first struck; hence, the main object was to save our lives from the impending danger. The raft being formed and launched into the sea, we jumped upon it and committed ourselves to the waves. It was a hazardous adventure, for the waves rolled over us, and there was danger of being killed when the raft struck the rocks, or of being drawn back into the sea by the receding waves. Nevertheless, we held on securely, and a few surges threw us upon the dark reef or rocks. Most of us were thrown down when the raft struck, but springing to our feet quickly, we succeeded in clearing the raft before it was drawn back into the sea.

When we assembled upon the dry rock, we discovered that one of our men—John Turner—was missing, and we concluded he was either entangled in the raft and drowned, or washed off while the raft was passing from the wreck to the rocks. He was not found that night, nor subsequently. . . .

Jack was up most of the night, prowling around on the deck over our bunks. From time to time Benson went on the prowl with him. I lay there, sinking now and then into uneasy dream and waking to the imagined cry, *Breakers! Breakers! . . . Where away?*

We ran up the sails at dawn, but we weren't sure what heading to make. There was no way of telling exactly how far or in what direction we had drifted, until we could get a fix at noon. So everyone became a lookout, each choosing a slightly different direction in which to stare till his eyes blurred.

At 10:30 A.M. we saw Takaroa! Just a short fuzzy line on the horizon. And by the time we could see it, we were less than ten miles away.

By eleven, we were abeam of its nearest point, but we still didn't know whether we were on the right heading for the pass. One must be absolutely sure about the location of such a channel. What shows above the surface of the sea has no real relevance to the shape of an atoll, which is in essence a great circular reef that has grown up around a sunken volcano. There may be one, or more, or no deep clefts in its circumference through which a ship can pass. What one sees is the "land"—never more than four feet above the high-water mark—that supports some sort of vegetable life. There are many stretches of reef that are awash at high tide, or even at low, but which would tear the bottom out of any boat that tried to ride over them. The best way to tell one of these phonies from a true pass is by the color of the water. That can only be judged from a considerable height. There was no way to get up our mast without dropping sail, and Jack didn't want to do that. So we coasted along the shore, looking for a landmark.

It's incredibly difficult to recognize on a shoreline what you read on a chart. What looks like an unbroken coast from a few miles offshore may be two quite separate islands, as at Hiva Oa and Tahu Ata, or a series of headlands and inlets. If one comes in too close, one may run on to a projecting underwater reef. If one stays too far out, one may never find the pass.

What we were looking for on the white sand beach, shimmer-blinding in the sun, was a wreck. The *Coast Pilot* said that the *County of Roxborough* was driven on the reef in the hurricane of 1906, and was clearly visible three miles northeast of the pass. It occurred to Benson and to me that a wreck almost sixty years old might be reduced to something hard to recognize as a ship from a mile or more away. (There is a wreck on the Oregon coast near our home, also dating from 1906, that has almost totally disintegrated.) So we put the binoculars on every dark object we passed. But they all turned out to be old coral heads.

As we got closer to noon, suspense began to tighten everyone's nerves. It was possible that we had missed the wreck, and therefore the pass, by approaching the atoll from a more obtuse angle than our plotting sheet indicated. In that case, we would have to come about and double back, and would arrive too late for slack water. Jack was talking about giving up and going on toward Manihi, when suddenly a point of land disengaged itself from the continuum of the coast, and, as we rounded it, we saw the wreck.

It was unmistakable! A great rusty hull, completely intact, sitting bolt upright with surf pounding at its stern. It might have been moored!

From then on, it was easy. We could spare part of our energies to marvel at the quality of the light and the color of the water. It is bluer than at Capri. (I read somewhere that it is because the rate of evaporation is so high. The faster, the bluer; the slower, the greener. That's why the sea is emerald near the poles.)

The pass, when it came, was as unmistakable as the wreck. We saw the little town—white walls, red roofs, and the spire of a Mormon church rising out of a clump of taller-than-average coconut palms. A few minutes later we were abeam of a wide stretch of smooth water that looked like a great river, leading to an inland sea. Both sides of the channel were defined by stripes of turquoise and sand-beige. The latter is a shelf of living coral almost at the surface; the former is a shelf of dead reef about twenty feet down. Wherever one looks in the lagoons and passes of true atolls, one sees the same bold pattern: beige, turquoise, and the ultramarine of the deeps. At Takaroa, the edge looks man-drawn, it is so sharp.

It was past the hour we had calculated as slack, and Jack was very tentative about our entrance into the pass. We dropped sail and tried it with the motor. It seemed able to handle the current, so we headed in. The beige reefs funneled in to a narrows, still ample for maneuvering, and we were close enough to have a look at the pier where we would have to tie up. It ran parallel to the channel, and was made of rough cement, with no sort of bumper to keep boats from scraping holes in their sides.

There were a dozen able-bodied men standing in a narrow strip of shade under the eaves of a copra storage barn, but none of them made a sign of greeting or offered any advice. It seemed a little uncordial, and once again, as at Ua Pou, I felt a slight stir of uneasiness. What if these short, dark, powerfully built Paumotuans did not want us to visit them? Norris shouted a *kaoha*, and then *ia orana*, which he had been told was a Paumotuan or Tahitian equivalent. I tried *bonjour*. Neither of us got any response.

Meanwhile Jack had executed a 180-degree turn in midchannel and was sneaking the *Aikane* up to the pier as gingerly as if she were made of eggshell. Norris and Benson jumped out—as soon as that was possible—and held us off, while I tried to place our two slim plastic bumpers in the most obviously threatened spots. They were much too chic for this situation; what we needed was some old truck tires.

Jack was giving orders about making the mooring lines fast to some stubby concrete posts that seemed to have been placed on the dock for that purpose, when the Paumotuans moved forward in a body. They were not smiling, and they did not return a second round of greetings. They were not reassuring to look at either, dressed in sleeveless undershirts and ragged cotton shorts, each wearing a different sort of battered headgear, a straw hat or a handkerchief, and each with a magnificent headband of shells so out of key with the rest of his costume that it looked stolen.

Some took the mooring lines from Norris's and Benson's hands and went about making them fast to other posts, most of them at a distance. Some came aboard and looked about for and found other lines. They said nothing because they knew in advance that we understood no lingua franca that they spoke. They did not know how to tell us that we were doing things all wrong; they only could do them right. And so they did.

When they were done, we were tied fore and aft with two ordinary mooring lines, and with four spring lines! Six in all! The wharf looked like a cat's-cradle, and walking along it was like skipping rope. They had used every foot of line we had aboard. (Jack suspected for a while that the whole ploy was a way of getting a look at new styles in nylon line.) But we were safe, no matter which way or how fast the current in the channel might run. We knew before the day was over how valuable their help had been.

Takaroa was the South Sea island of all our preconceptions: white coral sand, calm lagoon, palm trees tossing in a gentle breeze, warm night with a full moon—the works!

The village where we were moored was the only permanent settlement on the atoll, which is about thirty miles in circumference. Normally it houses about three hundred people, most of them in wooden houses. Every plank and stud of these had to be imported, and all were well on their way to liquidation by termites. A few of the larger houses, the Mormon church, and all the walls that separate dooryards from the public road were made of indigenous materials: coral rubble, shell plaster, and whitewash. These structures have real style (except that the church has a faint overlay of orthodox Utah architecture), and there is hope that urban redevelopment will take a cue from the termites and replace expensive ugliness with cheap beauty, as the tiny bulldozers make it necessary.

At the time of our arrival, Takaroa's normal population was swollen to one thousand by *la plonge*. Every able-bodied male in the archipelago (who was not off building the bomb base at Mururoa) was here, and many had brought their wives and children. The restrictions against diving for pearl and pearl shell had been lifted for three months, but only in a certain section of the lagoon of this island. When the three months were over, Takaroa would be closed to diving for perhaps as long as three years.

The French instituted this very strict conservation policy after World War I and the introduction of scuba when, for a while, it looked as if the beds of pearl oysters might be cleaned out all over the archipelago. Laws were passed prohibiting the use of any underwater breathing equipment, and diving by any but Paumotuans. A rotation system was worked out so that each diving area had years to recover from a season of exploitation, and, of course, the minimum size limits set. In addition, shell buyers were required to register with the government and be licensed. Each merchant has to contract with at least fifteen divers, who promise to sell their whole catch to him at a government-established price, in return for which they are insured against death by drowning or serious injury. (There are usually a few "free divers," who are not insured and who can sell to anyone for any price they can get. It was with them we did business when we wanted to take home some shells.)

There had been times (before Mururoa) when three thousand Paumotuans would show up for a dive, and Chinese merchants from Tahiti made a lucrative business out of supplying their needs. Entire stores were shipped and set up, including stocks of diving supplies, canned food, soft drinks, and what passes for ice cream in those latitudes, and billiard tables! Even at the time of our visit, the center of the migrant colony had something of the feel of a gold-rush town when the day's work is over and the evening's pleasures begin.

To police all the red tape involved in this operation, the government had sent out from Papeete a battery of *grosses têtes*: a game warden, whose job it was to see that no one dove outside the assigned area and that no undersized shells were brought up; a gendarme, who represented the power behind the regulations; an *infirmier*, who supervised public health and did what he could as a surrogate doctor; and the *chef*. The latter was theoretically in residence year-round, but actually his home was in Papeete. He divided his time pretty much as he liked between that home and his coconut plantation on Takaroa, except in the time of the dive. Then he had to be on location, and someone of his household had to be on duty to supervise the sale of beer, which was the only alcoholic beverage permitted to the Paumotuans. This function was performed during our stay by the mother of the *chef*, Mme. Manu Mervin, who was the closest thing to a queen we met anywhere in the islands.

Mme. Mervin was in her sixties, tall and beautifully proportioned, with heavy graying hair that hung, even when braided, below her waist. We never saw her dressed for anything but kitchen duty—barefooted, in a shabby printed cotton shift—but her air was so unconsciously regal that we were uncomfortable if she got up and moved about while we remained seated. Of typically mixed lineage (Danish, English, and Cook Islander), Madame spoke several languages well enough to conduct business in them, but her principal function was performed in silence. Her commodious backroom was not only a kitchen but also the beer parlor and lower-level municipal court. A drunken diver who applied to Mme. Mervin for another bottle of Hinano had to meet her eye, and most of them couldn't.

As a result, drunkenness was at an all-time low for the season of *la plonge*.

We met Madame first when we came to present our papers and passports, and she entertained us in her formal front parlor, decorated with shell treasures and family photographs, until the *chef* and his entourage returned from an inspection tour of the lagoon. By that time she and I had reached the recipe-exchanging level of instant friendship. The whole of our stay in Takaroa seemed, in retrospect, to be a working out of the gastronomic consequences of that first encounter.

It began with a picnic on which the four of us were guests of the four *grosses têtes*: Dédé (Ferdinand) the *chef*; François the gendarme; François the game warden; and Ricki the *infirmier*. Owing to the unusually low number of divers, the Four had not enough work to keep them busy, and too much time to brood on how homesick they were for the girls (or wives) they had left behind them in Papeete. We were the only real diversion that had turned up since the season started, and they decided to give us the full treatment. We were invited to inspect the diving operations and to go on an excursion to the wreck on the beach, where we would eat lunch. We accepted eagerly and asked what we could bring. Our own skin-diving equipment was the answer. Nothing more.

Our hosts called for us at the pier in two fine new launches with powerful outboards. They were government property, of course, and it would have been indiscreet to use them without at least a fig leaf of "official business," so two pairs of divers got the most cursory of inspections, and we got an illustrated lecture on how they go about their task.

Diving is done by teams of two or three men, with now and then a woman in the place of one, but never as a diver. An outrigger canoe is paddled (or motored) out to a designated spot in the huge inland sea of the lagoon. In quiet weather one person can hold the canoe above the diver and also handle the line that carries his weight up and down. In bad weather it takes one to handle the pirogue, and one to coil the line.

Divers wear black neoprene jackets (if they are rich enough to afford them) not because the water is cold—even at the working depth of 125 feet—but because they ease the pressure. For the same reason they wear goggles instead of masks. They protect their hands with gloves, and carry a knife. But their feet are bare; no fins! They get down by holding a stone weight that is secured to one end of a line, the other end of which is made fast to a thwart in the canoe. The coiling of this line is the critical skill in the above-water operation; it must run out without a hitch until the diver hits bottom.

He has a minute and a half to work: to get down, cut loose the nacre shells, deposit them in his basket, and rise to the surface. Anything over a minute and a half does damage to the brain, damage that is cumulative because it is due to oxygen deprivation. There are a number of old men wandering around all pearl-diving villages with foolish smiles, victims of their own greed or ignorance. Too many times they cut "just one more shell" and held their breath another twenty or thirty seconds. We saw half-a-dozen such pitiful cases in Takaroa.

When the diver is ready to come up, he tugs the line. His partner begins to coil it. The basket may or may not come up at the same time, depending on whether or not it is full. But the oysters are never opened until the day's diving is over. Then, when the diver is safely out of the water, the shells are opened, inspected for pearls (which are rare now) and for unusual color ("gold lip" shells, for instance, fetch a higher price). Some of the oyster meat is set aside for dinner; the rest is dumped overboard.

Moments later the sharks arrive and clean up. The sharks of Takaroa's lagoon are not ferocious, possibly because they are too well fed. They do not attack divers unless lured by some particularly delicious attraction; the blood of a freshly shot fish or a scrap of oyster meat will madden them. If one observes reasonable precautions, however, one may—and I did—swim in tandem with a fairly sizable specimen as safely as with a human buddy.

We tried to dive deep enough (with fins) to watch the divers at work. The water was marvelously clear, and I'm sure we could see at least fifty feet down. But at thirty feet I felt as if my head were going to implode, and I could still see nothing below but blurry sunrays, dissolving into blue. So we clambered back into the launches, and prepared to take off. Our hosts, in the way of cops everywhere, extracted a small tribute: a pair of fine shells for each of us. It was paid without apparent resentment, but we felt uncomfortable and offered the going price. "Not permitted," said François the gendarme. "These are contract divers. They can sell only to the Chinese."

Now, our hosts said, it was time to get food for lunch. We raced across the lagoon, bucking and bouncing in the chop until my spinal cord cramped in protest. In what seemed the very center, we stopped and threw out anchors on a huge coral head. It rose from unknown depths to within a few inches of the surface—something for the unsuspecting speeder to run on at full throttle! But perhaps there were no Takaroans able to achieve such speed who were also ignorant of the underwater landscape.

Everyone put on mask, fins, and snorkel, took gun in hand and went overboard, except François the gendarme, who had bad sinuses and did not dive. I decided to watch an expert hunt before I took off on my own, and I picked Ricki the *infirmier*, who turned out to be the best spearfisherman I have ever seen anywhere.

I followed him around for half an hour, so fascinated that I frequently forgot to go up for air until my head started to throb. Under the water, he looked like a marine animal. His dark skin took on a shadowy blue color, and his movements had the languid grace of a seal. Even when he surfaced for a breath, it was with a slow casualness that implied no urgency. His gun looked crude enough to be homemade, which was not the case. It had only one rubber and no safety, but it had a wooden stock that floated when released, and a very slender spear that went much faster than those of our American-made guns.

Ricki would take a breath, descend about ten feet, and swim along the face of the underwater cliff. Schools of small fish passed him without seeming to notice him. These same fish spooked when they got within a few yards of me, probably because my fins were working too hard. Even with a weight belt, I found it hard to stay down in that water. And having to go up for air more frequently than Ricki, I occasionally lost him.

Once, when I was looking for him, I rounded a sharp corner and came upon a magnificent underwater window, framing what looked like a prize aquarium: dozens of brilliantly colored and patterned shooting-size fish! I forgot to calculate such things as the probable depth of the window passage or the amount of air I had left in my lungs. I flapped hard with my fins and drove down and through.

The passage was longer than it looked, and narrower, and at the end I had to "motorboat" to get through. One leg touched the side, and I had a long coral scratch (not deep enough to draw blood but doomed to be infected, as all coral cuts are). At the time I didn't feel it. All I felt was the pounding of my heart and my head as my blood cried out for oxygen, and the wonder of the vision through which I moved.

By the time I caught up with Ricki, he had shot a small fish and was using it for bait. Violating all the rules about getting your catch into the boat before it attracts sharks, Ricki deliberately fixed the small fish on his spear, retreated behind a column of coral, and held the small fish out where an oncoming big one would see it. He held himself as motionless as possible in the current that swirled around the column, and moved the spear just enough so that the bait looked alive.

He had to go up for air a couple of times, but eventually the ruse worked. A large black and gray triggerfish came around the column and made for the bait. Ricki shot and had both of them. This time he wasted not a second getting his catch out of water and on its way to the launch.

I asked him later what would have happened if it had been a shark that came after his bait.

"I would have let him have it," Ricki said. "Everything but the spear."

After about an hour of such hunting, there were enough fish to satisfy Dédé, the majordomo of the excursion. (The crew of the *Aikane* had done very badly, thanks to our expensive spear guns.) We all got back in the launches and bounced away to a place on the lagoon shore opposite the wreck of the *County of Roxborough*. The launches were made fast to coral heads in shallow water, and we all waded ashore.

In the clear water through which we walked we could see squiggle-shaped splotches of brilliant color: malachite green, pink, gold, lavender, and lapis-lazuli blue. The wind ruffled the surface so that it was hard to make out exactly what the splotches were, but when we put on our diving masks we could see: the squiggles were the open lips of clams, deeply embedded in the coral that had grown with and around them.

"*Pahua*," said François the game warden.

"*Benitier*," said the other François, in French.*

Our hosts pried a few specimens loose from the coral and

---

* The shell books say "*Tridacna*."

opened them. The fleshy lips look less edible than any clam meat I have ever seen—mottled with jewel color and sooty black!—but they are as tender and tasty as a good pismo off the California shore. The shells are beautifully ruffled on the outer side, and the giant size (up to 250 pounds) is used for holy-water fonts in Catholic churches. (We had seen one at Omoa.) That is the size that is considered dangerous by divers, who occasionally lose a pry bar, or even a leg, in their clamped jaws.

We had come lightly provisioned (*à la* Marie Salomé) with a basket, a knife or two, a few limes, a loaf of French bread, and a jug of what the Four called *mazout*. This was Algerian red wine, and we all assumed that was its varietal name, until I looked it up in the dictionary and discovered it meant "fuel oil." We had a gallon, and two small yogurt jars to drink it out of.

Everyone was too thirsty from diving to begin with wine, so as we hiked across the narrow strip of land, François the game warden and Ricki knocked down some green coconuts and gave each his own "cooler." And to stave off hunger pangs, the other François hacked open a sprouting coconut and offered us each a chunk of *uto*. This is a substance that fills the cavity of a nut as it begins to form a new plant. It has the consistency of styrofoam and the taste of slightly sweetened pabulum, and is usually consumed by babies and toothless old people. But we rather liked it, which amused the Four no end.

Ten minutes of walking brought us to the site of the wreck. It was not quite as solid as it looked from the sea. The hull had rusted through in several places, and one could walk inside it. Several yachting parties had used it as a sort of Inscription Rock, but we refrained. (The "Kilroy-was-here" mania of the American amuses the Polynesian greatly, and ours were a little disappointed that their *popaas* were immune.)

Our "table" was set in the shade under the stern of the vessel, whose name can still be made out, and under it the word *Glasgow*. Lunch began with an appetizer of marinated *pahua* served in its own elegant shells. *Mazout* was poured into the yogurt jars (what yacht had left them here?), which circulated as loving cups. While the four guests sipped and nibbled, the Four were all busier than we ever saw them before or afterward.

Dédé constructed a barbecue: a circle of dry coconut husks

inside which he built a fire of driftwood, and covered it with carefully chosen pieces of coral rubble. François the game warden collected large leaves from a plant I didn't recognize, and "sewed" them together with the needlelike ends of coconut fronds to make plates and a tablecloth. François the gendarme was gutting and scaling the fish we had caught. Ricki was exploring. He called us to come and see a family of land crabs he had uncovered at the foot of a palm.

There were a half-dozen of the creatures, dressed to kill in a matching set of beautifully patterned *tun* shells. "They must go all the way to the lagoon for such shells," Ricki told us. "They do not grow on the outer reef."

The crabs' bodies had accommodated to the long spiral of the inner chamber of the shell. When Ricki managed to coax one out of its shelter, the poor thing was so out of proportion that it couldn't run away. Tahitians eat the soft coiled part of the crab raw. "It is very rich," Ricki said. "Will you try some?"

We said no. But it was the only local delicacy to which we said no, and perhaps we were mistaken. He and François the game warden ate a couple with obvious relish.

Half the *mazout* was gone before the main course was put on to cook. Dédé supervised that operation, laying the assorted varieties and sizes of fish each on a carefully selected part of the coral, as if there were different intensities of heat in different quarters. He squeezed lime juice on the fish as they cooked, but no other seasoning was used, not even salt. When he considered that a fish was done on one side—just done enough to be turned without falling apart—he turned it over by hand. It was permitted to cook a minute longer and then removed (by the tail) to one of the leaf platters. Luncheon was served when the platters of all guests were filled.

The fish were all superb. Our hosts insisted that each of us try at least one bite of each kind of fish, and declare our preference. Actually, there was a subtle but perceptible difference between them, but the *mazout* and the warmth and our weariness were beginning to blur the edges of all sensation. We gorged and drank and went for a swim to wash off, and lay down for a nap in the lengthening shadow of the stern.

Dédé must not have slept as well as the rest of us, for when we woke he was almost finished plaiting a basket of green palm fronds. Madame Mervin had asked for *pahuas*, and he was making a container for them—a remarkable suitcase-shaped job that would hold at least a dozen of the biggest clams we had.

"How many things can one make out of the coco palm?" I asked him as he worked.

Dédé began to enumerate, and the others chimed in: shelter (pillars and—if pandanus and bamboo were not available—walls and thatch as well); baskets; bowls for eating and drinking (from the husks); napkins and clothing (from the rough fiber at the base of each frond); pins and needles (from the sharp frond ends); hats and mats (for sleeping and for portable shelters); soap and cosmetic oils; food and drink . . .

"And bandage!"

Jack had a saltwater sore on his shin and had been pestered with flies. Ricki was applying a poultice of fresh green leaves that had some healing properties, securing it with a tough coconut-fiber cord.

The last stop of this marvelous day was at a diving spot close to the village, and here we almost had a tragedy.

We were diving in a sheltered corner between the long underwater arm of the pass and the shore itself. There was no current there, and fish and *pahua* were plentiful. At the far end of the reef arm there was a dangerous current, particularly on the fast ebb. At that time all the water that has piled up in the lagoon during flow is sucked out the narrow channel so fast that whirlpools are formed. These *opape* are feared by all the fishermen, and we had been warned about them.

None of us, including Norris himself, noticed that he was gradually working his way out of the sheltered area and nearer to the danger zone. Suddenly he felt himself caught in the current, swept around the end of the arm, and into the channel. He had time to cry out for help just once. Then he was using every ounce of energy to fight.

Norris is an excellent swimmer, but that was nearly his downfall. Instead of giving in and letting the current carry him, he tried to oppose it. He saw François the gendarme respond to his call, cut the anchor line, and start the outboard, and Norris tried to hold his own long enough for the launch to make it around the reef arm. But he felt himself being sucked under faster than the launch was closing the distance.

What saved him was a diver who had tied his pirogue to the reef and was fishing for his dinner. He shoved off a moment later than François, and had only a dozen or so yards to go. He shoved his oar practically under Norris's arm; Norris caught and held it, and was drawn free of the *opape*. He was safe, but badly winded, when François got to him.

The lesson we all learned from this had two parts: (*a*) if you're caught in a strong current, swim with it and try to angle off gradually; and (*b*) don't get into that sort of current in the first place, no matter how good a swimmer you are.

The next morning we took Jack's saltwater sore to Ricki's dispensary for treatment. All of us were beginning to have trouble of this sort: a small blister that appeared on legs or arms, gradually enlarged, broke, spread, and began to suppurate. Ricki's explanation was that the water in these atolls was *toxique*. No ordinary antiseptics are of much use against it, and the real cure is to stay out of it.

Jack's shin had got to the point where staying out of the water was not enough, and my coral cut was already threatening to beach me. So Ricki undertook to "operate," with all the gravity of a surgeon performing major surgery. There was a certain incongruity between his manner and his costume: a pair of blue swimming trunks, a hand-painted silk shirt, and a *tiare tahiti* behind the right ("seeking") ear. The operating room was the kitchen of a dilapidated diver's shack, and François the game warden officiated as surgical nurse, while he waited his turn for a haircut on the back porch, where a foolish old diver and a young one were amusing themselves playing Ricki's guitar.

Ricki's surgical procedure was orthodox. He anesthetized the sore with a squirt of ethyl chloride, and then scrubbed it with something that looked like tincture of green soap. When it was clean, he applied a potent mixture of alcohol, iodine, sulfa powder, penicillin, some sort of 'mycin—and, of all things, Mercurochrome! He called the mixture mercurochrome for short, and claimed that it would clear up any sort of infection, which we all doubted. But when he finally divulged the formula he used for mixing, we were awed into submission. Jack wore a huge wad of cotton waste, soaked in the pink potion, strapped to his shin for several days, and pronounced himself cured. I daubed my coral cut out twice daily from the little vial Ricki gave me, and was ready to sign a testimonial at the end of the week.

While I waited my turn in the surgery, I had leafed through Ricki's daybook records, awed by the variety of cases he was expected to handle with his fairly superficial training: broken limbs, fish poisoning, divers' headaches, and childbirth!—as well as superficial cuts and sores. I saw the name of François the game warden down for a visit the evening before—directly after our return from the picnic. No ailment noted.

"*Coup de soleil?*" I asked, sympathetically.

"*Coup de mazout,*" François answered and touched his head as if it still throbbed.

Before Ricki could get back to his duties as a barber, François the gendarme sauntered in to remind Ricki that it was time for the biweekly *inspection sanitaire*. Benson asked if he might go along, and that was how we learned about Ricki's real contribution to public health. Takaroa had in other years been threatened

Ricki the *infirmier* and Jack his patient.

with epidemics of all sorts of communicable diseases, whenever divers from other islands set up their migrant camp. But this year the camp was a model of cleanliness and good health habits that was forcing the permanent settlement to hump itself not to be outdone.

This miracle had been accomplished by imposing a regulation requiring every squatter to be responsible for the condition of his dwelling, the ground around it, and every living thing—animal or human—who shared either. Every piece of rubbish had to be gathered in the morning and dumped into the channel on the fast ebb. Every pig and goat was tethered. Every person too young or too old to care for himself had to be inspected, along with the premises, by Ricki and François, twice a week. I don't know what penalties had been set for infractions of this law, but I doubt that it had ever been flouted. For Ricki and François were a very effective set of guardians of the public weal.

Ricki was the smaller of the two, only middle height by American standards, but magnificently muscled, with the carriage of a Latin grandee. François looked like an Irish cop from the Bronx. Actually, his parents were born in Tahiti, but three of his grandparents were Irish, and the other was English. He was fat, blond, and blue-eyed, with skin that burned beef red even under the shade of a very wide hat. As they walked together through the town, they looked like the twin powers of Darkness and Light.

Benson was deeply impressed with the thoroughness of their inspection, and asked how long the results would last, after the dive was over and they were gone.

"About a week," Ricki said cynically.

"You think so? Don't the Takaroans take pride in the way the town looks? We haven't seen anything like it, not even in the U.S., in a migrant community," Benson said.

"Paumotuans are without pride," Ricki said. "Like Marquesans. Only Tahitians know what pride means."

There is no question about the pride of the Tahitians, bordering frequently on arrogance. They are the snobs of Oceania, and whatever resentment they harbor toward their conquerors is channeled into outspoken contempt for "lesser breeds without the law."

The *pahuas* we had collected for Madame Mervin were to be the base of a special dinner to which we were bidden—or thought we were. We arrived and were ushered into the kitchen at the hour specified. The Four were all there, lounging around the big table, but there were no places set for us. We sat down and were served rum punches, made from Madame's hoarded store of hard liquor.

Time passed. Nothing was said about eating. Gradually, it seemed to me that there was a strain in the air. There was also an odor of curry. We had been invited to eat curried *pahua*, and it smelled so good that our salivary glands were beginning to weep.

Finally I decided that frankness was the only appropriate tool, so I asked Madame if we had mistaken the day. If so, there was plenty of food aboard the *Aikane*. We could go home and come back when we were expected.

Madame shook her head and mumbled something I didn't quite catch. It sounded as if she had made the curry for us but had not expected us to eat it at her house. Before I could figure this out, she apparently changed her mind. She snapped an order at the Four in a language I did not understand, and Dédé helped her set places for everyone.

The tureen of curry was put on the table, and bowls of roasted breadfruit, and coconut cream. We were served and urged to begin—which we did. It was a marvelous dish, and we all said so. Madame beamed. She had included some nacre meat along with the *pahua*, and the spice was not the mixture of saffron and other spices that Indians call curry, but an herb garnered in the mountains of Tahiti, whose proper name we never got straight.

"Since you will not have the ingredients, I shall not teach you the making of this dish," Madame said. "But you will have it whenever you return to visit us, here or in Papeete."

About this time we noticed that none of the Four had been served. They were watching us eat with interest and appreciation, but their own plates were empty.

"Don't you like the curry?" I asked.

"Yes, we like it," said François the gendarme. "But tonight we eat something else."

"What?"

"*Fafaro*," said Ricki. "It is Tahitian. Very good for you. Very healthy. Especially after drinking too much."

I wondered why we were not being offered any of this health food, and also why the Four weren't getting theirs. The strain was beginning to interfere with our consumption of curry, and one or another of my companions asked me in English what the trouble seemed to be. Finally I asked.

"When are you going to eat your *fafaro?*"

They all said, "Later," in concert.

I must have looked as baffled as I felt, because Dédé explained that since most Americans did not like the odor of *fafaro*, they were holding off so as not to spoil our enjoyment of our own menu.

I translated this for my trio, and they all reacted as I did. We were not going to go on eating unless our hosts ate too. We put down our spoons. There was a quick and anxious consultation between Madame and the Four, in Tahitian, so that I could not follow it.

"You are sure?" she asked us in English. "The smell is like cheese. Like the camembert. It disturbs the digestion of those who are not used to it."

It would not disturb ours, we assured her. Slow smiles were spreading over the faces of the Four. Madame shrugged and went out into the darkness of the backyard.

"It is not the odor that one eats, after all," said François the gendarme. "If you are lovers of cheese, you will understand what I mean."

Madame returned carrying a large coconut husk suspended in an arrangement of fiber cords. A small blue saucer served as a lid to the hanging basket. When she lifted this, the odor hit.

It was dreadful. Norris made a loud gagging noise, and I was afraid he was going to vomit right there at the table. In a panic of outrage, I asked for a taste.

"You want to try *fafaro?*" asked the Four in wondering unison.

I nodded. Madame looked to her son for a suggestion, but he only shrugged. There was silence as she brought coconut over to my place and lifted out a fillet of red, raw fish. She laid this on a clean saucer; then one of the Four broke a couple of hunks of roasted breadfruit into a soup bowl and poured coconut cream on it.

"Now! Madame will cut a small piece of the *fafaro*, dip it in the cream, and eat, and then a piece of the breadfruit," Ricki explained.

"You are sure?" Madame asked me once more. "You wish to do this thing?"

I nodded and did exactly as I had been told. By holding my breath till the fish was in my mouth, I missed the worst of the smell. The coconut cream cut the taste, and so did the breadfruit, but even so, it was the hardest job of swallowing I ever did.

"*Voilà!*" said François the gendarme. "Does it not taste like camembert, as I have said?"

"It tastes better than it smells, no?" asked the other François.

"It is very healthy," said Ricki earnestly. "People who eat *fafaro* are never sick."

"How can you stand it?" Benson asked in an undertone. "Are you going to go on, or quit while you're ahead?"

I said yes to all the questions except Benson's last one. I was going to go on till I had finished my four-inch fillet. American honor was at stake. I was covering Norris's gaffe for the sake of . . . I really didn't know what.

But *fafaro* does not taste like camembert or liederkranz—or limburger—all of which I like. It tastes like nothing but itself, almost as bad as it smells. It is made of the best fresh tuna, cut in strips and soaked in seawater for three days. There is also a one-day *fafaro*, which is less pungent. And there are some schools of *fafaro* makers who don't change the water during the whole marinating period. Their product is said to be stronger than Madame's type, and the water is said to teem with creatures not to be eaten with the fish.

At any rate, my sacrifice was not in vain. We all ate together, and joy was unconfined. I acquired a reputation that I couldn't possibly have lived up to, but fortunately we sailed before I was put to another test.

As we began to make preparations to sail, we began to receive a stream of presents. It got really out of hand, and at one point

Jack said he was afraid to admire the scenery lest someone give us a reef.

We acquired such a stock of nacre and other shells that we had to empty several of the food lockers in order to stow the swag. There were some special problems, like how to protect a delicate tree of branch coral growing out of the hinge of a nacre shell. Benson and Jack finally lashed two of these treasures to slabs of wood and hung them upside-down in the chain locker. Jack's made it safely to land, but ours was smashed in the very last of all the storms we went through on our third sea leg.

Every time we paid a visit anywhere, we were presented with some sort of shell lei (and kissed on both cheeks). Some were magnificent and most uncomfortable works of art, others a bit grubby, the work of children in the primary class at the school (most of whom had guilty consciences about having stolen bananas from the bunch that hung over the *Aikane*'s stern, and who strung shells on monofilament to propitiate the angry gods).

The most addicted of the present givers was a diver named Martin, who lived on the point near where we were moored. He

Madame Manu Mervin and the pearl diver Martin, with his wife Joséphine, and child, Angélique.

was fifty-four, one of the oldest men diving that season, slim and healthy-looking, and careful not to push himself. His wife, Joséphine, was a handsome, fat, very dark woman, with a brilliant smile and gold rings in her ears. They made a rather odd-looking pair, since Martin weighed half as much and could pass easily for French. But they were very congenial, good parents to their own small brood and an assortment of more distantly related children. The pride of the ménage was Angélique, who was "*blanche*."

(When these people used the word "white," I discovered, they meant blond-haired and fair-skinned and nothing more. There was no connotation of race, superior or inferior, or social class. "*Une petite fille blanche*" denoted a particularly pretty child, nothing more. Such genetic accidents came up more often than one might have suspected, if one had not other evidence of the extraordinary mixtures that make up the present-day "Polynesian type.")

Angélique was blond and blue-eyed, and she was the daughter of Joséphine's medium-brown sister, who lived in Takaroa and had a husband, who was not the father of Angélique. Martin and Joséphine were delighted to have the little girl, and the arrangement seemed to satisfy all other parties to it. The child was always dressed in starched playsuits, imported from Papeete or perhaps from Paris, and Martin employed her as the bearer of his

Janet as navigator.

most valuable gifts to us. We never saw her coming along the wharf without something in her hands, while back behind the copra barn Martin stood in semiconcealment, beaming with pride.

The last gift Angélique brought us was a couple of *perles abîmes*, large, weirdly twisted gray pearls that were practically valueless on the commercial market but that I had made into a magnificent ring and pin when I got back to Los Angeles and found a sculptress who worked in gold.

Martin, incidentally, had other wives on other islands and some twenty-four children. He felt a fatherly affection and some responsibility for all of them, but they did not seem to weigh him down. He worked as hard as he felt advisable in view of his age, diving during the season and working as mate on a *goelette*, sometimes the *Taporo*, between seasons. He distributed his earnings according to need, and everyone seemed content. His son by an earlier "marriage" was diving with him, and if his relations with his stepmother were typical of this family, I should say the Mormons of Brigham Young's day could have learned much from their descendants in this distant parish of the church.

The last night before we were to sail there was a full moon, and everyone in the village was on the dock, fishing and singing and chatting. We were all in the cockpit, singing, when a very shy young woman came aboard and asked if she could speak with "*Monsieur le capitaine*." I interpreted for the interview that followed, which was actually a formal invitation to enroll in the Takaroa Yacht Club!

The young woman, whose name was Eugénie, presented her credentials: a card, very nicely lettered, that testified (in English) that she was recording secretary of this organization, and an official roster, in which the member boats were listed. Seven American yachts and one Australian had "joined" in the two years of the club's existence. Each had contributed a picture of their vessel, a crew list, and a short account of the circumstances under which they arrived at Takaroa, etc. The "etc." included where they were heading when they left.

We had no picture of the *Aikane*, but Jack pasted in a mimeographed invitation to her christening party, which contained all the relevant statistics. (He also took notes on other signers, whom we might possibly meet in our travels to come.) We all signed the book. Eugénie shook hands very gravely with each of us, and disappeared into the crowd on the dock.

We were up at dawn, and I cooked breakfast while the men made everything fast abovedecks. Before they were through, there was more cargo to stow, for friends were arriving with packages and letters for us to deliver, verbal commissions, and of course more presents.

François the game warden had written a letter to a friend who might be anywhere between Takaroa and Samoa. If we found it easy to deliver, fine; if not, we were not to "derange" ourselves. Madame Mervin had a package of dried nacre meat to be delivered to the Bank of Indo-China, where her daughter, Mme. Liza Manuel, worked. Liza (Dédé's sister) would be delighted to know us and to show us Tahiti. Angélique was sent over with a beautiful pair of gold-lip shells, which were contraband in the sense that Martin was obligated to sell it to his "Chinese." The man teacher at the village school had a small Odorono jar for me—full of seed pearls.

By sunrise we were ready to cast off. But we delayed a few minutes to watch the arrival of a small launch that none of us had expected to see again when it put out for Manihi three days ago.

It was, at that time, carrying the goods and chattels of the *chef* of Manihi, who had come to Takaroa for the dive, but who had got *feu*. This is a Polynesian word for a state of mind that the French profess to find very mysterious, but which seemed to me to correspond roughly to what we call "fed up." It is said to come on these islanders suddenly—inexplicably!—and there is no appeal from its finality. Perhaps the *chef's* ears were beginning to ache. Perhaps he had made all the money he wanted. Perhaps he rebelled against the *inspection sanitaire*. At any rate, he decided to go home—a journey of sixty miles across open ocean—with his wife, babies, sisters-in-law, nieces- and nephews-in-law, livestock, and outboard motors—and sundries.

We had never seen a boat loaded as his was. There were six forty-horse Johnsons aboard, only two of which were to be used en route. The other four were stowed "below," under the roofed space amidships. The length overall of the launch was no more than twenty-five feet, and it carried thirteen people, including babies, many rolls and bundles of baggage, much water and many coconuts and, for a while, two goats. Two wheelbarrows and four empty gasoline drums were lashed to the top of the "cabin." All the gear and the passenger list were arranged and rearranged, several times, with great care. In the end the goats were left ashore. But even so, when the launch finally pulled away from the wharf, it had no more than six inches of freeboard.

Our inquiries about the journey ahead brought us no comfort. There was no possibility of its arriving at Manihi by daylight. Also, the pass there had a strong current and a hairpin turn. But the sky looked clear and there would be a moon. If no sudden storm blew up, there was no reason to fear. There was no compass aboard, but they would be navigating out of sight of land for only three or four hours!

They had promised to radio the fact of their arrival, but they forgot. No one seemed concerned but us. I was infinitely relieved to see the evidence that these Vikings of the Sunrise could do what they said they could, as we set out on our passage through their Dangerous Isles.

Tahiti Bound

On the relatively short leg to Tahiti, Jack decided to give me some practice at stations I had not yet manned. For all the times I had been part of a team that changed the jib, I had never either raised or lowered it or the mainsail. Bagging or unbagging the Genoa or attaching the snap shackles to the forward stay had sometimes been exciting work, when the bow was bouncing and spray was flying, but I was quite aware that it was no challenge to an able-bodied seaman.

Now I was to have my chance!

I was to lower the jib. No physical strain was involved, but there was a built-in hazard. Norris had been chewed out so many times for having failed to coil the halyard so that it ran out smoothly when the sail was dropped, that he half expected it to foul. Naturally, it did. I was determined not to make the same mistake. Naturally, I did.

The halyard fouled when the Genoa was halfway down, and there it hung, flapping wildly, costing us "way" every second that I struggled with the knot, and threatening to put us into irons. I got the same treatment Norris got under such circumstances, and that led to an even worse goof a few minutes later.

It is easy to explain, now that I understand what happened, but if I had understood what was happening at the time, there would have been no goof. Jack had noticed a chafed place on the line that runs from the clew of the working jib, and had decided to reverse the line so that the chafed place would be at the "bitter" end, where there is no strain. He ordered me and Norris to "untie the jib sheet and change it end for end."

"What does 'end for end' mean?" Norris asked me in a whisper.

I didn't know, but I thought I could guess, and preferred that to exposing my ignorance. (I was still smarting from the halyard incident.) I did what I thought Jack wanted, but I thought wrong. The sheets were threaded all the way back to the cockpit before Jack discovered my mistake. He was outraged.

"I'm sorry," I said, when he paused for a last word from the condemned. "I didn't know what you meant."

"Then why the hell didn't you say so?"

It was one of those utterly logical, rhetorical questions that are not asked for clarification but for the purpose of underlining the enormity of a goof. I recognized the emotion behind it—exasperation—and that I had been guilty of it thousands of times in my life. But not till now did I recognize the effect on the victim who has no possible answer except "Because I am stupid—or lazy—or weak—or cowardly . . ." or whatever pejorative adjective best fits the case.

I retired from sail-changing with a badly damaged ego, and went back to Great-Grandfather's journal. He had approached the island of Tahiti, or Otaheite, as it was called in his time, from almost the same quarter, but in very different circumstances, one and a quarter centuries before us, and it was interesting to compare first impressions:

THE RESCUE

When daylight came, we perceived that we were wrecked upon a lagoon of coral rocks, extending several miles in semicircular form. Our ship was torn in pieces by the violence of the breakers: only a few timbers and spars remained fastened together, and the broken pieces of the wreck, together with the contents of the ship, were scattered promiscuously over the rocks. We were soon rejoiced to see the Captain coming to our relief with the boat. After taking the cooper from the isolated rock to which he had swum, he came around on the lee side, and landed on the rock where we were assembled.

Finding that our place of refuge was so low and small that it might be submerged if a storm should come on, we left it and proceeded to a larger rock that was several hundred feet long, about 60 or 80 wide and elevated 12 or

15 feet above the surface of the water. The first day was occupied in constructing a tent and collecting provisions which had been thrown upon the rocks. We succeeded in collecting spars and planks sufficient to build a tolerably good tent, which we covered with the torn sails of the ship. We also found several pipes of fresh water, and some bread that was still dry in the casks, and a number of barrels of beef and pork.

Altogether, we had provisions sufficient to last the crew for 50 to 60 days. Notwithstanding, our situation was still very critical. The rocks upon which we were cast, having neither soil nor productions, afforded no means of subsistence, after our stock should be exhausted, and the probability of being seen and aided by any passing vessel was very slight. The nearest inhabited island was Pitcairn's Island, distant 360 miles, and our boat would not carry more than one third of our crew safely. If we should go to Pitcairn's Island, no help could be obtained for those left on the rocks.

Mr. Norton proposed that a volunteer crew should be formed to undertake the voyage to Otaheite in the whaleboat. There was an American consul at Otaheite, and if the crew should be so fortunate as to reach there, he would send a vessel and afford every necessary aid to those who might remain at the place of disaster. It was truly a hazardous enterprise, and many preferred to take their chances upon the rocks. However, during the second day, a volunteer crew was formed, composed of the Captain, mate and six men. I had the good fortune to be one of the crew.

We spent one more day in making the necessary preparations for our departure. We made sails for our boat from pieces of the light sails of our wrecked ship, higher gunwales were fixed around the sides of the boat, provision taken in for 25 or 30 days, and being earnestly requested to commit ourselves in prayer to the mercy of God, we set sail for Otaheite, leaving our companions whom we had but feeble hopes of ever seeing again. . . .

We steered north, intending to run out our latitude and then beat west for Otaheite. By this plan we expected to reach some of the islands belonging to the Low Archipelago [the Tuamotus], and we would then understand our true position and be more certain to reach Otaheite. With the ordinary trade wind we could run about 125 miles per day, at which rate we expected to reach our destination in 7 or 8 days, but on the third or fourth day after our departure from the rock, the wind veered to southwest and increased to a moderate gale accompanied with heavy rain.

The gale continued two days, and though the weather was warm, we suffered much, because we had no protection from the rain, being compelled to sleep on the seats or in the bottom of the boat with the water three or four inches deep around us. Our bread got wet, and had the rain continued several days longer, we would have lost all. In consequence of the westerly bearing of the gale, we were driven easterly from our course, and passed the Low Archipelago or Chain Islands without seeing them.

Several days after the storm abated, we met with a Chilean brig laden with flour and bound for the Sandwich Islands [Hawaii]. We found that we had run much further than we expected, [and were] nearly two hundred miles northeast of the Chain Islands. We could not prevail upon the Chilean captain to take us to Otaheite, because it would affect his policy of insurance; but he was kind enough to supply us with some good bread and potatoes and some fixtures for cooking. He also gave us a quadrant by which we could determine our latitude, and with thankful hearts we parted from our benefactor and directed our frail bark once more toward Otaheite.

Having been driven so far to the northeast, we had to retrace a part of our journey, and were compelled to labor hard at the oars until we reached the southern part of the Low Archipelago, which brought us into the latitude of Otaheite. . . . These islands [the Tuamotus], unlike most others in the Pacific, are low. . . . The fact that they have been formed by the calcareous deposits of zoophytic animacules, affords indubitable evidence of the great age of our earth. [N.B. Great-Grandfather's voyage preceded that of the *Beagle* by at least twenty years.]

We landed upon one of the islands with some difficulty, obtained a good supply of coconut and vi-apples, and then steered westward for Otaheite, which we reached on the eleventh day after leaving the wreck.

I never had a greater desire to visit a place than this island, so justly [titled] the queen of the Pacific. As we moved slowly up Matavia Bay, wafted by the evening sea breeze, a holy enchantment appeared to surround the island. The mountains were more fantastical than any I had ever seen before; the stillness of the bay formed a lovely contrast with the roar of the breakers on the coral reefs which begirt this gem of the ocean; and the low cottages of the town, deeply shaded with breadfruit, orange and lemon trees, appeared to me at that time the very personification of contentment and peace. Probably a part of this enchantment was to be attributed to the fact that our arrival at this island would terminate all our sufferings consequent upon the wreck of our ship, and afford the means of rescuing our companions whom we had left on the rocks. . . .

[There follows an account of precisely how the expedition back to the rocks was organized, which ends with this paragraph:]

When Captain Hall arrived at the rocks, he found all the men in good health and condition except two, James Hutchins of Fairhaven, and Peter Stadt of New York. It is probable that the sickness of these men was caused by anxiety, for there were no local causes of disease, and the situation of the men was comfortable and safe so long as their provisions might last. . . .

Great-Grandfather graduated from Johns Hopkins Medical College before he shipped on the *Cadmus*, and I suppose his view of psychosomatic illness was typical of his time. I can attest that his view of Tahiti is accurate, allowing for what has happened to the low cottages under the breadfruit trees in 125 years.

At dawn on Easter Sunday, after sailing for twenty-six hours on a beam reach, we sighted Tahiti. There were clouds on the mountain core of the island, and all we could see were the very, very steep, very, very green slopes that run down to the short coastal plain. Along some of the shore we were passing there was a fringing reef, and the lagoon inside it looked idyllic. In other sections, the surf beat the toes of the mountains angrily.

Someone located, first on the chart and then on shore, Point Venus, where Captain Cook once observed the transit of that planet for the Royal Society.* Clear on the port bow was the rugged, almost Marquesan silhouette of Tahiti's twin island, Mooréa. There were rainbows all morning, and sudden shafts of sunlight pointing in the general direction of the opening in the reef that is the gate to Papeete's harbor.

We had been advised by Captain Amaru to radio for a pilot to see us in: "You have to pay for him anyway, and you cannot tie up till he shows you where, so you might as well have his help through the pass."

But although we called Radio Mahina at ten-minute intervals all morning long, on 2182, the emergency frequency that is monitored around the clock all over the world, there was no answer. By eleven o'clock we were abreast of the pass, and still calling. We had no detail chart of the harbor area, but the surface was calm, and Jack decided to feel his way in. Norris and I were posted as a bow watch to warn the helmsman if the reef suddenly loomed ahead. The theory was that since we were motoring very slowly, there would be time to go into reverse before we scraped.

The theory was unsound. The water was too murky and the change of depth too abrupt. Fortunately, the tide was high. We were over before we heard the sound. The *Aikane* shuddered lightly, like a lady who sees a mouse but is too well bred to make a fuss about it, and we were free, heading for the church steeple which (according to the *Coast Pilot*) marks the moorage used by sailing yachts.

We were not very far from it when the pilot boat appeared.

We were boarded by a French-speaking Tahitian who took the wheel with no comment about our having negotiated the pass without his assistance. After a minute or so I asked why no one had answered our call for a pilot.

---

* The archipelago is named for this event, the Society Islands. The French call the southeastern group les Iles du Vent, and the northwestern, les Iles Sous-le-Vent, but the whole is les Iles de la Société.

"What frequency did you call?" he asked.

"On 2182."

"That is the emergency frequency. You should not have used it. You were not in distress."

"We don't have your other frequency," I answered defensively. "Besides, we might have been in distress. And no one answered!"

"Mmmm," he said absently. "*C'est bizarre.*"

It was exactly the equivalent of "No kidding" in its infuriating indifference.

He was a pretty indifferent pilot in other ways as well. He took three passes at bringing us into the position he had chosen for us in the line of visiting sailboats, and in the end a man from a small schooner (the *Okeanos*) had to row out in his dinghy and take our mooring lines ashore. About twenty minutes later, the same pilot brought in the *Magnolia*, which we had last seen in Taiohae. He managed to foul her stern anchor line with ours so that neither of us could leave the harbor without taking the other along.

We knew better than to venture ashore, even though we were touching it, until we had been cleared by the *fonctionnaires*. So we broke out the wine and settled down to enjoy the parade of Easter costumes along the Quai Bir-Hacheim, the girls in their pastel sheaths and the men in their dress uniforms, military, naval, or Légionnaire. Across the Quai we could see the handsome new post office, where perhaps there was mail. Perhaps a check from my publishers, an advance on the novel I had finished just under the wire before we sailed . . . or a rejection . . . or a request for revisions. How remote the whole thing seemed! And yet only two months ago I had been totally immersed in the lives of an embattled family of New England abolitionists a hundred years ago, southern Quaker ladies and their Negro nephews, sin and slavery, and the anguish of the Puritan conscience on the horns of a political dilemma. The writing seemed as remote as the events themselves. . . .

We were boarded by three irritable bureaucrats who resented having their Easter interrupted. They revenged themselves by taking three hours to complete their interrogation of us, and one of them lifted our passports as he left. Someone would inform us, he said, as to whether or not we could have them back again. He didn't say when someone would do so.

The crew of the *Magnolia* had by now heard rumors, which they relayed to us: The American consul had been ordered to pack up and go home; a jet liner full of American tourists had been turned back at the Faaa airport; tourists who had no visas (like the *Magnolia* crew) were to be sent away in three days, while Americans who had sixty-day visas (like us) were to be sent away in ten.

We couldn't understand. Was it possible that war had been declared while we were out of radio contact? Or was the whole thing a delayed *Poisson d'Avril?* Or had M. Plantec, of Atuona, got through to General de Gaulle?

Papeete

I remember reading somewhere of Gauguin's disappointment on arriving in Papeete, which he had imagined as an isolated and unspoiled paradise, to find it a shantytown full of Europeans.

We had something of the same sense of letdown, although we had not fought as hard to get there and had fewer illusions, thanks to informants like M. Bertrand. Even so, the backside Papeete presents on one's water-borne arrival is disheartening. The water itself is disgusting, opaque, foul-smelling, and mixed with all sorts of other liquids, including oil. (Perhaps it is really no worse than the East River or the harbors of San Francisco or Los Angeles, but we had got used to an element as clear as a pane of fine crystal in small amounts, and blue as gem sapphire in depth. We were spoiled.)

On the shore, across the Quai Bir-Hacheim (which was full of noisy mobilettes, taxi horns, dust, potholes, and exhaust gas twenty out of every twenty-four hours), stood a line of one and two-story buildings that could have been Tijuana's water-front, if Tijuana had one. Souvenir stores full of cheap Japanese imitations of Polynesian handicrafts, travel agencies full of posters showing half-naked brown beauties bathing in streams on which gardenias floated; beer parlors; food and general-merchandise emporiums whose windows were so grimy that one could hardly make out what order of articles were on display; and a collection of upper-floor "hotels" that gave a strong impression of being something else. The racket was devastating after the relative silence of the sea: not only the traffic noise, but also a rattle of steam hammers from across the harbor where some naval installation was under construction, a cacophony of boat horns and whistles, all of them angry, and the sounds of building—cement mixers, electric saws, and hammers from almost every side street!

Papeete was a phenomenon one could hardly apprehend without outside aid. I had to read *Time* to discover that "it is one of the world's most expensive cities," that the number of vehicles had increased eight times in a single year, that restaurant and bar profits were up 200 percent, and that it had been suggested in the Assembly that prostitution be legalized and professionals imported from Marseille before the Tahitian *vahine* is irrevocably corrupted and the Tahitian family destroyed. We did not need *Time* to discover that all this had radically affected the Polynesian character. Even before we stepped ashore we were aware of the generalized hostility that is "human nature" in the big cities of the West, but a rare aberration in the island world through which we had just passed.

The post office was closed on Easter Monday, and by Tuesday morning we had worked up such a thirst for mail that we didn't stop for coffee. We braved the mobilette traffic and stormed the great glass doors before they were opened. We were not the first in line, and the lines moved very slowly. But by the hour of the morning coffee break—about 10:00 A.M.—we had our pockets full of letters. Mine included the news that the manuscript of *Sisters and Brothers* was, on the whole, acceptable but that there were "rough spots." My editor hoped—very tactfully —that I could find time to do the necessary work at once. Otherwise, what with the slowness of communication at this distance and the even greater slowness of printers, it would be a year or more before the novel would come out.

I resolved to begin right after lunch. I dug out my portable typewriter, found the flimsy carbon of the MS I had brought along, and began to study the editorial suggestions. But the gentle breeze that kept the cabin comfortable scattered the loose pages so that I had to spend more time improvising paperweights than I did reading. Also, the interruptions were incredibly varied and numerous. During the hour and a half in which I tried to work, I jotted down the following incidents:

1. The *fonctionnaire* who had heisted our passports dropped by to say that there was as yet no decision about them;

2. A young Australian boat bum came aboard, introduced himself, had a look around, and invited us to cocktails aboard his ketch;

3. An American boat bum, ditto;

4. Another American wanted to bum a ride to Hawaii, if we were going that way;

5. A sailor from the *Taporo* dropped by to tell us that his daughter had been operated on in the big government hospital here and was doing well;

6. Three more boat bums who were—or said they were—looking for the *Magnolia*, took time to look around and give advice on where to buy clean diesel (and how to filter it anyway, just to be sure), where to buy cocktail ice, and other nautical matters.

That afternoon I went with Benson to call on M. Georges, an impressive gentleman whose rank seemed to be roughly equivalent to Minister of Education for the archipelago. He read our letter of introduction and listened to our account of *l'affaire Plantec*, and asked in what he could serve us. Benson said he would like to talk with some teen-agers, both in and out of school. M. Georges was silent, thoughtful. Then, abruptly, he excused himself and called the Governor.

I understood every word of the conversation that ensued except one. M. Georges described us as American psychological pedagogues, reported that we had had some difficulties with the Sisters of Atuona, stated his opinion that we were actually looking into what we said we were looking into, and then said he did not want to be *foudroyé* for assisting us. (Back at the boat I looked up the word in my dictionary and found that it means to be struck by lightning, or blasted.) Apparently the Governor was willing to hold his lightning, so M. Georges made another call and summoned a psychological pedagogue who would act as our guide—a M. Mansard.

While we waited for M. Mansard to arrive, we explored with M. Georges the reasons for the passport crisis and M. Plantec's hostility. In the first place, he explained, French Polynesia had become the dumping ground for all the bureaucrats thrown out of work by successful independence movements in other parts of the French empire. "If they did not come here, they would have to return to France, which would be insupportable." (It was not clear whether he meant insupportable to the bureaucrats or to France, or both.)

In the second place, M. Georges explained that there was resentment of the way we and the British had shut France out of the atomic club. "After all, we had the most valuable information—the work of men like Joliot-Curie—which we turned over to you when the Germans occupied. Naturally, we expected consideration when the Germans were driven out. But you have treated us like children who may not be trusted with their own fate. Therefore, it has been necessary for us to make our own atomic weapons. It has not been easy. There have had to be sacrifices. But we are proud that we have succeeded—by ourselves! unaided!

"Now that we are ready to test the results, suddenly the number of American tourists visiting Tahiti is tripled. And if you will pardon my great frankness, one would have to be enormously stupid to mistake some of them for vacationers."

At this point I made a tactical blunder; I pointed out what seemed to me a logical contradiction between accusing the United States of maintaining a selfish monopoly on atomic know-how and accusing her of spying to get information. M. Georges reacted with indignation.

"It is the logic of madame that is faulty! If there were nothing to be learned from us, why would you send spies?"

Despite this contretemps, we were much indebted to M. Georges and even more to his deputy, M. Mansard. The first of many favors we owed the latter was the solution of my literary problem. He took me to a hotel used almost exclusively by official (French) visitors. Here I was able to rent a charming bungalow with bamboo walls and a thatch roof, a working refrigerator, and a hot and cold shower. If there had not been such distractions as *tamure* dancers, giggling and chattering as they plaited gardenia girdles, or the crew members from the *Aikane* dropping in for a shower around noon or a Happy Hour drink with ice cubes! I could have worked around the clock. Even so, I managed pretty well. I got up early, after having dreamed dutifully about my characters, and went straight to the typewriter, erecting a sound barrier to hold at bay the sounds of birds, *vahines*, and visitors to the swimming pool.

By noon I had usually exhausted the vein, so I was available as interpreter between Benson and M. Mansard in the interviews with students from the Lycée Paul Gauguin. The results of these interviews confirmed Benson's hypotheses about the relationship between self-sufficiency and the "problems" of adolescence. These young people had none of the naïve self-confidence of the boys at Atuona. They were full of unfocused angers. One blamed his parents for "not trusting me enough." Another blamed his for having given him too much liberty too young. They were less anxious about marriage than the teen-agers in the study Benson had brought along, but on all the other sensitive areas—cosmetic problems, spending money, clothes, job and career opportunities, and so on—they were just like their American equivalents.

The most insightful response Benson got was to a question about the reason why the *bandes* of juvenile delinquents along the waterfront stole and mugged and got jailed only to go back to their delinquent ways when released. Our *lycée* students began by giving as their own opinion explanations they had read and heard: for example, that the lack of parental love was the root of all evil. But one of the older boys contradicted this flatly.

"You know nothing of these *copains*," he said. "They are my friends. I go to see them in jail. They do not steal to eat. They could go back to their homes if they wanted only to eat. They stay in Papeete because it is a greater world, but they want to be someone in that world. Someone of note! You remember last week they beat up that soldier? Do you think they were angry with him? They did not even know him, and besides it was dark and they could not have recognized him if they had."

"Perhaps they were angry against the French in general, and the soldier wore the uniform—"

M. Mansard was beginning to feed answers, despite Benson's express request that he refrain. But the young man would have none of it anyway.

"They are not angry, I beg to assure you. It is that they are bored! There is nothing to do! They like some excitement! That is all!"

I had finished my work, and Benson had finished his, and Jack and Norris had had enough of Papeete at the end of a week. But we had radioed to San Diego for a replacement for the voltage regulator and a couple of sail battens, and they had not yet arrived.

We killed time like other tourists, shopping in the Chinese-owned supermarkets (Donald's was a total failure as far as re-provisioning was concerned), gossiping in one of the sidewalk cafés, observing the "natives" from a distance, and getting to know only our fellow exotics—mainly the other members of the boat set. I tried to set down a few impressions of the women, to compare with the women of other island communities.

The one notable difference was the overwhelming chic of the Chinese-Tahitian ladies who seemed to occupy most of the desirable commercial positions. The male (French) gossips in the cafés said harsh things about these elegant beauties: that they were coldhearted and grasping; that they married Tahitians (in preference to the French) only to acquire land. In this way valuable property, which the French themselves were prohibited from buying, was coming under the domination of Chinese families whose commercial chromosomes are strong enough to invalidate the recessive Tahitian tendency to let things slide. Fortunes, if not dynasties, were being built right under the noses of the "master race." The Tahitians, on the other hand, said harsh things about the French, who married Tahitian women only to turn them into French bourgeois, raising children who do not consider themselves Polynesian and are incapable of living comfortably in the old ways.

The only Tahitian lady we met bore out this latter thesis. She was the stately and gracious Madame Manuel, daughter of Madame Mervin, to whom we delivered the package of dried nacre meat from Takaroa. It did seem a bit *infra dig* in the elegant and exotic décor of the Bank of Indo-China, but Madame received it graciously and observed all the amenities, just as her mother had said she would. She and her French insurance-executive husband called on us on the *Aikane* and invited us to a Sunday excursion around the circumference of the island.

"We would have preferred to entertain you in our home," Madame explained, "but both of my maids have just left. I am all day at the bank, and it is all I can manage to look after the children. The house is a mess!"

(As she had four boys and a six-year-old hoyden of a daughter, one could understand her dilemma.)

That Sunday excursion was a real treat; without it we would never have had any impression of the Queen of the Pacific except from the angle of vision least likely to show off her beauty. Thanks to the Manuels and their un-French Volkswagen, we saw the whole of the exquisite coastline; the crumbling but impressive *marae* (temple) on the west coast, the view of Papeete's harbor and Faaa airfield from the high hills behind them, the view of Mooréa from Punaauia, where Gauguin lived and painted, the view of Tahiti Iti from the beach at Mataiea where he lived earlier with his thirteen-year-old *vahine* (the nearest thing he ever found to the Eve he sought), and finally the handsome new Gauguin Museum, which does not have a single original painting or carving—a fact that I believe would amuse and delight the painter's angry ghost.

The one Tahitian touch in the day's excursion was a stop at a small scattering of houses a few hundred yards from one of

Madame Manuel and her children and Janet at the Paul Gauguin Museum on Tahiti.

the exposed beaches. Madame excused herself; she had to have a chat with the mother of the two maids who had wandered off from the ménage. It was necessary that the mother understand that Madame could no longer be responsible for their conduct. I got the impression that she had regarded the girls as "charges" as much as servants and that she felt a guilt at having failed to carry out her end of the bargain, although nowhere near so disgracefully as the girls had failed on theirs.

While she explained herself, we walked through the yard of the house next door—a real Tahitian bungalow, so Madame said. It was a dollhouse, a small square dwelling, set high on coconut posts, with walls of beautifully woven mats and a roof of pandanus thatch, gay pareu-print curtains blowing at its two windows and open door, surrounded by a green, green lawn, blooming shrubs and flowers, and shaded by a grove of hardwoods. This, if one had to live in Tahiti, would be the place and the way to live, we thought.

During our ten days as members of the "yacht colony," we had a chance to observe the working out of the old saw about no small boat entering and leaving Papeete's harbor with the same crew. There was no longer any problem about the *Aikane*'s foursome sticking together, but we were the only example of domestic stability along the Quai. Four of the *Magnolia*'s six had decided to separate. The crew consisted of the skipper and his girl on the one hand, and a family with two young daughters (and a cat) on the other. The trip down from Guadalupe to Taiohae had taken them thirty-four days, as against our nineteen! It was rough on everyone. The little girls and the cat were confined to cramped quarters under the bow for most of that time, with bilge water sloshing around under the slats of their four square feet of deck space. The two men divided the wheel watches, eight hours on, eight off! The women didn't stand any watch at all. There was a rumor that the men's endurance had been bolstered by a plentiful supply of marijuana, but I found that hard to credit.

At any rate, whatever held them together had given out. The family with the cat had decided to get off and enjoy a couple of weeks in Tahiti and Mooréa and then get back to the States as best they could. The skipper was looking for a couple of new hands to finish his projected voyage to Australia. Jack (and several others) felt that someone ought to warn the young man the *Magnolia* was not seaworthy. It is bad form to put down another man's boat, but the *Magnolia* was so odd that there was always a crowd of Tahitians on the wharf, staring at her stern in awed disapproval. She had been converted to sail from her original vocation as a sardine trawler by the simple expedient of pouring a lot of cement into the bilge. There was no keel at all, and all the experts along the Quai predicted that the first heavy sea that hit her abeam would turn her over like a turtle.

Then there was the steel-hulled ketch *Wunderkind*, which Benson and I would have liked to buy. Its skipper had decided he wanted to go back to Detroit and his executive desk. He had fired his co-pilot, a New Zealand boat bum, and the ketch was advertised for sale at a give-away price—in the *Journal de Tahiti*, *The New York Times*, the *Los Angeles Times*, and *Sea* magazine.

A few slips away in the other direction was the sloop *Solano*, which was also losing half its crew of two. The skipper, whose name was Leo Woyschner, had decided he'd rather sail alone than endure any longer the company of his mate. Leo was said to be an excellent sailor but too antisocial to be cooped up with another human being for any longer than a Happy Hour.*

The most sensational piece of harbor gossip about ship-jumping (involuntary) concerned the huge two-masted schooner *Goodwill*, which arrived a few days after we did, and dwarfed the whole colony. One hundred sixty-four feet long, she had brought down the American astronomers and all the gear with which they intended to observe a total eclipse of the sun from two islands in the Scilly and Cook groups. The *Goodwill* had been leased to the National Science Foundation for this trip,

---

* Less than a year from the date of our meeting with Leo, someone sent a newspaper clipping that detailed his suicide at sea. He was sailing someone else's boat from Los Angeles to Honolulu with a completely inexperienced young man for a mate. A few hundred miles from Oahu, Leo went quietly mad, jumped overboard in a calm sea, and refused to be rescued. The green hand didn't know enough about maneuvering the boat to argue the point. He was blown slowly away from the swimmer . . . and picked up two days later by a search-and-rescue vessel from the Coast Guard. Leo was never seen again.

but the owner and some of his friends had come along as part of the crew—just for the adventure and the ride!

The trip down was rough. It took only eighteen days from Los Angeles, but the winds were adverse, and several times the stern was "pooped." The captain was new, and most of the crew were green hands, recruited from United States Employment Service offices and college coffeehouses. Apparently the owner needed some relaxation after the strain, for he began to amuse himself at Quinn's—the notorious waterfront dance-bar, which did its drab best to look like a den of iniquity. His behavior put a severe strain on the already difficult relations with the French authorities (who had originally refused permission to the American astronomers even to set up shop on the target island they controlled). The man in charge of the operation was forced to exercise his authority and to have the *Goodwill*'s owner sent back to the States. Several of his friends were staying on, but it was rumored that they were on probation.

Our old friend Captain Amaru paid a courtesy call one afternoon. The *Taporo* was on the ways, having some of the rust scraped off her hull, and he had been approached with an offer to skipper the *Goodwill* on the last leg of her journey. The French atoll of Bellingshausen, where half the observation team was to set up shop, is one of those that has no pass whatsoever in the fringing reef. All the delicate instruments would have to be carried in whaleboats over the barrier in the sort of surf ride that only skilled Polynesian mariners can manage. Captain Amaru had chosen a crew for the purpose, and his hands were already itching for the feel of the schooner's gigantic wheel. But Donald, that faceless corporate entity that dominated so many destinies in Polynesia, said no. He was needed to keep an eye on the rust-chipping. Captain Amaru was an embittered man, and nothing we had to say or to drink was much consolation to him.

The day after his visit we got an official notice that a parcel from the United States had been received and was waiting for us at Customs.

We reported for duty at once and spent the rest of the day (and part of the next) fighting the battle of *bureaucratie* (red tape). Bureaucracy is not natural to the Tahitian character, and the effort to adjust to it results in really unique levels of snafu. For example, we were required to fill out a form of which there was not a copy in any of the offices in the huge rabbit warren of the *Douane*. We were advised to find a Chinese—that is, a merchant—who imported goods for resale. The fact that we were not importing goods for that purpose was dismissed as irrelevant. Only an importer would be likely to have the forms, we were told. (*Les papiers* was the term, and it seemed to mean forms in general, not any particular sort.)

We did find a Chinese merchant, waited out his two-hour lunch period, and got a form. It was headed "goods for resale," but when we got it back to the office, the word "not" was inserted in the proper place, and everyone was satisfied. Everyone, incidentally, was a collective singular for nine different *fonctionnaires*, each with his own office, desk, and rubber stamp. By playing the game with straight faces, we finally made it through the whole team and out to the locked shed where our $14 parcel was impounded. But before he could lay profane hands on it, Jack had to sign a declaration that accepted several dire penalties if he were ever to return to Papeete with these "imported objects" in his possession—even in use on the boat.

It was a cloudy Sunday morning when we finally prepared to weigh anchor (no mean task, thanks to our *bizarre* friend the pilot), and I caught myself feeling like a resident of Los Angeles off for a weekend at Catalina to escape the traffic, the noise, the neighbors, the pace and tension of city life.

Was Tahiti really that un-Polynesian? Well, Papeete was. Of the old, unspoiled Tahiti we had seen very little. It seemed to have drawn into its shell like a mollusc, and whether it was alive or dead inside no ten-day visitor could know.

As we sailed on through the Societies—Mooréa, Huahiné, the double island Raiatea-Tahaa, and Bora-Bora—it seemed to me that the things that make Polynesia and its people beautiful were evident in inverse proportion to the penetration of European and/or American "culture." The more creature comforts (and military and industrial development), the less loveliness. Partly because the invaders themselves—tourists, soldiers, bureaucrats, and businessmen—were generally unlovely, and partly because the effect of the two cultures on each other is to soften (very slightly) the abrasive quality of the Western and to erode (very considerably) the substance of the Polynesian.

But all is not yet lost. Our farewell to Papeete had good as well as evil omens in it.

By the time we got our anchor line unsnarled from the *Magnolia*'s, a rain squall hit, and Jack decided to wait it out. While we were having a cup of coffee belowdecks, there was a sudden raucous cawing of a Volkswagen horn and a babble of children's voices. Before we realized that it was we who were being paged, we were boarded by a bevy of Manuel children, accompanied by Madame. They had made and brought five exquisite plumeria leis, one for each member of the crew and one to be tossed into the water just before we sailed out of the pass to ensure our eventual return.

While we were going through the kissing ritual that accompanies the giving and getting of leis, we were hailed by a hitch-hiker, who introduced himself as Yves Gabin, the purser of one of the big UTA jet liners. He had flown in from Los Angeles the night before. His two daughters (Parisian secretaries) were spending their vacation on Mooréa and would be expecting him, but he had overslept and missed the day's only excursion boat. Could we possibly give him a lift?

We did. And our farewell to Papeete was the beginning of a friendship that helped us penetrate the shell of tourism on Mooréa as we could hardly have hoped to do without such help.

Mooréa and
Les Îles Sous-le-Vent

Captain Amaru had told us that his favorite of all islands was Mooréa and that his favorite of all her bays was Papetoai. But Yves's daughters were staying at a small native hotel called (by *popaas*) the One Chicken, on Pao-Pao Bay, which is also known as Cook's. That was where we moored the first night.

Yves took us over. He ordered the proprietor and his wife around as if they were part of his own staff, ordered the dinner we were to be served, promised to cook the omelette himself, and got us included in an expedition to catch the fish course. Daniel, the proprietor, had a new *éparveil* (a large circular casting net, about twenty feet in diameter, weighted lightly around one edge) and he wanted to try it out. I drew the job of paddling the outrigger canoe, while the men worked the shallows along the edge of the bay. Daniel moved a few yards ahead of them, the net bundled in his arms, wading with a slow gait that hardly disturbed the mirror reflections. His little grandson followed along the beach.

All at once Daniel lifted an arm. Everybody stopped. He had spotted a school of small fish. The boy on the beach tensed like a sprinter at the start of a race. Daniel nodded to him and to Yves, and at almost the same instant made a single sweeping pass with his right arm. The net flared out and settled slowly onto the water. The boy rushed into the water, shouting, splashing, and throwing pebbles. Yves began to stamp and shout and splash; the other three men got the idea, and followed suit. As the weighted edges of the net slowly settled, the fish were frightened inside it. When the weights reached the bottom, all the helpers began—with feet and fingers—to draw the net closer and closer around the imprisoned school until Daniel signaled that he was satisfied.

He gathered the whole catch up in his arms, found a small opening in the tightened edge, and began to shake a cascade of living, wriggling silver into the open mouth of a bamboo fish trap, called a *nase*. We had seen these handsome containers used as lampshades or flower baskets, but never being used as originally intended. Daniel filled his half full, and buttoned down the lid. Then, grasping it by both ends, he shook it violently a minute or so, dipped it in the water and let it drain, shook again, dipped again, and finally opened the lid and poured the fish into the outrigger. They were scaled, rinsed, dead, and ready to be cooked.

They were served to us less than an hour later, gutted but not beheaded, and fried so crisp that they looked and tasted like French-fried potatoes with only the faintest overtone of fish.

The other memorable dish of that meal was the dessert. Mooréa is a vanilla-growing community. The new crop was drying in every backyard in Pao-Pao, when the wind was right the perfume was enough to set us drooling. Daniel's wife gave me a year's supply of the long black beans and the recipe for the custard she made of green coconut jelly.

COCONUT CUSTARD À LA VANILLE

> Young coconuts—enough to provide you with as much of the delicate jelly that lines the husks as you will need to serve your party. About 1½ coconuts per person, on the average.
> Vanilla beans—an 8-inch bean should do for a custard that will serve 4.

The preparation is mainly a matter of getting the green coconuts cracked so that one can scrape out the jelly. Chop a whole vanilla bean, very fine, and mix it into the jelly. Let it stand overnight, if possible in a refrigerator. Any reasonably cool place will do.

The One Chicken did not do much business as a hostel. The Gabin girls occupied one of the only two bungalows available; when their father was in residence, the hotel was full. But its dining room was always crowded on a weekend night, when dinner was served to soldiers, sailors, and airline employees who came over to dance the *tamure* with the local belles.

The girls who drifted in during the evening were not particularly beautiful, but when they danced they put even Atuona's Philomène to shame. The star of the evening was a woman in her forties, the mother of eight, including three teen-age daughters who were on the dance floor, and a three-year-old boy who sat under the table all evening, drinking orange pop.

Mama was missing most of her front teeth, but she had kept her figure. Yves invited her to dance, and he did very well for a *popaa*—much better than the doctor in Atuona. Mama encouraged him for a few measures, goading him on with provocative little grunts. But eventually she lost interest, in him and everything else around her. She began dancing by and for herself, executing figures we had never seen before, hand movements with the slow religious grace of the Hawaiian hula, knee bends that took her right down to the floor in a regal obeisance, while her hips were undulating in an orbit that might have been called planetary.

Later in the evening we made a "research trip" to the posh Bali Hai Hotel, up the shore of the bay, to see the *tamure* dancers they imported to entertain the weekend tourists. The whole village of Temae was hired to perform what amounted to ballets, magnificently costumed and choreographed. Some told legends, like that of the voyage north to discover Hawaii; others reenacted the creation myth in one of its variants. The enterprising Americans who ran the Bali Hai claimed to have sparked a real renaissance of the ancient Polynesian religious rituals by providing an audience for them, and it may have been true. What went on at the point in the choreography where male and female began their work of populating the newly emerged earth was indescribable—at least, by me. I had never thought of the *danse du ventre* in the light of a religious act before, but of course the Greeks did. I wonder how the rites of Dionysus would have grabbed a Polynesian audience.

On our second day at Mooréa we took the *Aikane* through the smooth inside passage to Papetoai Bay, to compare its perfections with Pao-Pao. Both are paradisiacal. Deep fjords like the Marquesan inlets, they are backed by greener, but no less spectacular, mountains, and protected by reefs that calm the waters to mirror—except when a williwaw blows down from the heights. The slopes are less precipitous than the Marquesan, and there is a wider, lusher coastal plain. More coconut palms, more flowers, in general a gentler, more Eden-like feeling. But between the two Mooréan bays there is little to choose except isolation. There are two posh hotels on Pao-Pao (not counting the One Chicken), and a continual coming and going of excursion boats from Papeete. Papetoai seemed undefiled.

While Norris and Jack tried to teach the Gabin girls how to swim, Benson and I went diving to try out the new spears we had bought in Papeete, guaranteed to work in these waters. The hunting was not good, but we brought back two monstrosities: an "abominable Acanthaster," a many-legged starfish covered with terrible spines; and a gigantic brown-splotched moray. The Acanthaster was mine. I spotted him on the face of a low reef wall and poked him with my spear. He promptly curled himself up into a menacing puffball and rolled with the current like a western-plains tumbleweed. When I tried to pick him up, one of the spines went through a hole in my cotton gloves. The prick turned blue, and the finger throbbed all night and was numb for weeks. (Daniel said I should have held the wound against one of the suckers by which the Acanthaster holds on to the rocks, and let it suck its own poison out.)

The moray was a real adventure. I first saw him sticking his ugly head out of the face of the reef above which I was snorkeling. I didn't want to risk my new spear by shooting into the coral, so I swam away and got Benson, who is a better shot than I. He maneuvered a few minutes, during which the moray continued to peer around. Then Benson pulled the trigger. The spear and the head disappeared at the same instant. The line went slack. For a moment we both thought he had missed and that the spear had buried itself in the sand below.

Then the reef began to "explode" from within. Little puffs of "smoke" began to emerge from small openings as much as twenty feet distant from each other. Benson tugged on the line and found that it was not free. It led into the reef face at the point where the moray's head had been. Somewhere inside the coral labyrinth the big eel was going through convulsions that stirred up sediment and expelled it by various circuitous routes. Eventually, he would die. But would we be able to get the spear out, with or without the prey? The whole of the two-and-a-half-foot shaft had disappeared. Was it possible that it was not bent like a fishhook by now?

We snorkeled around, watching, for nearly ten minutes. Things seemed to have quieted down inside the coral. Benson tugged gently on the line. It gave a little. He pulled harder, and out came the moray! Pinned cleanly through the brain by a perfect shot, but still very much alive, and almost six feet long, swimming with a ponderous grace in the direction the "leash" was pulling!

I was not comfortable about swimming ashore in this kind of company. There was nothing to stop him making a sudden dash for the man on the other end of the leash. But I was afraid to take a shot at him with the other gun, lest, instead of finishing him off, I simple enrage him. Jack was rowing around not far away, encouraging his beautiful pupils. We hailed him. They got safely to shore, and Jack took the gun from us, towed the beast in to the beach, where we killed him, took his picture, and threw him away.

Back at Pao-Pao we were roundly abused for this wastefulness. Despite his nasty face and disposition, the moray is delicate and delicious when baked—or so said Daniel.

We put the Gabin clan on the boat for Papeete and followed it out the pass. As it turned east, we turned west, heading for the Iles Sous-le-Vent. We could see Tahiti clearly on the horizon astern, and it seemed a good idea to vent all our accumulated spleen at the bureaucracy we were leaving behind us. So we called Radio Mahina, intending to tell its deaf ears, in English, what we thought of the whole operation. To our amazement, a calm and pleasant voice came in:

"*Radio Mahina. En quoi peut-on vous servir?*"

I was so flustered that I could hardly muster enough French to explain—not very convincingly—that we were trying out our set's *propagation*, which the voice assured us was excellent. It wished us a *très bon voyage*. I said thanks, and blushed for the better part of an hour.

Huahiné, the first of the Leeward Islands, was like Papetoai, unspoiled and exquisite. We entered the pass at the main settlement, Fare, and anchored about a mile from the main wharf. (We had taken on a stowaway copra rat at Takaroa, which had eaten its way through a lot of cake mix and started on the back cover of Bowditch before we finally got him. Se we were keeping our distance from places where copra was stored for shipment.)

There was a very handsome ketch (the *Elusive*, out of Seattle) moored in the area where we began taking soundings, and

The Island of Huahiné.

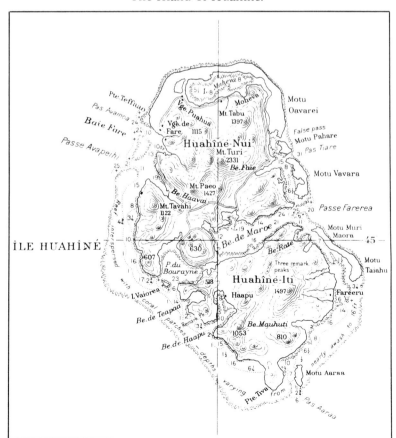

before Jack and Benson were satisfied with bottom below us, we were hailed.

"We're going to run some friends over to Bora-Bora," shouted a friendly American voice, "so you take this anchorage. See you when we get back."

For the next two days we lived on top of the best shelling we had ever known. The water there was about twenty-five feet deep, and the bottom was pure white coral sand, shelving gently up toward the beach a hundred yards away. There was a full moon, and the water was so warm and so calm that we could go shelling at night, when the big fellows were out on the prowl. We had an underwater flashlight, but found that even without it we could make out a wavy track on the sand. The only trick was to guess in which direction to follow it. At one end there was almost bound to be a large miter or auger or a flea-bitten cone exposed or hidden in a mound of soft sand.

And there were other delights on the shore.

On the point nearest us was a small coco-palm plantation that was being gradually invaded by the lagoon. We came upon a freshly fallen tree, and had—at last!—the ingredients for a Millionaire's Salad, the recipe for which begins: "Find a healthy tree of suitable size, and fell."

MILLIONAIRE'S SALAD

    The heart of a healthy palm tree
    Assorted fresh vegetables, like cucumber, radish, scallions, green pepper (all optional)
    Marinade of oil and good vinegar
    Fresh-ground black pepper and salt

Preparing this dish is work for a woodsman. Saw off about three feet of the top of the trunk, and hack off the tough outer covering. When you have what looks like an oversize celery stalk, start peeling off layers, tasting each (or trying for tenderness) before discarding. When you have reached the fiberless, tender embryo fronds, start slicing. A good-sized heart, sliced thin, will feed at least 10 gourmets a great salad course. Other fresh, raw vegetables simply add bulk, and point up the superiority of the palm.

Marinate for an hour or two, and chill, if you can.

The *Elusive* returned from Bora-Bora before we had finished exploring the shelling grounds or the quiet little village of Fare. We were invited for "cocktails on the afterdeck, when the sun is over the yard arm." Something about the phrasing warned us; the men shaved, I set my hair, and we cleaned the detritus out of the *Lili Aikane*. But even so, we all agreed later that we felt like "hillbillies" when we scrambled up the boarding ladder and met the Wilsons.

Jim and Martha looked like the subjects of an article in *Holiday*, and so did their ship. They were running what amounted to a free interisland taxi service for their Polynesian friends. There had been three overnight guests on the run to Bora-Bora, and two new ones on the run back. But the galley was immaculate; there were fresh hibiscus blossoms in bowls in the salon; the guest bunks were made up with fresh linen (blue, monogrammed, and ironed!). All sorts of nibble food was laid out in carved bowls on cushions on the shaded teak afterdeck. Jim was wearing spotless white shorts, and Martha's muumuu was ankle-length and elegant. Her shell lei was magnificent, and when we commented, she told us it was a gift of Madame Mervin from Takaroa.

Jim turned out to be the founding father of the Takaroa Yacht Club. While he and Jack discussed the organizational problems of that and an even newer club Jim was fathering in Bora-Bora, I made a sneaky tour of inspection. There was no hired help aboard. Martha and Jim had brought the *Elusive* all the way down by themselves, getting relief from continual watches by more generous use of the automatic pilot than we had made. On their interisland hops they frequently had the help of guest pilots, from whom Jim was learning a great deal. ("If Steve Ellacott tells me to head straight for the reef, that's what I do," he was saying to Jack in the awed voice of a man who has seen a demigod at work.) But for the most part, they did it all: the maintenance, the repairs, the chores, and the hosting. It was awesome, and the effect of the *Aikane*'s crew was a flurry of housekeeping and person-preening that took nearly a week to subside.

We were heading next for the great double island of Raiatea-Tahaa, and the Wilsons said they would see us there or at Bora-Bora, where Jim was determined to enroll the *Aikane* in the Yacht Club.

As we raised sail outside the pass, three island shapes were clear and bold on the horizon ahead: Raiatea, Tahaa, and Bora-Bora (which is actually another twenty miles to the northwest). The sky was full of dramatic storm clouds, and suddenly a complete double rainbow arched its back from the volcanic core of Raiatea to its sister cone on Bora-Bora. Nature is always doing that sort of overacting in these islands, and it is hard to resist the temptation to read omens.

A single enormous fringing reef encloses Raiatea and Tahaa, both of which are good-sized islands with more than one settlement. Raiatea is the larger, over thirteen miles long, with a 3400-foot mountain at its western end. The only large town in the Iles Sous-le-Vent is Uturoa, which is situated at the southeastern tip of Raiatea. It is the site of a new *lycée*, much larger and more fully staffed than Taiohae's, but not as venerable as Papeete's. There was a newly instituted daily plane service to Tahiti, with a trickle of tourists that has doubtless by now swelled to a stream. Travel folders we had picked up in Papeete advertised the new branch Bali Hai Hotel, with "sidetrips to see the fabulous fire-walkers of Mount Temehani . . . climb the extinct crater . . . water-ski in the lagoon . . . fish outside the reef. . . ." It seemed only a matter of months before the Matson Line would begin to bring the air-conditioned octogenarians in.

We entered the lagoon by one of its two passes, and found a place to moor as close as possible to the market section of Uturoa. This was going to be our last chance to reprovision for the long sea leg to Hawaii, for Donald's of Tahiti had really let us down.

The shops were already closing when we had squared away, so we hiked up the shoreline to have dinner at the Bali Hai (with thick steaks of New Zealand beef, flown in fresh three times a week!) and then, a mile or so farther on, to use a letter of introduction from M. Mansard, of the Lycée Paul Gauguin, to M. and

Mme. Beaulieu, of the faculty of the new school. This was the last and the luckiest of all the uses to which we put Benson's professional project. The Beaulieus not only fell in with the spirit of the inquiry, but formed an instant but lasting friendship with all four of us.

As their guests, we boomed around the lagoon in a launch, looking for select shelling spots, explored one of those slow freshwater, flower-decked rivers we had seen on the travel posters. (There were no half-naked Tahitian beauties bathing under the vine-draped trees, but Gabrielle Beaulieu in a bikini was not a bad substitute.) They also took us on a moonlight hunt for *chevrettes*, a delicious freshwater crawfish that we ate afterward, cold with mayonnaise, and hot in a curry-and-tomato sauce.

Our guide on this expedition was a neighbor of theirs, the first Polynesian female we had met who lived up to the reputation of the species. She was in her middle thirties, still energetic and attractive, and she responded to what she took for an amorous advance on the part of one of the male hunters by explaining

Benson with bananas.

in perfectly understandable English that she never took a lover "for a single night only, or even the weekend," because she was "sleeping with" her father and did not want to disrupt a satisfactory relationship for anything too transitory. The effect of this declaration was to inhibit all the unattached men from so much as a look in her direction for the rest of the night.

The *chevrette* hunt was, as a result, more decorous than is usual. We wandered around in the dark for a couple of hours, shining flashlights into the rills of a many-branched brook and looking for pairs of eyes *"qui brillent rouges."* When one spotted a pair of these tiny red headlights, one stabbed with a long cane, equipped with several blunt tines. Those who were quick—or lucky—pulled a salmon-colored, wriggling crawfish, unharmed, from their tines.

We did most of our shopping at a grubby-looking but exceedingly well-stocked Chinese establishment named Moo Fat. (Donald's of Uturoa was high-priced, poorly stocked, and staffed by a quartet of sulky, unaccommodating teen-agers.) We did pretty well with most of our list of staples, once we gave up expecting familiar brands. The one exception to this was the problem of peanut butter. It had turned out to be as essential to Norris's sense of well-being as cigarettes, and for a while it looked as if the French had no equivalent. There were no friendly brown jars on the shelves, even at Moo Fat's. My requests for *beurre de cacahuète* got no response. But finally I saw a woman actually receive a jar of the precious stuff from the hands of the clerk who had turned me down.

I crept up to her, and pointed. *"Comment s'appelle-t-il?"* I whispered in a conspiratorial tone.

She looked at me as if I were mad. "Skee—pee," she said.

We got plenty of good coffee, canned paté, excellent canned string beans, bully beef, cheese, and hardtack. We filled all our empty gallon jugs with Algerian wine. Other more basic items: detergent, paper towels, toilet paper, and powdered milk were either unavailable, of appallingly bad quality, and/or ludicrously overpriced. My card file system had worked well enough in one way: that is, I had an accurate list of our needs with a minimum of time lost in inventory. But in the end, I had to throw the list away and buy what there was.

The night before we moved on to Tahaa, the *Elusive* came by. The Wilsons were taking another set of friends from Huahiné to Maupiti (a dot of an island fifty miles to the west), but they would see us in Bora-Bora.

"Can you make that wild pass at Maupiti?" Jack called as the space widened between us.

"I don't have to," Jim called back. "Got Steve Ellacott aboard! He can make it drunk and with his eyes bandaged! See you next week!"

The distance between Uturoa and the nearest point of the island of Tahaa was less than five miles, not worth putting up the sails, but it was quite an adventure. Our chart of the area showed such a maze of underwater obstacles that working out a passage was like solving the problem of the Minotaur's maze. When my third effort ended in a cul de sac of coral from which there was no exit, I gave up. (On paper, that is; it was the day's navigation problem, and I was back in class by this time.)

Jack had consulted several self-appointed experts, each of whom had recommended a route, but no two had agreed. So, finally, he plotted his own best guess, and sent me up the mast in the bosun's chair to keep watch for uncharted reefs.

It was not a comfortable or a dignified position, hugging the mast like a green rider clutching the pommel of his saddle, unable to sit gracefully to the gait of his mount. But the view was worth a good deal of discomfort. The surface of the huge lagoon looked like a gigantic enlargement of one of those rainfall or population or temperature maps that come first in an atlas, splotched with concentric "free" forms in contrasting colors, from purple to tan. I could see islands joining hands surreptitiously at a depth of ten or fifteen feet, as if they were conspiring to trap some deep-keeled vessel. Other islands, more forthright, were reaching for the upper air. Being born! One had recently been baptized by the rooting of a single stunted palm. In another year or so, it would have a name.

When we got close to the western face of Tahaa, the channel was clear. I was dropped (gently) to the deck, and we began to look for a good place to anchor and go ashore.

The island of Tahaa was still almost untouched by the cancer of tourism. There are no very good harbors along its shoreline, and no real towns. Just valleys full of coco palms and coffee bushes, with here and there a cluster of three or four bamboo-walled houses. Others are set out over the water on stilts, with matching privies, also on stilts.

We finally tied up at a cement dock, reassured by the absence of any copra shed, and tried to dive for our dinner. There were no fish, and we were afraid to eat *pahuas* that lived near this sort of sanitary plant, so we ended by buying our dinner from a floating fish market. A twenty-foot launch came through the pass on the western face of the reef, announcing its approach by a blast on a conch shell. Housewives all along the shore emerged from indoors and gathered on the rickety little piers that jut into the lagoon. The launch stopped whenever hailed. By the time it was close to us, we saw the transaction: a beautiful big bonito was unhooked from the tail rack that ran the length of the launch. There must have been nearly a hundred of the blue-silver beauties in the day's catch!

We stood on our bow and waved frantically, and the launch came to us. The price was fixed: thirty francs * for a whole fish, which must have weighed five all-meaty pounds. The exchange was made with all the efficiency of a supermarket cash register, but as the launch pulled away the traditional took over. The teen-age apprentice took up his post at the prow and blew another blast on his shell. We could see women coming down to their piers all the way up the shore until the island turned a corner out of sight.

We barbecued our fish on charcoal, which we had brought from Los Angeles. A large crowd—perhaps fifteen—spectators gathered on the pier to watch. Apparently they had never seen fish treated this way. Breadfruit, yes. They nodded approval of our efforts in that department. But the fish simply baffled them, and my efforts to give a demonstration without a common language made me so self-conscious that I botched the job.

FISH BARBECUED WHOLE

**A fresh fish, 3 lbs. or more
Fresh (if possible) herbs**

* Polynesian francs, at less than 1 1/5 cents each.

Cooking oil
Salt and pepper

Gut the fish and carefully slit the back from head to tail along the dorsal spine, making the cut penetrate almost to the central backbone. Oil the flesh inside and out and stuff the body cavity with fresh herbs. (Or sprinkle with dried herbs: tarragon, basil, marjoram, or a blend.) Leave the fish on the grill over a hot charcoal fire until the outer surface is charred, so that it will not break into pieces when you turn it to the other side. Turn it only once. Brush the upper side lightly with oil before turning. If you have fresh herbs, use them as a brush.
Serve in chunks and eat it off the burned part.

I turned our bonito too soon, and the results were messy. No one on Tahaa learned anything from watching the *popaa* lady and her pretty but useless portable fire.

Pai-pai pass, the exit to Bora-Bora, was a real thriller. Great combers hit the reef on either side of the opening with a force that shook the air, while an offshore wind blew their hair back and made rips in the deepwater channel that led from the lagoon to the sea. There was a crazy little shack of bamboo poles and palm thatch standing on the edge of the reef on the port side; apparently deserted, awash even at low tide, it looked as if it had been blown there in some particularly strong wind.

Jack had the chart on his knees and the compass in sight all the way out because the angle of the combers played tricks with our eyes, and what looked like the channel on the surface would have led us right on to the reef.

The same illusion (in the opposite direction) plagued us once we had crossed the open water and were coasting alongside the reef at Bora-Bora. This went on for a couple of hours because we had to make half a circuit of that island to get to the single pass—Teavanui—that opens into its lagoon. I was sure the whole time that we were gradually being drawn into the field of the rollers that were pounding themselves to mist on the reef, beyond which we could catch little glimpses of the still lagoon and the beautiful Hotel Bora-Bora, from whose windows that day's planeload of tourists were doubtless watching our slow progress and thinking how picturesque a sport sailing is.

The Teavanui pass is the most hair-raising entrance we ever attempted, and it was well we saved it for the last.* It must have been the one Jim Wilson was talking about when he said, "If Steve tells me to head straight for the reef, that's what I do." That's what we did. The underwater coral arm reaches much farther out on the north side than on the south, from which we were approaching, and even the chart says of the surf that it "breaks heavily" on both promontories. We sailed straight for a jagged brownish wall that was alternately bared by the sucking back of a giant surge, and buried in foam.

Jack sounded cheerful as he assured me that we were not as close as I thought, but he stuck to his chart. Finally, when I had closed my eyes to await the shock of collision, he put the wheel over. I felt the *Aikane* execute a smart right turn. By the time I felt safe enough to open my eyes, Benson and Norris were dropping the sails.

The surge was quieter, but the sound on the outer reef behind us was not. It was like a series of dynamite charges from the depths. We were still in uncomfortable proximity to the reefs on both sides. The channel looked to be a mile long, and the chart showed a turn in it—under water!

"Look at those channel markers!" someone said in alarm. "Isn't it red-right-returning? We're way off, if it is—practically on the rocks."

"I'm lined up with the range markers and the right heading," Jack said, no longer so cheerful.

"Range markers may not be any more reliable around here than navigation lights. I'd go by the—"

"We're all right! There are the black buoys. We're between the black and the red, so we're all right."

"But red is supposed to be to starboard, and black to port!"

Jack kept on the course advised by the range markers, and told me to look the matter up in Bowditch. We were well into

---

* According to several authorities, the pass at Maupiti is considerably worse. Once you have committed yourself to the entrance, to look back is to risk the punishment of Lot's wife.

the lagoon and out of danger before I found the answer. There are two systems of buoyage, the Lateral, and the Uniform, and they are diametrically opposed to each other in the matter of coloring! "It may be said that, very generally, European countries follow the Uniform system of 1936, and most other countries follow the system proposed in 1889."*

Bora-Bora turned out to be just what everyone had told us: the quintessence of all the delightful features of South Pacific islands of both types. It has a handsome rugged volcanic cone, freshwater rivers and waterfalls, and lush valleys, and it also has a clear lagoon in which pearls of all colors can be grown, an abundance of edible fish and shellfish, little motus—tufts of palm, perched here and there on the wide fringing reef—and an airstrip that brings tourists in from Papeete twice a week. It is also a port of call for Matson liners on their deluxe cruise schedule, but now and then one of these behemoths runs on to the reef on the starboard side of the channel.

The corruption of the beautiful people of this beautiful Eden may have begun with the American military occupation during World War II, but it is being compounded by the French military occupation on weekend passes from Papeete or Mururoa. All the smaller hotels around the main anchorage of Teavanui Bay seemed to turn into whorehouses late Friday afternoon and continue in that line of business until noon Sunday. The clientele of the Hotel Bora-Bora was of a different class: jet-set tourists, who usually move in pairs or larger groups and who corrupt manners rather than "morals." But on a Saturday night both sets of invaders met in the dining-room-turned-dance-hall of the Hotel Bora-Bora, and celebrated an orgiastic rite that has replaced the old dances and drumming as the religion of the place.

We anchored in front of one of the lesser hotels and went

---

* It will come as a surprise to many American navigators to know that we are out of step with the rest—or a large part of the rest—of the world in this matter. While I was trying to check out the details of which countries had stuck with us and the 1889 system, I consulted a whole roster of authorities, including a very obliging gentleman in the office of the Captain of the Port (of Portland, Oregon). Neither he nor anyone else I could find had ever heard of the "deviation" of "most European countries," so my friend called Coast Guard headquarters in Washington, D.C. The authorities there suggested that perhaps the problem I raised was "the result of a misplaced marker." The possible consequences of such parochialism are awesome.

ashore to report to the *gendarmerie* and to look for mail. Despite a letter of introduction from François, the gendarme of Takaroa, we were not welcomed with any great cordiality, not invited to go diving, fishing, or picnicking. In fact, we were snubbed. But the mail compensated, at least as far as I was concerned.

The revisions of the novel that I had airmailed from Papeete had got safely around the world and onto my editor's desk, and he had found them good. As far as they went! There was one editorial request I had resisted. Ever so delicately I was urged to reconsider. I rented a bungalow on the shore, hardly fifty yards from the *Aikane*'s moorage, and went back to the nineteenth century, while the men aboard sanded and varnished and played in the aquamarine water like porpoises.

One very pleasant result of this short stint at the typewriter was that I met two American women who had the next bungalow—two wives from the *Goodwill* crew, who were waiting for the schooner to come back from her mission of depositing the scientists on Bellingshausen and the New Zealand protectorate of Manuae. That accomplished, the entire crew was to have a holiday on Bora-Bora while the astronomers set up shop and waited for Eclipse Day.

By the time we got to know these ladies, they were a little concerned about the whereabouts of the *Goodwill*. The communication plan agreed upon in advance was that Radio Mahina was to maintain daily radio contact with the ship, and to forward messages—including their established time of arrival—to Bora-Bora. But no messages had been received in the several days they had been there. Remembering the calm, pleasant voice that had wished us a *très bon voyage*, we offered to call Radio Mahina direct for them. (They had been working through the operator at the Hotel Bora-Bora, who seemed to be interested only in reservations and who regarded their choice of another hotel as apostasy.)

We tried every day, morning, noon, and early evening, for three days running, but we never got a reply. It was *bizarre*, but not surprising.

While we were waiting for the *Goodwill* to appear, the *Elu-*

sive did. The Wilsons were able to introduce us to the fabulous Steve Ellacott, who had got them in and out of the pass at Maupiti. Steve is half English and half Tahitian, and speaks English and French, as well as Tahitian; his wife is half Tahitian and half Swiss, and speaks no language we knew except that of the gracious smile and nod. Their home is on Bora-Bora, where Steve is in charge of a government-subsidized experiment in the growing of cultured pearls of different shades in colonies of imported Chilean nacre shells.

Since we were by now "old friends" of the Wilsons, Steve included us on his tour of inspection of the pearl nurseries. "I will also show you where the big *moules* grow, and perhaps, if the wind is right, we will dive with tanks on the outside of the reef. You would like that?"

That excursion inside and outside the Bora-Bora reef was the underwater climax of the voyage for me. We had been hoarding our two tanks of air and our scuba equipment for emergencies, but in Bora-Bora there was a compressor that could replenish the used-up tanks, so we felt we could afford it. Also, while skin diving was exciting enough in the quiet and relatively shallow gardens of the lagoons, scuba was essential if one was to plumb the dangerous depths outside, so it was not "wasting" the air.

The four of us joined the Wilsons, another American couple (also sailing folk), Steve, and a rather sulky young man named Pierre who held some sort of official position at the Hotel Bora-Bora as well as a government job diving for Steve. (Steve had split an eardrum several years before, and did no diving at all.)

The first stop of the day was an official inspection of the nacre nurseries in a sheltered part of the lagoon near the tiny Motu Tapu on the southern side of the pass. Only Pierre was permitted to go down. He used full (and very expensive) scuba equipment, but he was only down a minute or so. His report (in Tahitian) seemed to satisfy Steve, who said that we might as well use up the rest of the tank of gasoline, which would carry us around to the *moule* beds and back to the pass and give us a good hour outside.

The giant mussels grow in an underwater environment unlike anything we had seen until then: a forest of brittle white antler coral on a bottom of coral sand so fine that it rose in clouds that obscured vision whenever it was disturbed. The *moules* were jet black and deeply buried in the sand. By the time anyone got a knife down—often as far as a foot below the surface—and severed the tough byssus fibers, he was usually swimming in milk. If one had to come up for a breath before finishing the job, it was easy to lose the prize, large as it was. And many of these giants measured over two feet from pointed hinge to flaring lips. (The hinge muscle, incidentally, was all that we ate, and it was delicious—rather like a good scallop. But I have been told since that the meat of the mantle is also edible and choice.)

When we had taken aboard all the *moules*, antler coral, and other souvenirs that we wanted, we reversed our course, returned almost to our moorage, and headed out the pass. The surf was not as high as on the day of our arrival, but it was scary enough. When Steve picked a spot and threw out an anchor, about a mile from the pass, I suffered a sudden change of heart about the whole operation. Until that moment I had been ready to fight for my "right" to "my own" tank and regulator. Jack and Benson had already used it for a short exploration at Huahiné, when I had a cold and couldn't dive. Norris had never dived with scuba before, and this was no place to learn. So it was my "turn," and I intended to say so if anyone challenged me.

But by now I almost wished someone would. There were three other tanks aboard: one belonging to Jack, one to the other American family, and one to Pierre. Jack and Benson had already decided to divide the air in Jack's tank, and to pair off with the man of the American couple. That left me to buddy with Pierre, who was going to use his thirty minutes fishing on the reef face.

"You can take your gun if you like," he said to me in a tone that implied doubt that I knew what to do with it.

I began to "suit up" (without a suit). The straps of my tank had been adjusted to fit the last man who wore it, and I was in a hurry, so I never really got the tank firmly and comfortably on my back. I also forgot my snorkel and the socks that kept my fins from rubbing. But somehow I made it to the rail and plotzed into the water in the spectacularly graceless way I had been taught in my scuba class, a hemisphere away in a pool in North Hollywood, California.

Once the bubbles cleared, I could see Pierre already about thirty feet down, signaling me to follow. The water was pleasantly cool and as clear as air, and the floor of the sea below me looked like a color picture of the moon. I started down, and immediately my ears began to ache. After all, it had been nearly two years since I'd scubaed, and I would have to clear them slowly, I thought, so I took my time, breathing regularly and swimming in a slow descending spiral, enjoying—and trying not to be frightened by—the view.

As the floor slanted gently upward in the direction of the reef, gullies appeared in it, but no fish or other life. Everything was pitted, scarred, dead; the predominant color was that of wet cement, streaked here and there with rust or yellow chartreuse patches of algae. Weightless as an astronaut, and about as clumsy, I made my way slowly down, seeing only what was under my mask. I had already found that I couldn't turn my head, because the tank had slipped up and the sharp edge of the valve cut into my cerebellum every time I moved my neck. I couldn't see Pierre, but I supposed he was behind or above me.

Ahead, the reef was visible now, rearing like the wall of an embattled fortress that has been breached in many places. There were passes wide enough to swim through, except that the current reversed itself every time a wave broke on the surface, forming dangerous whirlpools and making the water milky with minute air bubbles. I was being tossed—gently enough—by those currents even at this distance, and I found that it was all I could do, by working my fins steadily and constantly, to hold my own. I couldn't stay in one spot, either. I tried to, because I finally saw a small coral "flower" I wanted to break off, but even when I held on with one hand, the current tumbled me and banged the tank against my neck, which was already getting sore.

And Pierre was nowhere to be seen. Neither were the fish that were supposed to be so plentiful out here. It must be the wrong tide or time of day or wind . . . the *wrong*—!

It struck me suddenly that it was wrong for me to be there alone, as wrong as a scuba diver can be. I had been carefully following all the other rules and lessons, but I had forgotten the basic dogma: Never dive without a buddy. "It's not my fault," I told myself. "He didn't wait for me. I couldn't come any faster without breaking my eardrums." It was just like Pierre, I thought. He was really an unpleasant character, obsequious and smiling as long as we were paying guests in his hotel dining room, rude and uncooperative when we came to buy a tank of air. . . . But the problem was not essentially one of Pierre's character; it was what I ought to do about my situation at the moment.

"When you lose your buddy, come straight up to the surface." That was Lesson Two. But I couldn't surface here; too close to that terrible surf! The next best thing was to swim as close as possible to the boat, and then surface. Cut down the distance I would have to swim against the chop, which was going to pound the loose tank against my neck. (Swimming on the surface with a tank under the best of circumstances is like dragging a cross up a watery Calvary.) The trouble was, I had only a general idea of where the boat was: that is, a hundred yards or so *off* the reef. I tried swimming "straight away" from it, and after going for what seemed far enough, I found I had managed to swim in a circle and was back in sight of the great breached wall again. More tired than before, and with less air!

As a matter of fact I was running out of air—at this depth— and there was nothing to do but start coming up. I took another "bearing," and started away from the reef, this time on a long slant up toward the surface. The air came more easily as the pressure was relieved, and I was careful to rise no faster than my exhaust bubbles, so I made it to the top with none of the horrendous consequences of panic I remembered from Lessons 3 to 6. (Like "spontaneous pneumothorax" or the bends.)

I surfaced about fifty yards from the boat, took a look around, and saw no one in the water, put my face back in and started swimming, using up the last of the air and remembering— with anguish—that I had no snorkel. When I ran out of air, I was going to have to swim crawl! And with seventy pounds of excess baggage banging me in the brain! It served me!

Before I had covered half the distance, I felt a tap on my back. It was Pierre the deserter, whom I could cheerfully have drowned—full of angry excuses and explanations that I couldn't hear well enough to contradict.

The one line I caught, as I was being ignominiously hauled

over the stern of the launch, was that my husband and *M. le capitaine* were at that very moment searching the face of the reef for me, and that if anything went wrong with them, the blame would be entirely mine. Nothing went wrong with them; in fact, they got a look at the reef they would otherwise not have seen. I don't think anyone was really much frightened by my "disappearance" except Pierre, and I hope his fright was painful enough to teach him better manners, next time he is called upon to buddy a backward partner into the depths.

The day after our dive, the *Goodwill* came in and tied up at the old United States submarine landing around the point to the north of us. Our ineffective efforts to close the communication gap served as a social introduction to the "working guests," friends of the owner who acted as his deputies and labored in certain key posts of responsibility—without pay. Even on this "shore leave" they worked hard for many hours of the day, but they all liked to dive, and one evening we took a launchful of them to the mussel beds.

There were only about fifteen minutes of daylight left when we finally located the spot, but six men with scuba brought up twenty-six enormous *moules* in that quarter of an hour, and we all went back to clean and eat them on the *Goodwill*.

It was our first close-up look at any sailing ship of that size, and we were awed. The engine-room was a two-story affair with its own power plant. The galley was supplied from a walk-in freezer locker. There was a grand piano in the main salon, as well as a banquet table on gimbals! Two men had to work from a crow's nest on the mast to thread or unthread the slides when the mainsail was raised or lowered, and God only knows how many hauling on the halyards! The boom was so thick that its inertia would tear the mast out by its roots in a jibe. (The captain put it another way when he commented to us, "She sails just the same as your vessel, except that if I make a mistake, someone's apt to get killed.")

We spent one more day, mailing my manuscript, buying coconuts and breadfruit and bananas (nothing was for free in Bora-Bora), and saying farewell to the fabulous underwater world. The *Goodwill*'s Boston Whaler came by in the afternoon and gave us a lift out to the Motu Tapu, where we found two downed palms, and divided the loot. One of the lady "working guests" (one who had washed dishes for fifty-three people three times a day all the way down from Los Angeles) lucked on to a gigantic golden spider conch in the shallows. Benson found and shot a puffer fish, which we later skinned, inflated, and dried. I found dozens of small escapees from the cultured pearl nurseries—all too young to have pearls. But the real high point of the excursion was something we ought to have filmed in color.

I was swimming along the surface over a fine sand bottom when all at once, at a depth of no more than fifteen feet, I saw a coral head, shaped like an overripe cauliflower about ten feet in diameter, and colored a lovely pink-mauve. In and out of its delicate flower heads darted thousands of small turquoise-colored minnows. When I started down to have a closer look, the minnows all sank into the coral, and disappeared. When I moved away, the pink rose bloomed turquoise again. It was like a slow-motion camera study of the opening (and closing) of a chrysanthemum.

The morning of our scheduled start on the long sea leg north to Hawaii, we were blasted out of our bunks at dawn by the *Elusive*'s horn. The Wilsons had taxied Steve Ellacott's wife over to visit her cousins on Huahiné and returned by moonlight, and all aboard were revoltingly wide-awake.

We explained that we were weighing anchor at eight, said our good-byes, and then it occurred to Jack that it would be a good idea to check our ship-to-shore radio (which had just failed to raise Radio Mahina again). Jim had one of our frequencies on his ship-to-shore, so he promised to call us as soon as he was moored in Steve's bay—which was out of sight around a point to the south.

While we were eating breakfast and getting things secured around the cabin, Jack kept trying to get Jim, but there was no answer. I could see that he and Benson were a little worried. Of course, the trouble might be on Jim's end. Still, one ought to be sure. . . . We were starting out on a 2300-mile voyage, and might want to send, as well as receive. . . .

"Tell you what," Jack decided aloud. "It's a little before eight. Let's get the anchor up and go around by the *Elusive* before we head out."

I was too busy in the galley to pay much attention to what was going on on deck, but it seemed to be taking longer than usual to get under way. I heard the motor that turned the winch run a while, shut off, then start again. Finally, I stuck my head out the companion hatchway just in time to hear Benson say to Jack, "All we're doing is pulling the bow down. The anchor must be fast on something down there. We're not going to break her loose this way."

They tried several other maneuvers that I didn't understand and that didn't succeed. By this time the Hotel Noa-Noa's dock was filling up with *bon voyage* wishers who had got themselves up to wave us away at 8:00 A.M. It was getting to be embarrassing.

The water was so clear that we ought to have been able to see what we were fouled on, even though it was seventy-some feet down, but the surface was already rippled with wind. We had refilled one of the scuba tanks for just this sort of emergency, but although Jack thought he could make it down seventy feet without hurting his ears, he doubted he could free a badly fouled anchor alone at that depth. We could, of course, have cut the chain and left the anchor there. We had two others. But all of our chain was payed out, and that would have left us unable to anchor anywhere, till we got to a place we could buy heavy chain.

The obvious solution was to hire a diver, but whom? Steve Ellacott has given up diving since he broke an eardrum; none of us wanted to negotiate with Pierre, even if he were competent to do the work (which was doubtful). We were still trying to come up with a better idea when the *Elusive* appeared. Jim had come to tell us that he wasn't receiving us on his set.

We explained our new problem, and as its seriousness sank in, a look of pure bliss came over his face. He said he would have us free in no time! He would simply couple the *Elusive*'s powerful engine to the chain in such a way as to pull on the anchor without pulling the *Aikane*, throw in his clutch and break us loose! He went about the preparations for this operation with an intensity of concentration that reminded me of a surgeon.

By now there was quite a crowd on the dock, and the Noa-Noa's bar had opened to accommodate the thirsty ones in it. Advice was being shouted to us, but the throb of the two engines drowned it out. When the chain was attached to Jim's satisfaction, a hush fell. Jack and Jim both gunned their engines at the same instant. Black smoke poured from both exhausts, and ours made a big smudge on the *Elusive*'s gleaming white hull. Jim's look of rapture faded as he examined the damage, but he was still undaunted. We tried it again—and again.

All we accomplished was to bend the bronze fitting on the *Aikane*'s bow, over which the anchor chain runs. People who were watching from the shore told us later that the *Aikane* looked as if she were standing on her nose, preparing to dive.

About this time, I had a brainstorm. Not a mile away was the *Goodwill*, with plenty of divers, plenty of tanks, and a compressor to replace any air that was used up. Jim was about to motor over to ask for assistance, when we saw the *Goodwill*'s launch rounding the point, heading our way.

We hailed them and they came alongside. There was no scuba aboard, but almost before we had explained our problem, the Gordons, father and son, were on their way back to the *Goodwill* for their gear. (John Gordon was an executive in a manufacturing company back in Pasadena; aboard the *Goodwill*, he and his wife were in charge of the galley, and their son functioned as part of the paid but green forecastle crew.)

While they were gone, Benson assembled all the tools they were likely to need, and secured them to a line long enough to reach the bottom. The trick about the repair—if one was to be undertaken—was going to be slacking off the tension of the chain so that the Gordons could work it, and at the same time keeping the *Aikane* from drifting too close to the reef in front of the hotel. The water around us was full of swimmers now, most of them equipped with mask and snorkel, and anxious to be helpful. It was decided that they would function as spotters, keeping the Gordons in view as they descended, and passing the information to us.

Jack and Jim had a new scheme: to couple the *Elusive* and the *Aikane*, hull to hull, so that the two propellers could be operated like the twin screws of a big ship. They would thus be able to hover like a helicopter right over the spot where the divers were.

There were a lot of last-minute instructions that I missed; then the divers were over the side. The spotters went into action. Jim and Jack played with their Siamese twins and kept the chain slack. Watchers yelled a warning when we drifted in too close to shore.

It seemed like forever.

Actually, it was less than ten minutes. The spotters began to wave frantically to us. Benson tugged at the chain. It had gone slack and could be raised easily. A minute later the Gordons came up.

"Be careful with that other line," John yelled, as soon as he had the regulator out of his mouth. "The anchor is attached to it. Don't foul it up!"

There was a babel of advice from the snorkelers, and in the confusion we managed to do just what John had warned against. The anchor on its way up caught on a coral head, and John Jr. had to go down once more to free it. He was breathing the last of his tank when he came up the second time. But the anchor came up too.

What had happened, as John explained later, was that we had snagged the only coral head in sight anywhere on the bottom. "Your chain was thrown around it in a perfect half hitch! You'd tightened it with all that pulling, of course. But what I couldn't believe, even when I saw it, was that the anchor was lying right next to the head with the chain leading it right into the coral! As if you'd threaded a needle through and put a button on the far end!"

The snagging had probably happened a few days after we secured our anchor in what we hoped was good sand. The scope we let out brought the chain right across the head, and it lay there working its way—or wearing its way—down till it reached the bottom. Then, as we swung around with winds and tides, we made a great circle that "threw a hitch." The only way to cut this Gordian knot was by unbolting the anchor. After that, it was easy to pull the chain through the head and unwind the hitch. But it was hard work, and air is used up very quickly at that depth. The Gordons had done very well to make it on one pair of tanks!

We tried to express our gratitude, but John waved it away almost brusquely. "Glad to have had the chance," he said. "I like to dive, and you can't go down that far without a reason."

By now the bleachers crowd seemed to be moving toward us en masse, in dinghies, life preservers, everything but water wings. It was getting distinctly anticlimactic. So we taxied our rescuers back to the submarine dock and bade farewell to the Wilsons by radio. (We were reading each other on the sets now.) Jim and Jack promised to call each other on 2638 every night at seven, and to try again at nine and eleven, if there was any difficulty in getting through. It gave us a feeling of "home ties" that was pleasant, if not very meaningful.

Precisely at noon—four hours behind schedule—we headed out the pass under sail.

North to Flaming Hawaii

Our course was ten degrees east of north, although our destination, Hilo, on the big island of Hawaii, lies a little west of north. We had to get "easting" before we hit the northeast trades of the other hemisphere.

The first men who sailed this course from Bora-Bora to Hawaii did so in the second century after Christ. They had no compasses or other navigational aids; they steered by stars, none of which was fixed like our polestar. Their vessels were great double canoes, perhaps a hundred feet long and twelve or more feet wide, propelled by lateen-shaped mat sails, and steered by a long sweep oar. Very probably there was already some knowledge of islands far to the north, as vague as the evidence on which Leif Ericson sailed for Greenland or Columbus sailed for the New (*sic*) World. Archaeologists believe now that the Hawaiian chain was first settled from the Marquesas but that those settlements had died out by the time the Tahitians came. Only the legend remained, preserved in an ancient chant that tells of the trickster god Maui, that he: ". . . *tae na to'erau, na Nu'u hiva roa e na aihi ahuahu Hawaii*" (sailed north to great Nuku Hiva and to flaming Hawaii).

Who were those voyagers who first watched the cone of Bora-Bora's central volcano fade astern? A small exploring force sent to seek a new home for a tribe? Or was it a well-equipped expedition, with women as well as men, food plants, and domestic animals? Why were they leaving the Eden of les Iles Sous-le-Vent? Is Michener right when he guesses that they were refugees from religious persecution? Or was it something more prosaic that sent these "Vikings of the Sunrise" north?

Overcrowding, the exhaustion of thin soils, or perhaps simply a collective itchy foot?

I tried when I was alone on watch to steer by the stars, shifting from one to another as they moved across and up. But without a polestar the task seemed impossible. I remember reading that an old Samoan once kept a European chronicler up all night long, reciting lists of stars and the uses to which they could be put in navigation. The memory of men who don't rely on writing is as much superior to ours as a dog's sense of smell. Or, for that matter, a Polynesian's sense of smell. Steve Ellacott told us that he can smell land as far as ten miles away to leeward, and I believe him.

On the subject of the Polynesian instinct for seamanship, we had heard an interesting postscript on the saga of the *Taporo* sailors, hired for the unloading operation at the two observation atolls. They were the *Wunderkinder* of the whole international scientific operation. The American astronomers and all their gear went over the reef at Manuae in longboats without a single mishap, and the job was finished a day and a half ahead of schedule. But on the return trip to Papeete, the *Taporo* men disgraced themselves by getting into a fistfight on their night wheel watch. It turned out, when the combatants were pulled away from each other's jugular veins, that they were fighting for a chance to stand behind that magnificent spoked wheel and steer the ship.

And that story provoked night thoughts about the Americans on the *Goodwill*, the paid hands and the working guests. There was something about the behavior of the latter group that nagged at my mind like the meaning of a particularly clear dream that fades on waking. The phrase that kept recurring was John Gordon's: ". . . You can't go down that far without some reason." Man has to use his powers—physical and psychological, as well as mechanical—for some purpose he can respect, and at something like full capacity.

Was that why the working guests aboard the *Goodwill*, and boat bums in Papeete, and people like the Wilsons, were so unlike other American tourists we saw in the same latitudes? They came from the same cities, classes, and professions as the impatient, helpless, demanding, discourteous snobs who embarrassed us to the point of trying to conceal our nationality in posh bars and restaurants and hotels. But the Wilsons and the Gordons and all the others whom we met at sea or along its margins, out of reach of repair shops, supermarkets, laundromats, and all the other "comforts and conveniences" that make up the American way of life for the middle class and its betters at home—these people had taken on the characteristics that we are always touting as our national virtues. They were resourceful, efficient, daring, obliging, outgoing, unassuming, and profoundly democratic.

Why? Were they a different breed of cat? Or was the difference a function of the life they were leading?

The contrast between the performance of the working guests and the paid hands on the *Goodwill* was illuminating. Some of the latter were old pros who did their jobs and pocketed the pay without complaint. But the rest were college boys who had signed on for the adventure and were being paid the going rate to learn skills they didn't have and didn't respect. They were full of umbrage and unconscious snobbery. One of them said in my hearing once, "We are the Tahitians of this voyage." What he meant was that he and his fellows were discriminated against (not being invited to relax in the owner's quarters or to eat with the owner's friends—that is, the working guests) in a way that would have been appropriate for members of a lesser breed without the law.

The work that, temporarily at least, ennobled those who chose to do it and committed themselves wholly to it seemed to be spiritual food not available in ordinary life ashore. A middle-class job (or career) does not use the whole person of most men or women, and it may be that the unused powers fall prey to dry rot. Perhaps what smells so obnoxious on the spiritual breath of many American tourists is the end product of an atrophy of the soul.

The first few days at sea were a reminder of how quickly one goes landlubber. I was frequently mildly seasick as I hung over my swaying stove, although we were on one of those rare and beautiful beam reaches. Not being in the best of moods for coping with fishy foods, I didn't nag, and the men didn't bother to throw a line over. Instead I served cold lunches of canned pâté and dressed up canned vegetables to suit my taste for the sour.

BEETS VINAIGRETTE

1 can sliced beets
Sliced raw onions, same quantity as of beets
Vinegar, salt, pepper, herbs to taste

Open a can of beets and drain the liquid (which can be used for many other purposes, including drinking straight, when chilled); combine the beets with thinly sliced onions; pack into a jar with a screw top and fill the interstices with vinegar—seasoned to taste. Let stand at least 6 hours in a cool place. Makes a fine substitute for a hot vegetable or a salad—or both.

If straight vinegar makes it too sharp for your taste, dilute it slightly with some of the beet liquor.

The beam wind blew itself out before the third day was up, and again we were on a wind that did not appear on Jack's chart. Worse, it was fitful, and we had to motor many hours out of the twenty-four. Jack began to complain that we had lost all the easting we had gained, that we might very well be too close to Flint and/or Caroline Island, that the fuel we had aboard would not get us to Hilo if the wind didn't come round.

The sea was so calm at night that the vibration of the motor wakened big jellyfish as we passed close over them. It looked at times as if we were plowing through a field of buried lamps. The bow wave had a gleam that looked like moonlight, but the moon didn't rise until nearly dawn, and was sliver slim.

We were beginning to fish again, and one evening we were all sitting in the cockpit to watch the line that had been rigged with a new lure, when Jack pointed off the port quarter and said:

"Look! A flare!"

We all whipped our heads around. Benson and I both thought we saw a last white gasp of light, but we weren't positive. Norris said he had missed it. We tried to take a bearing, and the consensus was 300 degrees, but no one was positive of that. In fact, no one but Jack was positive that there had been a flare.

Jim Wilson had seen such a flare on his way down the year before. He decided to alter course as soon as he saw a second flare and could take an accurate bearing. But the second flare never came. It bothered Jim considerably that he had continued on course without ever finding out who or what it was.

Norris and I stationed ourselves at the bow and fantail to watch for a second, if it came, while Benson and Jack tried the radio. It was just about the hour of our nightly, and so far futile, effort to reach the *Elusive*, so we tried 2638, and when nothing but static came through, switched to 2182. Nothing there either. We broadcast our position, and asked for an answer from any vessels within reach of our signal. No answer.

All of us had been reading the Navy manual on *How to Survive on Land and Sea*, as well as assorted Conrad novels, so our minds were full of tales of gaunt castaways floating helplessly out of the steamer lanes, and of decoy signals sent up by piratical Lascars or desperate Malayan revolutionaries. The only comfortable explanation of a single flare that any of us could think of was that it might be a signal from a "mother ship" to call in her fishing boats. But if that was the case, why couldn't we hear them talking to each other, as we had on other evenings while trying to get through to the *Elusive*?

Finally we decided a clear conscience was more important than a good day's mileage, so we altered course and tried to get as near as possible to the spot from which the flare must have been sent up. The men calculated that it was between three and four miles to the north-northwest. We motored on a heading of 300 degress for thirty minutes with the speed indicator showing six knots. (Once again I realized how difficult position is to establish on a limitless expanse without landmarks and how basic to survival the art of celestial navigation is at sea. I vowed to begin all over again, regardless of the humiliation and frustration of my first attempts.)

When we were where the men thought we ought to be, we

cut off the motor and blinked our masthead lights. It was dark by this time, and by turning on the spreader lights we could illumine the mainsail and make it visible for twenty miles. We did that, and blinked the lights. Benson even tried blinking Morse code, though he didn't know how to spell any useful words. We tried the radio again.

The silence—comparatively speaking—was creepy. The sea made obscene sloshing noises against the hull, and now and then a nasty-voiced bird would fly over. I wondered what Steve Ellacott would have made of such an omen. The nearest island to where we thought we were was 113 miles west. Could it be that our navigators were wrong?

After an hour things were so calm we could see star tracks on the surface. Jack asked our opinions on whether or not we should resume course. It was really foolish to slosh around all night, losing time and drifting who knew where. But what if the flare was the only one they had aboard some waterlogged raft? What if its crew was paddling as hard as they could toward the beacon of our sail? What if we turned on our motor just in time to drown out their faint hail? What if they had to watch us disappear into the darkness, knowing the odds against another vessel appearing in time to save them from slow, agonizing death?

It sounded corny, but we all knew it was possible. So we dropped the main and hove to, leaving the masthead lights on. The wind came up very brisk and appealing at 2:00 A.M., and Jack had to fight his impulse to make the most of it. But we waited till dawn—by which time the wind had died again—slatting around so that real sleep was impossible, haunted with nightmares about being cast away.

In the first light, I was raised up the mast in the bosun's chair. I could see at least twenty miles in all directions, and there was not a blob that could be a boat anywhere. Feeling foolish, but very virtuous, we turned on the motor and headed back to ten degrees.

Despite the anticlimactic ending of our night's adventure, it was good for us. There had been some strains developing under the surface of our by-now habitual politeness. For one thing there was no longer enough to do to keep us all busy all the time. The setting of daytime watches and the conclusion of navigation classes had left us with leisure time for the first time since we left home. But even more crucial from the point of view of morale was the relaxation of anxiety. The stage fright of the first sea leg was over. We did what we had to do and knocked off, without placating the gods that governed our fate by little extras (like taking shots ten times a day) or worrying. We were on the verge of being bored.

But the flare had reminded us that there were worse fates than being cooped up in a comfortable cabin for a few weeks and that we were still totally interdependent, no matter how dull we might find each other when the going was too smooth.

The library became really popular at last. I finished *Hawaii*, decided to have a try at Joyce's *Ulysses*, and began in secret to review the directions for the noon latitude shot.

The very next night there were clouds on the horizon at sunset, and a rainsquall hit us at dark, on my watch. We were running with the Genoa, which we ought to have dropped, but no one really took this change in the weather seriously, so Jack told me to fall off to 330 degrees. We tore along at over seven knots, with the lee rail awash, and just about the time I came off watch, the wind died.

Another squall hit on the 12:00 to 2:00 A.M. watch. This time the men struggled forward and dropped the jib, getting freshwater showers for their pains. All our bedding got wet because we weren't properly battened down, and our wool blankets smelled like some beagles I have known.

By the time the sun came up, we were back on something like our old course, making an average of six knots, heeled over so far that movement fore and aft was a gymnastic feat. It was obvious that we were in for a blow of some duration. The seas were building up, and we were taking them over the starboard quarter. All hatches were properly battened down now, and plugs screwed into the ventilators. But things were pretty wet before we got the ship tight, and there was no way to dry them out. Besides, when a really big sea broke over the main cabin, one of the ventilator plugs leaked (it needed a gasket); water ran down the tilted ceiling and into the transom bunk, which was turning into a swamp.

I was cooking in my safety harness again, and as little as possible. But appetites were not adversely affected by all this unwonted exercise, and I had to concoct dishes that stuck to the ribs, despite a growing number of shortages. Eggs were gone; bread was almost gone; the last heart-of-palm salad was behind us; all the bananas had come ripe at once, and many had spoiled. It was no weather for fishing. So we broke out the dried legumes and sausages.

LENTIL AND SALAMI CASSEROLE

> 1 8-oz. pkg. of dried lentils
> 1 large onion (or equivalent amount of dried onion bits)
> ½ any good hard small salami (approx. 1 lb.)
> 1 large can tomato sauce
> Marjoram, garlic, salt, and pepper

Soak the lentils for several hours, if possible overnight. Sauté the onion (if raw) and the mashed clove of garlic in oil, add bite-sized chunks of the salami, and heat through. Combine with the soaked and softened lentils, tomato sauce, and spices and simmer in a heavy pot with a good lid for at least an hour. Serve with salad or a sour vegetable dish. (cf. Beets Vinaigrette.) Red wine is appropriate.

Once or twice, within a day or so after the flare, we heard Jim very faintly and intermittently on 2638 at the late night rendezvous hour. We couldn't make out most of what he was saying, but we did hear one phrase that indicated he was giving up the whole program. It underlined the feeling of isolation that the flare had stirred.

Then came the eclipse. We were well out of the zone of totality, and there were high clouds obscuring the sun at the time we knew the telescopes on Bellingshausen and Manuae and the observers flying above them were on the alert. I was at the wheel, and the wind was down a little, but still enough to move us along at better than six knots.

Benson came up with the bubble sextant in his hand and began to try for a hole in the cloud cover. Jack and Norris were below, having given up hope. It seemed to me that there was a perceptible darkening of the sky, but it was possible that it was only a thickening of the clouds. Or the projection of a wish.

"There it is," Benson said, and took the wheel so that I could look. Through the heaviest of the filters I stared at a slender gold crescent, rather like a new moon. It was not as exciting as I had expected.

We kept the radio on for the rest of the day, hoping for news of the official observation. Had the skies over the atolls been no clearer than ours? If so, the whole effort and expense had been futile. Only the observers aloft would get any data, and their instruments were a good deal less sophisticated than the gear that had gone over the reefs at Manuae. Until this point we had been able to tune in on the *Goodwill's* afternoon news bulletin, but today there was only static.*

We recrossed the equator at 4:00 A.M. on May 31. It was the nether end of my night watch, so I roused everyone. We had some uniced champagne and a slice of pound cake, made from a mix. It was delightfully quiet, after the pounding of the last few days. We played the tape of the *Threepenny Opera*, and watched a constellation I had never found before. There was such a confusion of sparkles in the night sky in these latitudes that I didn't usually manage to impose any patterns on it, but this night I was able to make out the great snaky curve of Hydra, right up to its heads.

I was deeply asleep in my warm but soggy blankets when, about 7:30 A.M., there was a sudden *Geschrei* from the cockpit: a bell clanging, men shouting, sails flapping, buckets clanking, and so on. I had taken an aspirin bought in Papeete, which I suspected of containing some sort of tranquilizer, and I couldn't

---

* The news, for which we had to wait till we got to Honolulu, was that there was cloud cover over Bellingshausen (the French island over which so much difficulty was raised) but not over Manuae, which was governed by New Zealand, and more hospitable.

come really awake even when I was on my feet and struggling down the clothes-strewn center aisle.

On deck, the three men seemed to have gone mad, like sharks with the blood lust on them. Benson was hauling in the biggest and shiniest bonito I had ever seen. Jack was tearing the hook out of its mouth before it was well aboard; and before Norris had clubbed the first catch into passivity, a second was flapping wildly around on the fantail. I pleaded feebly for moderation, but no one heard me. The only reason we didn't take on a third and fourth oversized fish was that we ran out of the school.

We caught these beauties on a 180-pound test monofilament, backed by regular clothesline. The lure was an oversize white "candy bar" with a double hook, attached to a steel leader that only a good-sized shark could bite through. Our reel was made fast to one of the stanchions, rigged with a rubber snubber to take the shock of the strike and a bell that clanged when the snubber was stretched. It had taken three months and five thousand miles of almost totally unsuccessful trolling to produce this unsportsmanlike apparatus, but we were by now fishing to eat.

We ate for a whole week off those fish, and felt ourselves in a position to make some authoritative judgments about their often-disputed merits. Offshore fishermen in California often consign their bonito catch to their mulch piles. Perhaps there is a different variety in the deeper waters. In any case, it was our consensus that bonito is a boon to travelers afloat. There are some problems about its preparation, however, and there follows a compendium of what we learned about:

EATING BONITO

1. If you are going to keep this fish any length of time, with or without refrigeration, you must discard the darker flesh, which gets "fishy" after a few hours.

2. Cold or hot, bonito is best when served with a well-seasoned sauce of some kind. The meat is too dry and compact to be served ungarnished. Also, it is not good steamed or poached.

3. When very fresh, it makes excellent limed fish—*sashimi,*
céviche, or even *poisson cru.*

COLD BONITO

Carve a big slab of solid (cooked) meat into serving-sized
portions. (Remove all dark meat, bones, and skin before cooking, and chill the cooked meat well when it is done.) Serve
with a *rémoulade,* made by adding to mayonnaise, garlic (or
garlic powder), capers or chopped sweet pickles, mustard and
tarragon. Let the sauce stand for an hour or more before
serving.

CURRIED BONITO

Chunks of previously cooked and chilled bonito
1 can condensed mushroom soup
1 large onion sliced and sautéed, or a portion of dried
onion bits
Curry powder to taste

Heat the fish through in the soup, thinned slightly with
water. Add the sautéed onions. (If dried bits are used, heat
them in the soup.) Add the curry powder, and mix just before serving. Good with white rice or bean thread, either of
which must be cooked separately and almost completely before the curry is started.

BONITO "AIKANE"

Thin steaks of raw bonito (2 or 3 per serving)
1 slice of onion per steak
1 pkg. dried mushrooms, reconstituted
1 can (medium) tomato sauce
Oil, lime juice, bay leaf, herbs, salt, etc.

Cut the steaks about ½ inch thick and marinate in the oil
and lime-juice mixture with seasonings for about 2 hours.

Soak the mushrooms in water for the same length of time—at least. Arrange the steaks in a shallow baking dish with an onion slice and a mushroom on top of each. Cover with tomato sauce thinned with the water from the mushrooms. Bake about 20 minutes. Serve with rice—or grits, for variety.

The wind let down completely for one hot night just above the Line, and we motored on and off, with short, hot squalls at irregular intervals. We were on a course of 360 degrees now, averaging something like four knots.

During the day it was sultry—real doldrums weather—and we tried to air the damp bedding. It seemed to dry out several times, only to "slime" up again at night. We were learning some of the subtle forms of revenge that the sea takes on creatures born for life ashore.

Then—almost before we were sure we were in the doldrums and had time to worry about fuel consumption—the wind picked up and began to blow a mild gale. It started on my 6:00–8:00 P.M. watch. By nine it was clear that we would rip the Genoa if we left it up all night, so the men put on their safety belts and worked their way up forward into the howling, spray-splashed darkness, leaving me as emergency helmsman.

All sorts of things were going on in the sea around us. A school of bottle-nosed dolphins was playing what looked like a game of water polo. They dove at us, passed under the hull, doubled back, criss-crossing and trying to rush the goalposts. Not only were they luminous in the troubled water—like streaks of submerged lightning—but they stung big jellyfish into giving off green depth charges of light.

I was drenched by the warm rain and the not-so-warm salt spray, but not uncomfortable and rather proud of the fact that I was holding us into the wind, as ordered, falling off just a little and coming up again, keeping the tension off the sails. Then Norris came into view, buckling and unbuckling himself in a correct but awkward fashion along the port lifeline.

"Is Jack back here?" he yelled.

Obviously, Jack was not. And if he wasn't up where Norris had just come from, there was only one place I could think of where he could be!

For one frozen moment I tried to remember the procedures for man overboard: Take a bearing. Note the time. Yell a warning. Throw over the life preserver and the Minibuoy. And come about . . . head for the reciprocal. . . .

There was no one to give me the order to execute that maneuver. No one to carry out the order if I gave it. Norris had disappeared again into the darkness forward. I shouted for Benson, but I knew my voice wouldn't carry against the wind . . . even if he were there. . . . They could all have been overboard! How long should I wait?

If it had been daylight or reasonably calm, I could have got to the automatic pilot switch and liberated myself to go forward and see what was wrong. But if I did that now, and if the men were struggling with some balky piece of equipment on the bow, any sudden lurch of the boat might topple them. I had a sour taste in my throat and a prickling sensation from what was probably a cold sweat that the rain washed away.

Then something drew my eye to the windward rail. (I had been staring at the place where Norris had appeared and disappeared.) There was Jack, buckling and unbuckling himself along, swearing outrage at some piece of stupidity or carelessness. I never made out what the crime was or who the criminal. It might even have been me. I didn't care then and haven't since.

What puzzled me even in retrospect is how three men working within no more than eight feet of each other can lose track of each other. But obviously, under the proper circumstances, they can.

The wind became a permanent member of the crew, beginning with that night. And the sea did its best to sign on. Big seas came at us in a rhythm so regular that if there was a slight remission in the pounding, it created a momentary suspense. And despite everything we could do to lock it out, now and again the unwanted guest slipped in.

One night when I was asleep flat on my back in my own berth, I got a faceful of water through the locked hatch. There was just enough play in the lock to let a thin sheet in when the wave struck horizontally! Everyone's bedding was irrevocably wet by this time, and so were most of our clothes—despite the two suits of top-grade oilskins that Benson and Jack shared with

Norris and me.* It was our own fault; we admitted it. Next time we would know better and take care not to get wet at the start of a blow. But for the present there was nothing to do but try to take preventive measures against the salt itch. Coconut oil helped a little, and as a result the cabin smelled like the copra hold on the *Taporo*.

But the most impressive thing about the storm was the noise. The wind actually did whistle in the stays. Once I mistook it for some sort of signal, and went on deck to see who was sending it. There was a tremendous whooshing as water poured over the deck above our heads, and now and then a slam, as if a giant hand had struck us a glancing blow. There was quite a different sort of slamming, combined with a thud that shook the ribs of boat and crew when we cut through a big wave and fell into the trough on the other side. The really dismaying sound, as far as I was concerned, was the one that came from the mast. It could be heard most clearly from our berth—an awesome snap-crackle-pop, like the cereal commercial.

Sitting in the head one morning, I suddenly saw what went into this sound effect. The mast of the K-43 goes up through one corner of that tiny room in a slot formed by two of its walls and the short side of the counter. If one put one's fingers between the mast and any of these surfaces, they would have been painfully pinched when the sway narrowed it from about an inch to something near contact.

The head, incidentally, had begun to stink for the first time. I suspected that one of the males was too stubborn to sit in approved sailor fashion, but I couldn't summon the sangfroid to voice a protest. If there had been any sort of ventilation, it wouldn't have been so unbearable, but of course all ports—even on the lee side—were locked.

It was almost impossible to sleep in our berth for a number of reasons, only one of which was the proximity of the head. There were other smells that collected there—cooking odors, for one. Also, with the vessel on a constant cant of at least fifteen degrees from level (and up to forty-two degrees at

---

* We had both practiced ill-advised economy measures in this department. Norris's bargain pullover lasted one month; mine lasted two.

times), the sleeper on the high side rolled down and crushed the sleeper on the low side against the oak ribs of the hull. Benson rigged a sort of bundling board of canvas in the center, and we used cushions from the dinner table to pad the ribs. It got to be so complicated to get in or out of the sleeping slots that it wasn't worth the trouble for anything less than a four-hour stretch.

But there were not many alternatives available. Even the quarter berth was wet and on the high side. The transom berth was on the low side, but it was still irrigated by the leak in the ventilator plugs. The prize place was the long side of the dining-table settee, but it held only one. Next best (if you had or could get a full suit of oilskins) was the lee side of the cockpit.

In spite of the discomforts, spirits were good. The days were bright and the nights starry. Appetites were astonishing. We were beginning to use up staples we had overstocked at the start, like cereals and pasta, and the following concoction, which was rich enough to gag me, was a substantial hit with the three other eaters:

SPAGHETTI SOMEWHAT TETRAZZINI

    1 lb. pkg. spaghetti, cooked in half-fresh, half-salt water
    1 can condensed cheddar cheese soup
    1 can white sauce
    1 small can mushrooms (buttons or pieces)

Cook the spaghetti to the *al dente* stage, and drain. Make a sauce by combining the canned ingredients (diluted with a little of the mushroom liquor, if desired) and pour over the pasta. Serve with a tart salad or canned vegetable: beets or string beans or even celery vinaigrette. Wine also helps to cut the richness of the main course.

By the fourth day, the storm seemed to have become stronger. The speed indicator never showed more than seven knots, but the men were sure it was broken. By everyone's navigation (even mine) we had made 180 miles in a twenty-four-hour run, which meant that we averaged seven and a half.

Both the boat and the crew were getting tired. The Genoa had been ripped, mended, and ripped again, before it was struck for the duration. Then we noticed a number of broken ties on the main. Jack had decided to reef anyway. (The first time we had got to use the fancy roller-reefing gear!) But even when one-third of the big sail was neatly rolled around the boom, there was a broken tie out of reach near the peak.

No one was getting enough sleep. We crawled from bunk to bunk like a pack of wet sled dogs looking for a better hole. Benson slept on deck during my watch—to give me moral support—but he slept so soundly that I couldn't wake him the one time I needed him to help trim the sail. I tried to get the cockpit bench during his watch, but the competition was as keen as a game of Jerusalem chairs.

The cabin looked like a laundry room most of the time. Not only were there heaps of wet pants (mostly Norris's) to crawl over, but pareus and bed sheets hung up to air, if not to dry, billowing weirdly as the boat lurched. Everyone and everything smelled. I finally complained about the head. Everyone denied

Stormy weather.

my charges. An investigation was made, and the trouble turned out to be a gasket that had worked loose in some vital part of the apparatus. Nothing to be done till the sea calmed. If ever.

I was running out of "filling food" that was reasonably easy to cook. Bread was what the men craved, and finally I devised a substitute that I could manage without too many bruises:

CORNMEAL DODGERS or JOHNNYCAKES

1 cup of cornmeal, yellow or white
Boiling water to bring it to the consistency of malleable mush (salt water mixed with fresh, as always)
2–3 tbs. of fat, depending on taste and the condition of arteries; bacon drippings preferred

Stir salt (if you use any) and sugar (if you use that) into the cornmeal. Stir in boiling water, a little at a time, until the mixture can be patted into cakes. Mix in the melted drippings. Form cakes and lay on waxed paper. Drop them, one by one, on to a well-greased hot skillet, and fry until they can be safely turned. Open when they are brown on both sides (and done through) and fill with butter, margarine, or jelly. They can also be baked in the oven, in which case they don't have to be turned.

Baking, difficult as it was under these conditions, turned out to be worth the trouble because of the effect on everyone's morale. Also, it was easier than cooking on top of the stove. As long as I used a container at least twice as deep as would have been necessary under normal conditions, I could do anything—even angel food—from a mix. We had an ample supply of assorted mixes, unused till now, and at the rate we were going the men calculated that a ration of half a cake a day would get us safely to Hawaii.

Sometime during the fifth consecutive day of the storm, it occurred to me that I was afraid.

I was lying in my padded cell under the bow, listening to the mast, which by now sounded like a volley of pistol shots. I had already asked a few discreet questions and had some idea of the possibilities of trouble from that quarter. A laminated mast, Jack had explained, rarely snaps under strain from one side; it explodes. As the force of the wind against one side increases, it is translated by the stays into an increasing down pressure. If this builds up past the resistance of the mast, it bursts apart! And it is impossible to repair it. The best one can do is to jury-rig a replacement, usually the main boom.

If anything like that should happen to us, we would lose most of our ability to point, he said. We would have to forget about Hawaii, which lay dead ahead of us on a course of 340 degrees, and run for little Johnston Island, about six hundred miles to the west. I loked at the big chart and saw the dot of Johnston, and nothing else till the Marianas. Dots are not easy to hit when one can only run before the wind.

When I went on watch next time, I noticed—or thought that I noticed—that the shape of the waves had changed. It was odd and unwavelike. Peaks like the crags of Mooréa or Ua Pou were unnatural for water, and showed a menacing disorientation at the heart of things.

I tried to cook my way out of the cowardice that was overcoming me, and succeeded at least in creating a comic diversion. We had by this time eaten bonito in every way I could think of except in a *paella*. There was no saffron aboard, but there was a can of powdered mole. I made a hot sauce out of it and a can of chicken broth, and warmed in it chunks of good, hard salami and cooked fish and some leftover canned ham. When all this was piping hot, I turned my attention to the rice.

The stove was swinging wildly, despite its gimbals, so I had to find a place to park the stewpot. It fitted nicely into one half of the double sink, which had been used for similar purposes many times. I had unscrewed the lid of the big plastic container in which we kept the instant rice and was measuring out the first cupful, when the *Aikane* lurched so sharply that the jar got away from me. It slid down the counter, toppling as it went and spewing a fountain of rice grains—into the pot, onto the floor, and even behind the stove.

Norris came by and inquired who was "just married," but he got no laugh.

I was still down on all fours when another sea paw curled around and into the open companion hatchway. Instead of sweeping, I bailed the rest of the rice.

Before I had finished my cleanup, I was too tired to stand— if that is the word for what we did on our feet in that sort of a sea. My ribs ached from having swung too long on the flying trapeze of my safety harness. So I decided to finish the dinner preparations sitting on the floor, well braced, with my back against the refrigerator and my feet against the pan closet under the sink. This worked so well that I forgot to be cautious.

When I came to a point at which I needed something from the pan closet, I got to my knees and ducked to be able to see into its depths. The boat pitched into a wave trough, and I pitched headfirst into the pans. Just like the White Knight, but with no Alice to pull me out.

The *paella* was not bad, considering the substitutions for traditional ingredients, but it was the last time I cooked to quiet an internal storm.

The sixth night was miserable. I had lost the game of Jerusalem chairs, and was forced to try my padded cell. The mast was shooting off volleys, and I couldn't sleep. I heard eight bells, when Benson went up to relieve Norris. That gave me two hours before my own watch. I needed to sleep in order to function responsibly. But I heard one bell; then two, then three . . .

At about twenty minutes to two, I crawled out of my burrow and began groping about in the dark for the various articles of clothing I had laid out. Some malignant power had tossed them all into different inaccessible corners. Halfway through the process of robing, I found myself considering raising the white flag.

It had never occurred to me to confess that I was frightened because I couldn't see any alternative to enduring what was going on. But sometime during the evening I had tuned in on an argument between Benson and Jack, which I realized had been going on for some time. Benson's position was that we didn't have to take this sort of beating; all we had to do was to fall off to the west and ease the strain on the boat and ourselves by riding the troughs between the big seas. Jack didn't want to.

He gave so many different reasons that it seemed likely that none was his real one. For instance, he said that we could never get back the easting we would lose. (Benson's answer was that we could tack back, without losing time.) Jack said we didn't have enough fuel to motor back east into this sort of storm. (Benson said we had plenty of fuel.) Jack said the extra mileage would mean a long delay. (Benson insisted that we would gain enough speed to make it up.) Besides, what difference did it make whether we were a day or two or even three late? We had no schedule to meet. No one was waiting for us at Hilo. We were not racing. There was no bet to be won or lost. If the wind kept up, we were liable to set some kind of record for this passage, but it wouldn't be official. So what was the hurry?

I had a feeling that what was really at stake was a bet Jack had made with himself, perhaps not even consciously. The challenge of the voyage for him was somehow connected with taking whatever came without deviating from course or schedule, once set. This seemed to be a matter of principle and took the place (for Jack) of the small risks Benson got his kicks out of running. Jack was very critical of Benson's "foolhardiness" in small matters, and I had been inclined to agree with him till now. But what Jack was doing seemed foolhardiness of a rather different order: a stubborn refusal to compromise with nature when there was nothing to be lost by compromise.

Also, I sensed that there was resentment building up between them as a result of this, their first serious difference. Jack seemed to feel he was being urged to downgrade his seamanship, and Benson to resent on my behalf the discomfort and anxiety I had not managed to hide. It struck me that my refusal to cry "uncle" was part of my defensiveness about being the woman aboard, whereas the really useful function of my womanhood was to do just that. If the men were all imprisoned in various "games" that prevented their acting rationally, maybe I would be doing them as well as myself a favor by forgetting to save face and just saying "Stop!"

I spent my two hours at the wheel rehearsing the way I would do that when Jack came to relieve me at four. But I funked it. What had seemed only sensible in the noisy darkness seemed only craven in the light of dawn. If the wind didn't go down during the day ahead, I would surely speak the word by night. . . .

The wind didn't go down. We flew along all day under the reefed main and a storm jib. The latter was a sail Jack was particularly fond of because he had designed it in collaboration with Kenneth Watts, the sailmaker of Torrance, California. It looked like one end of a lady's scarf, and I gathered that the excellence of its "performance" had to do with a steadying effect. But it was hard for me to imagine a progress less steady than the one we were making.

There ought to have been radio contact with Hilo by this time, but there wasn't. Nor with anything else in this howling water-wilderness. I had a tennis shoulder from holding the wheel over, although I was using my feet more than my hands for that purpose.

As night came on, my resolution hardened again. The noises from the mast were absolutely deafening. I lay there in my bunk waiting for the splintering crash that seemed inevitable until at last it was my turn to go up. It was easier on watch. I couldn't hear the mast, for one thing; and for another there was a sense— illusory, of course—of being in control of something. My two hours passed like the last two days before a vacation. The wind didn't let up and the seas didn't go down.

I began to rehearse what I would say to Jack when he came up. That I would say something this time I felt absolutely sure. I might hold out another day, but the mast couldn't. (I had twice caught Benson making covert little sketches of jury-rigs, and the fact that he no longer mentioned the problem proved he considered it serious.) I owed it to the others to have the courage to be a coward.

Eight bells struck. I murmured the best of my opening lines and waited for Jack.

But he didn't come.

I heard one bell—half-past four. He was oversleeping his watch for the first time on the trip. I called him. No answer.

He must be truly exhausted, I thought, which showed that he too was under more strain than he would admit.

For another half hour or so, I felt sympathy for the sleeper, but as my second hour of extra watch began, it turned gradually to righteous indignation. Jack had an alarm wristwatch, but he had lent it to Benson and me. He didn't need it; he had a captain's "internal alarm," he said. Well, we'd see about that now! No one, not even Norris in his old, three-hour watch days, had ever been this late! We'd see now who was responsible, long-suffering, and whatever else the male sex in general and captains in particular were supposed to be! Never mind about me! I'd take up the slack! Stand four hours of watch if necessary! I was almost sorry for Jack when I thought of how deeply shamed he would be when he woke and found that the woman aboard had borne his burden!

It was five fifteen when he finally appeared in the companionway, yawning, neither shamed nor overwhelmingly grateful, but very relaxed indeed.

"It looks as if it's calmed down quite a bit," he said, as he unbuckled me from the safety belt that held me in place. "Anyway, we're in motoring range of Hilo now."

"Could we motor into port if the mast broke?" I asked.

Jack nodded and yawned again. It didn't seem to be the moment for the lines I had rehearsed. I postponed the scene for a second time and went below and to sleep.

At noon we took down the storm jib and put up the working jib. There was still the possibility that the wind might pick up again, but it was certainly down from its peak. There was still no radio contact with the Coast Guard at Hilo, and it was possible that we were not as close in as the navigators thought. We were still taking big seas over the cabin, and Jack wasn't ready to shake out the reef. But there was a subtle feeling that the worst might be over.

I noticed it at Happy Hour, or even a little before. We had always laughed immoderately over that single drink—fashioning an escape valve out of a form of semicontrolled hysteria my mother would have called "the sillies." But by this point in the storm, the sillies took over every time the four of us were close enough to converse, and on the flimsiest of stimuli. On this particular afternoon it was excruciatingly funny that Norris, who had only one pair of dry shorts and one clean T-shirt left, "dressed" for drinks and had hardly been given his tumblerful of beer when the *Aikane* bucked and he came up dripping. We laughed till our eyes blurred, Norris included. And every added comment, no matter how reminiscent of Bob Hope or a TV commercial, set us off again. Storm fatigue must be something like battle fatigue, and we were our own USO troupe.

It was possible, of course, that the war was not over, that the next enemy attack would catch us off guard. (Jack had decided to take a chance and not change back to the storm jib for the night.) If the wind picked up again, I was not going to wait for the end of my watch. I was going to speak my piece the moment fear stirred in me! But at 7:00 P.M.—halfway through my evening watch—I saw the long slope of Mauna Loa on the horizon ahead and to port. At first I thought it was part of the sunset-silhouetted cloud formation, but I called Jack and he put his glasses on it. Land was there, only ninety miles away!

There was a great buzz of activity during the last hour of my watch. Benson tried to get a fix by shooting two stars in the short civil twilight, but only Sirius obliged. Jack's final verdict was that we were a bit east of where he wanted to be, after all. We altered course slightly—it seemed almost wicked after all the beating we had done to keep our easting—and headed for the harbor of Hilo, well up on the eastern face of Hawaii.

At the end of my 2:00–4:00 A.M. watch, I saw lights of the first vessels we had seen since the *Goodwill*. Probably fishing smacks out of Hilo. And a few minutes later, when Jack came up, we both made out a strange rhythmic flash of light on the horizon. Jack started timing it, and counted six seconds between flashes: the interval of the giant million-candlepower beacon on the south point of Hawaii—the cape where according to Michener the first Polynesians landed on their long sail up from the island we had left. It would have been impossible to see even that strong a beam from thirty miles away, but it was reflected off the low-hanging clouds.

I held the wheel for an extra quarter of an hour while Jack

tried again—and failed again—to make radio contact with Hilo on
2182, and I wondered, now that it was all over, whether I ought
to confess how close I had come to chickening out. But I didn't.

When I woke in the morning, we were motoring along the
eastern face of the big island. All we could see was a monotonous
black cliff a hundred or more feet high (solid lava, as I later
learned), topped by very green, gently rolling fields. It didn't
look like Polynesia; it looked like the States. It took a while to
know why. Planted fields! We hadn't seen a planted field from
the sea (or anywhere else) since San Diego. And barns! Not
many, but distinctive enough to alter the whole character of the
scene. Red or brown barns, with galvanized-iron roofs.

And suddenly I was galvanized by the possibility of laundromats ahead! Places where we could wash the salt out of our
clothes, sheets, and blankets, and dry them in electrically heated
and rotated dryers. Lying there in my stuffy berth, wrapped in
my salt-slimy blanket, I felt the first surge of homesickness. I
could hardly wait to breath the perfume of detergent and hear
the melodious clank and whirr of washing machines.

The Big Island
(and Others)

We made contact with the Coast Guard when we were well inside Hilo's protected harbor, close enough to see the search-and-rescue vessel that was answering our call.

"Where have you been all the time we were trying to raise you?" we asked. "Up to an hour ago you were dead!"

"That right?" drawled a pleasant southwestern voice, in exactly the tone of Papeete's "*C'est bizarre.*" "Well, we do have some trouble with transmission here, now and then. Magnetic interference."

There were other aspects of our welcome that were unpleasantly reminiscent of Papeete. Bureaucrats are bureaucrats even in *aloha*-cultured Hawaii. The Health, Customs, and Immigration officials took their time about showing up, and brought plenty of red tape in the briefcases when they did show. They took away our pompelmous and coconuts. (The former were irreplaceable, the latter not so.) They soberly inspected the dinghyful of garbage—shells, coral, glass floats, and so on—and rummaged through the dank confusion of our drawers and lockers until the smell drove them off. The manners of the Immigration man reminded me so strongly of his counterpart in Tahiti that I almost expected him to go off with our passports.

But at last he returned them, and nodded reluctantly. We were in! Inside America! Free, and ready to be washed.

The rest of our *aloha* was in delirious contrast. Two quite separate sets of strangers came down to the dock to see whether there was anything they could do! People in Hilo who live on high hills keep watches on the harbor mouth; when a sail is

259

spotted, they put the binoculars on it. If it is not a local boat, a greeting party is sent down. The watchers are sailors, or ex-sailors, themselves, people who sailed here from the States (in some cases via the Marquesas and Societies) and decided to settle down. They have all the zeal of recent converts, and I have never been so pleasantly proselytized.

The Coast Guard commander (we were moored at his dock) gave us the keys to the shower room, and by the time we were all desalted, we had been given the keys to one small car and offered another. Jack had made a call to his friends in the I.L.W.U., and they had offered a third vehicle.

We took the first we could lay hands on, loaded it with laundry, and headed for town. There was no one in the laundro-mat nearest the post office when we arrived, so we loaded every machine in the place and went over to check General Delivery. I had a letter from my editor. The Bora-Bora revisions were fine. The job was done. If they hurried (*sic*) on their end, the book could be out by next March. (It was June 8.)

We spent five days on the big island of Hawaii, which is like a sample book of ecological alternatives. The north cape, where the big sugarcane fields are harvested almost without human intervention, is like the Maine coast in summer—bright, windy, and a little chill. The high country on the slopes of Mauna Kea looks like Texas, with clumps of prickly pear dotting the grasslands, herds of range cattle, and authentic cowboys tending them. On the way to Kilauea, the active volcano, we drove through tropical jungle, complete with sound effects, and we had just left behind us lava beds more desolate than the surface of the moon. The people who inhabit this "vacation paradise" of an island are just as variegated as the landscape: *haoles,** both resident and transient, Portuguese, Japanese, Chinese, Filipino, Samoan, mixtures of all these with each other and with Hawaiian, and finally a very few pure Hawaiians. The result of all this mingling and mating is an almost comic range

---

* *Haole* is the Hawaiian word for "foreigner" but it is applied only to Americans or Europeans, with the exception of second-generation Portuguese. The connotations escaped me, but I am sure that, on balance, they are at least as uncomplimentary as the American terms "native" or "kanaka."

of size, shape, and skin color, and a great many extraordinarily beautiful people.

The Hawaiians are the most impressive. Especially the women. Very tall and sometimes very fat, they walk barefoot in ankle-length muumuus on the streets of downtown Hilo with the carriage of queens, or ride horseback, sidesaddle, with the same straight-spined dignity. They have imposed their sense of beauty on most of the other women around them, and women from America's Midwest, who would have been condemned to tailored suits and unnaturally shaped shoes for life at home, walk barefoot and muumuued with uninhibited pleasure, if not with native grace.

We were told everywhere in the islands that the native Hawaiian is losing out on all fronts because "the Hawaiian character lacks the essential component of competitiveness." But it seemed to me that the Hawaiian had managed to impose some of his "natural" virtues on the polyglot personality that is taking his land from him. *Aloha* is Hawaiian, and it has infected everyone except the most recently arrived in-migrants and the tourists. It makes itself felt in the customs of social intercourse and its tone: in the cordiality of welcome, of hospitality, of gift-giving, of feasting and public celebrations, and, of course, in leave-taking. It surpasses even the *kaoha* of the southern Polynesians, and I doubt if we could have stood up under another five days of exposure to it.

The high point—on our fourth day in Hilo—was a *luau* arranged by Jack's I.L.W.U. friends, and cooked on the grounds of their elegant new hall.* The production number in this banquet-cum-pageant was the roasting of a whole pig. Ours was sent down from the north cape, disemboweled, singed, and scrubbed before we met him, sitting up like a begging bear in a large refrigerator in the union-hall kitchen. With him came about one thousand pounds of carefully selected lava rocks (pretested to assure that they would not explode when heated).

---

* This hall is used not only by the union for meetings and various types of celebration (birthdays of members, etc.), but also by the P.T.A., the Rotary International, the Boy and Girl Scouts, and at least once by the local unit of the National Guard. The mind of a Californian boggles at the implications of peaceful coexistence among these elements.

The first act of the drama (not counting the preparation of the pig, which we didn't see) was the digging of the pit, which became the *imu*, or oven. It must be large enough to hold the animal, other foods such as yams, chickens, whole fish, and the hot rocks, without crowding, and it must be dug in well-drained, not soggy, ground. The earth that was removed was piled carefully to one side for later use. The bottom of the pit was scraped level; a good-sized log was placed upright in the center, with other hardwood stacked around it till the cavity was at least half full. The rocks were washed clean and piled on top of the wood, bringing the level up to that of the ground. When everything was ready, the upright log was removed and a lighter—an oil-soaked rag bound to an iron rod—jammed into the hole, so that the kindling at the bottom was ignited first. Once the fire was going strong, everyone went off to do other chores, leaving it to burn itself almost out—about three hours.

The second act began with the removal of any unburned wood from the pyre. The hot rocks now covered the whole bottom surface. Banana leaves (or pounded banana stumps) were placed over the rocks, and the pig was lowered onto them in a basket of chicken wire. The pig had been prepared for this moment by having its abdominal cavity sprinkled with rock salt and then filled with a dozen or more of the clean heated rocks. Other foods were piled around the porker, and the whole covered with another heavy layer of banana or *ti* leaves. On top of this the men piled wet burlap bags; on top of them a stout tarp; on top of it, dirt. The mound was then sprinkled lightly with water. By this time steam had been generated down below and could be seen curling up from accidental escape valves. All these were plugged with earth and tamped before the curtain fell on that act. There was a five-hour intermission.

We missed the third-act curtain. The pit was already open when we arrived. The only detail I caught was that the burlap bags had been carefully placed upon the earth around the pit edge so that none of it could drop in on the feast that was to be unveiled. It took four young longshoremen to bring up the chicken wire basket and move it to an improvised table, where a cadre of wives was ready to shred the pork into serving portions. There was no problem about carving; the pig fell apart at the touch. All that was necessary was to tear the meat into portions without burning one's hands, and these ladies were experts at that. No vulture every picked a carcass cleaner in less time.

On the long tables set up in the open-roofed patio of the hall were platters and bowls of all the accompanying garnishes and side dishes, cases of beer and pop, and a few bottles of *okolehao,* a strong *ti*-leaf brandy used to spike a wide assortment of mixers. One of the most popular offerings was *sashimi,* cut from loin of yellow tuna (which sold in local markets for $2.50 a pound!). Other exotic delicacies were: *opihi,* limpets gathered from surf-washed rocks and marinated for several days in soy sauce; *lomi-lomi* salmon (see below); *lau-laus* (a Hawaiian tamale, see below); and poi, the one-day and three-day varieties, warmed over in a double boiler and then chilled.

LOMI-LOMI SALMON

> Fresh, raw salmon—enough to serve your guest list, or salted (but *not* smoked) salmon. (If you use fresh fish, soak it in brine overnight, and wash out the salt before using.)
> Firm ripe tomatoes—approximately the same amount
> Shredded scallions
> Lemon slices—optional

Remove skin and bones from the salmon and then shred it or dice it into half-inch cubes. Chill it thoroughly. Dice fresh tomatoes and chill them, separately. Just before serving, toss the fish and the tomatoes together. Garnish the serving bowl with the green onions and lemon slices.

LAU-LAUS (10)

> 2 lbs. beef (chuck will do)
> 1 lb. fresh or salt salmon (cf. above)
> 2 lbs. pork, with a little fat left on

> **1 lb. fresh or frozen (thawed) spinach**
> **Salt**
> **20 ti leaves at least 15 inches long, on aluminum foil**
>
> Cube the meats and fish into 10 portions each. Remove the central rib of the leaves so that they are flexible, and lay them in crossed pairs of two. In the center of each pair put a few spinach leaves. On this place one cube of each of the three fillers and some salt. Rock salt is good. Cover with more spinach. Then fold the *ti* leaves around to make a tight packet. Bind it with strong string, and steam for at least 3 hours. There is no reason not to include this in the *imu* load, but it can be done in any steamer.

Dessert at a proper *luau*, we were told, is some confection made of coconut cream and pineapple spears. The carving skill that is wasted on *imu*-cooked *pua'a* (pig) goes into cutting spears inside a ripe pineapple without spoiling the outside, which is used as a serving dish.

By the time Jack was ready to leave Hawaii, I felt that the alternative to immediate escape was a sojourn in a convalescent home and a strict fast. We had eaten and drunk so much marvelous food and liquor that my jeans were uncomfortably tight. We had visited the homes of owners, managers, and workers, union halls and picket lines, a prison farm lost in the clouds, an automated cane field, a sugar mill, the newest super-posh tourist resort, and a totally integrated public school system. My head was stuffed with the strong impressions tourists acquire and store uncritically, but they were so mutually contradictory that it would take weeks to make sense of them.

All the contradictions were represented in the party that assembled on the dock to see us off. The guest list covered the social and racial spectrum: sandy-haired Coast Guardsmen from Oklahoma and North Carolina; the *haoles* of the sail-watching fraternity; families of I.L.W.U. members—Japanese, Portuguese, pure Hawaiian, and Filipino; the crew of a ketch that had just tied up next to us—three Americans from California and one Mexican from Baja California; a Hawaiian nightclub singer; a bearded faculty member from the branch of the University of Hawaii; and a Hawaiian-*haole* "society lady" whom we had never seen before, who came bearing a double-ruffle orchid lei—a gift for me from her sister, whom I had met at the other end of the island.

We made a splendid exit, hoisting sail before there was any reason to, for the benefit of the youngsters in the crowd. Looking back at the group on the dock, it seemed to me that it was breaking up too swiftly. Had I imagined it, or was there a perceptible strain under the surface of the prevailing *politesse?* When all these people—each of whom had been extraordinarily cordial to us—were gathered in one spot and forced to rub elbows in our confined space, were some of them uncomfortable? And if so, who?

We had found the beginnings of anti-Semitism in Hilo, and a strong hint of a brand-new prejudice forming against Negroes who are moving there from the States. It would be a pity if the tidal wave of migration from the mainland were to wash away the Hawaiian spirit of mutual respect and put gravel in the *aloha.*

We sailed shorthanded across Alenuihaha Channel from Hawaii to the island of Maui. (Norris had asked for and got permission to fly on ahead to Honolulu, where he had old friends he wanted to visit.) The channel is a funnel into which the trade winds pour; the current runs hard in an oblique curve; the result is a surface like a roller coaster.

I stood my usual night watch, aware that steering was not easy with the big ones piling up behind and sliding under us with a heave. Way back on the fast run to Nuku Hiva I had learned not to look over my shoulder at times like this, so I watched the compass face and listened to the clock's bells and the snores of the men. (There is something about the sound of other people snoring while one is on watch that is profoundly flattering.) I had never felt so much a member of the fraternity. I didn't even mind the loss of a couple of hours between-watch sleep, for without Norris we were on a two-on-and-four-off pattern.

But in the light of day, when Jack and Benson saw the rollers, they voted unanimously that it was too big a job for a woman at the helm. For the first (and only) time, I was ordered away from the wheel!

I started to argue that the seas were no bigger by day than they had been at night, but I changed my mind. Both the men were as euphoric as boys with a new surfboard, and the truth was I was tired. I just sat there in the cockpit with my legs propped up and my journal on my knees, not doing anything but looking at the scenery. Not even worrying about lunch.

Maui is much more rugged and dramatic than Hawaii, whose huge volcanoes cheat the eye by the consistency of their slope. The great extinct cone of Haleakala forms the core of Maui. Waterfalls pour through breaches in the cone, making the black lava walls green in wide stripes that merge into the jungles at the cliff's foot. A cloud hung over the top of the mountain as we rounded the cape at the southwest extremity and entered the "roads" of Lahaina, where missionaries and whalers once fought for control of Hawaiian bodies and souls. On our port beam was the small, uninhabited island of Kahoolawe, and then the larger island of Lanai, almost entirely given over to pineapple culture. Far ahead on the horizon we could see the "leper island" of Molokai.

There was no room for us in the small yacht harbor of Lahaina; it was too full of trimarans, built in Oregon. We wangled a temporary berth, wedged between two boats that fished for black coral, great spindly bushes of which are brought up from depths of three hundred feet and made into jewelry here. The town of Lahaina is—or was then—being reconstructed as a sort of Disneyland attraction for tourists who fly over from Honolulu for the weekend. It was "authentic" but not attractive, at least to us, and the huge, half-empty hotels up the coast were positively repellent. We were turned back at the door of the dining room of one because a member of the party had rubbed a blister and removed his sandal to ease it. One might as well have been in Los Angeles or Palm Beach.

Our one good piece of luck in Lahaina was Tommy Ka, a young sculptor, who converted our big helmet conch into a trumpet and taught us how to blow it. His grandfather, who lived at Hana on the south end of Maui, had used one to direct the *hukilaus* (communal fishing expeditions) by standing on the cliffs from which he could spot schools of fish in the bay and guiding the men who carried nets much like the *éparveil* Daniel used on Mooréa. One blast on the conch meant "go to the right"; two blasts meant "go to the left"; and he could blow a high harmonic that meant "You're there!"

By the time Tommy had finished his demonstration, all the stray dogs in Lahaina were sitting outside his studio, howling softly as the overtones of the trumpet tormented their inner ears.

The passage from Maui to Oahu is the finish line of the TransPac race where many boats suffer knockdowns. We had guests aboard who had flown over from Honolulu and kept themselves on the verge of seasickness all the way home by telling us tall tales of tragic accidents. It came as a shock (to me, at least) to learn that if the *Aikane* were knocked down by a sudden gust, she would not necessarily right herself. Worse, she would sink like the lead in her keel if not righted promptly. I had had a naïve notion that we would float almost indefinitely, which had been some comfort to me in tight moments, but I felt able to dispense with it now.

The first view of Oahu is impressive, though not so impressive as any one of the Marquesas. We sailed along parallel to the surf of Waikiki, close enough to watch the surfers climb up on their boards and start in on the crest of a comber. The city looked like Miami from the sea, but the mountains and the clouds behind the tall buildings looked like El Greco's "View of Toledo." If man must build structures that scrape sky, it's good to have something close by that keeps them in perspective.

The *Aikane* went up on ways to be scraped, painted, varnished, and mended wherever she needed mending. Some of the work was done by hired hands, but the crew took some responsibility, too. I sanded all the combing, the exterior of the cabin, and as much of the mast as I could reach. We had left San Diego with three coats of heavy-duty varnish on these surfaces and done some patch varnishing at Takaroa, but even so, sun and salt water had worked their way down to bare wood in spots.

Benson had research to do in the library of the University of Hawaii; I had shopping and provisioning to do, the Bishop Museum and some old friends to visit. Our week of shore leave was like a foretaste of the readjustment to "normal life" that lay ahead of us at the end of the third sea leg. But there was one more port of call before that: Kauai, the Garden Island to the northwest that everyone said was the loveliest and most Tahitian of the whole Hawaiian chain.

Two hours before we were due to shove off, Benson and I were in a store in the huge new shopping center up the water-

Janet and Benson at Puna Luu on Oahu.

front from the moorage, buying a "boat present"—a new set of plastic tumblers for Happy Hour. While we waited for them to be gift wrapped, I overheard a conversation about tidal-wave alerts. It was not interesting enough to keep me eavesdropping, and when our package was ready I forgot even to mention it to Benson. We started out of the store and stopped for one last ice-cream soda.

Just as we got the straws to our lips, I heard a siren. It wasn't very close or very loud, but it kept on and on. No one at the counter paid any attention to it. Neither did Benson. Finally, I asked the waitress what it was.

"Tidal-wave alert," she said.

"You mean now? There is one right now?"

She nodded a little disdainfully, as if it were not good form to make a fuss about such things. Benson and I looked at each other, trying to absorb the implications of this piece of news. It might not mean anything much to the other soda drinkers, but none of them lived in a small house, floating on the tide that might suddenly swell into a disaster.

We paid our check and walked—did not run—to the exit, through the parking lot, out onto a boulevard that was absolutely solid with cars. Only pedestrians were moving, so there was no use getting into a taxi. We walked faster and faster, clutching our package and beginning to sweat.

The siren never stopped wailing.

As we came into the complex of ways, shops, docks, and parking lots that surrounds the yacht basin, we merged into a river of foot and car traffic. The owner of each of the thousands of boats there was trying to get to his craft and get her out to sea. We would never have made it to ours if someone hadn't given us a lift. As it was, Jack and Norris were casting off when someone shouted to them that we were on the way. We broke into a run, and finished with a great leap that almost cost us the plastic present.

For the next half hour we were part of an extraordinary parade. Everything afloat was heading out to sea. Far to starboard we could see another, even larger, procession, headed by the *Lurline*, the Swedish ship, *Oriana*, and the Russian oceanographic vessel *Vityok*, which had just brought in an officer for emergency surgery. In our parade line were big schooners like John Ford's *Aranel*, a brig built for the filming of *Hawaii*; Chinese junks, sloops of all sizes, catamarans, trimarans, power launches, and sailing canoes. It looked like Dunkirk.

The radio was doing a countdown and explaining the situation. The shock had begun in the Aleutians and was due—if it came at all—to hit Kauai at two minutes before 3:00 P.M. and Honolulu five minutes later. It was just three now. The beach was absolutely deserted. Helicopters were buzzing the sands, looking for stray surfers or sunbathers to bully to safety. The water off Waikiki was free of boards for the first time. (Even at night there seemed to be a few enthusiasts out there waiting for a wave.) The radio reported that the first and second floors of all the big hotels along the beach had been evacuated; guests were being detained in emergency waiting rooms above. All traffic had stopped on Kalakaua and Ala Moana boulevards. Similar precautions were being taken on the two islands worst hit in the 1960 disaster: Hawaii (on the Hilo side) and Kauai.

Then it was 3:06.

Nothing had happened, neither here nor in Kauai. Two minuttes passed, and Hilo was safe, too.

With a curious feeling of anticlimax, we came about and started back. The surfers were in the water by the time we came abreast of the gathering place of the big waves. We passed and greeted a few friends and acquaintances. The jokes were pretty

The *Aikane* moored off the Yacht Club at Honolulu.

forced and feeble. Everyone felt a little as if he had been "had."

We had a lovely night sail from Oahu to Nawiliwili Harbor on the near end of Kauai. But it was the Fourth of July, and the harbor was horrible with the din of hydroplane races. We tied up at the dock and fled to the nearest town, Lihue, to order supplies for the long voyage home: meat and chickens, to be frozen; six loaves of superior whole-wheat bread at 55 cents a loaf; pancake flour, cake mix, peanut butter, paper towels, detergent, and canned bacon. Food was plentiful but not cheap on the outlying islands. If something grew locally, it grew abundantly and was given to the visitor in embarrassingly generous quantity. But if it had to be dragged over from the mainland, via Honolulu, it was a luxury item, priced out of the reach of common folk. Fish (both saltwater and fresh), frogs' legs, crabs, lobster, papayas, mangoes, avocados, and coconuts were free for the catching or asking. (Marie Salomé would have said it was possible to live without money, even here.)

I had been reading a book called *Six Months Among the Palm Groves, Coral Reefs, and Volcanoes of the Sandwich Islands,* written in 1874 by a remarkable Scotswoman named Isabella Bird, and recently reissued in paperback. She got the difference between this island and the big one in a phrase that cannot be improved upon: "Hawaii is all domes and humps, Kauai all peaks and sierras." The core of Kauai is a 6000-foot mountain called Waialeale, a volcano that has been extinct so long its crater has silted up and turned into a swamp in the sky. The rainfall up

Benson and Jack on board.

there is something over 450 inches a year. More and larger streams than those on Maui come leaping down the mountain walls, and the ravines below are so choked with jungle that no one can walk or ride up them. Even the humblest houses in the settlements along the coast are fenced with high hedges of begonia and hibiscus, and the summer homes of rich *haole* families from Honolulu are set like English manors in acres of mowed lawn. Orchids grow wild, and so do ginger lilies and lobster-claw flowers.

We sailed from Nawiliwili to Hanalei on the north tip of the island, and did a little exploring and diving. The underwater scenery is almost as beautiful as Bora-Bora's. We found no particularly good shells, but it must have been our bad luck, for we saw plenty on display in the homes we visited. Our only interesting "bag" was a trap (illegal) full of lobsters that were mottled green and cream right down to the ends of the thin legs. When cooked, they turned scarlet, as a good lobster should, but the free-form blotches remained on the meat.

We rode as far as one can in the direction of the Na Pali coast on the northwest (lee) side of the island. The only way to penetrate this area is by outrigger or helicopter. The headlands drop sheer into the sea, and the valleys between them are guarded by equally unscalable precipices. The tribes who live here were never conquered, either by *haoles* or their neighbors, and lived in splendid isolation up to a few years ago. Now they are invaded by bands of tourists who have just had lunch in the luxurious hotel that overlooks Hanalei Bay; cool, dry, and unwrinkled, they step out of their whirlybird taxis, take a look around, and whirl up and away again. I wonder if the inhabitants have got anything of value in return for the loss of their privacy.

On July 6 the food we had ordered was driven up from Lihue, and stowed. We did our last laundry ashore and went for one last (unfruitful) dive. The wind we wanted came up in the afternoon, and at five o'clock it was brisk.

We weighed anchor and headed north on course of ten degrees (magnetic—twenty degrees true).

All the Way Home

The first five days of the home-bound voyage were absolutely miserable for me. Perhaps I was psychosomatically resisting the imminent end of the adventure, or perhaps I was seasick. (The wind was brisk, though erratic, and we were beating—but not nearly so hard as on the trip up from Bora-Bora.) At any rate, it took all the fortitude I could muster to take my wheel watches, my morning longitude and noon latitude shots, get my "fix" and plot our position on my little blank sheet, and cook one (main) meal a day, swinging by my uneasy midriff on the safety harness. If the voyage to the Marquesas had started in this fashion, I would have been tempted to get off at Guadalupe and hitch-hike home.

We caught only one fish during these five days—a small but very beautiful *mahi-mahi*, the fish dolphin, not to be confused with the mammal dolphin, otherwise known as a porpoise. The "dying colors" of this creature have become a literary figure of speech. They are gorgeous enough when alive: a brilliant metallic blue-black and silver flank streaked with gold! Out of water and gasping for breath, the *mahi-mahi* goes through a muscular convulsion that makes ripples of iridescence—pink, green, yellow, blue, and violet—run along its flanks like an aurora borealis. The shape of the fish is curious: its head is squared off in most unfishly fashion, and it is so thin in comparison to its depth and length that it gives the impression of being a bad job of taxidermy.

Our specimen was too small for a main course, even for three, so I tried to make *poisson cru* of it. It was not very good. Considering the fuss that is made in fancy California restaurants about "fresh *mahi-mahi* fillets, flown in from Hawaii," we had expected something more interesting.

The old struggle for "easting" or "westing" was replaced now by a campaign to get as far north as possible before turning east. The Pacific high was reported to be somewhere around the thirty-fifth parallel, roughly the latitude of Point Conception on the California coast. Jack's plan was to reach the high as directly as possible, pick up a strong westerly wind, and run straight for the Channel Islands on a course of about ninety degrees.

On the sixth day we seemed to be coming into the high. The airs were light, the weather heavenly—warm enough to strip down for a tanning at noon, but clear and chilly enough for a sweater on watch at night. We were beginning to have to motor at intervals—which gave me a relief from the effort of bracing myself against pitching even during sleep and from having to wrestle the wheel with arms and legs. My inner turbulence subsided.

On the seventh day, we came into "glass-ball country." This is a sort of aquatic dustbin into which the waves and winds sweep the detritus of the whole ocean. Glass floats that are torn loose from fishing nets anywhere in the Pacific usually end up here, and we had been forewarned that we would need a good dip net to take advantage of the souvenir-collecting opportunity. Our advisers had managed by holding the lightest member of their crew by his heels. But I refused to be used in the capacity, so Benson had devised something out of the handle of a mop, a wire coat hanger, and some old nylon gill net. We had all gone through "scoop drill" in Hanalei. When we sighted our first glass ball, visible from a quarter of a mile away, bobbing gently on a glassy sea, there was a rush for the weapon.

From then on, for as long as we were in the hunting grounds, the competition was fierce. The rules of the game, arrived at without discussion by an uneasy consensus, were that—all other things being equal—the spotter of a ball had property rights to it, whether or not he actually retrieved it. (The helmsman could not leave his post to retrieve, and he was frequently the first to sight. Also, there was some reluctance at first to give me my turn with the net. The men acted as though I ought to be content with the boodle and let them have the fun of bagging it. But after one of my "superiors" had missed an extra large ball that I had spotted, and we had to make a big circle for another dip at it, I claimed and got my turn.)

Actually, a successful dip was more of an achievement than it looked. One had to brace for the moment of contact when the net hit one of the eight- or twelve-inch (diameter) heavy glass globes, and hold against the forward movement of the boat for several seconds before lifting it clear. How much of a physical strain this was depended largely on the helmsman. If he didn't come in close enough, the angle became too awkward even for the men. If he got too close, the ball would slide away along the hull. Some things about the sport reminded one of jousting, but it was much more productive.

Our total for the first day was nine floats, three of them with part or all of the original netting, two empty beer bottles (Japanese), one detergent bottle (American), and a lot of plankton that looked like waterlogged newsprint.

On the eighth day we knew we were in the high, and made our turn to the east. Our latitude was a few minutes above or below the thirty-fifth parallel and the longitude was about 150 degrees west. The weather was so beautiful that we began to try all sorts of esoteric navigational tricks: I got a moon shot of the lower limb (in civil twilight) that worked out very close to the consensus on our position. Benson finally got and worked a fix from two stars: Venus and Arcturus. The plotting of position on our tracking sheets had become usually simple now that all lines of position were at right angles to the course, and under these conditions I was as good a navigator as anyone else.

The eighth day out was also Bastille Day, the great fête of the islands we had left below the Line. We washed and dressed (*sic*) for dinner. The menu was built around a lamb curry, made from the last of our fresh meat from Lihue, and a *guacamole* of the last of our gift avocados from Kauai:

GUACAMOLE

Ripe avocados (half a medium-sized fruit per person)

Raw scallions
Green or red peppers
Lemon or lime juice (or vinegar)
Salt, pepper (black or red), garlic powder (optional)

Peel the avocados and remove the seed; crush the meat to a paste, lumpy if possible, and mix in the lemon juice. Chop the raw vegetables quite fine and mix them in. Then season it to taste. If hot peppers are part of the raw ingredients, go easy on the condiments. A little zing of chili is desirable, but the avocado flavor is delicate, and can be lost if the seasoning gets out of hand.

We were still in the high on the ninth day. Ball hunting was great: the total count was twenty of assorted sizes, one blue light bulb of unknown, but foreign, manufacture, and one serum bottle with Russian writing on it. The glass balls were "occupied" by several interesting species: some tiny blue pelagic crabs; goose barnacles; and a sort of ropy webbing so tough one couldn't break it by hand, studded with tiny glass-like beads. The goose barnacles, observed closely, were the strangest of all the types of life we ever stumbled on: a beak formed of two sharply pointed shells at the end of a long, sinewy neck. The necks writhed slowly, and the beaks opened and shut to let a set of curly "feathers" reach out for food or draw back for safety, the total effect being somehow as un-natural as if a swan's neck and head were being operated inde-pendently of its body by a mouthful of its breast feathers.

The big excitement of this day was a school of basking whales. We saw the first spout at quite a distance and mistook it for a school of dolphin or tuna. Then we saw another spout, then another. We couldn't believe there were really whales under those geysers till we saw the great flukes come up and disappear in a graceful curve—black against the glare of the water.

We revved the motor down to its quietest and tried to sneak up on the closest of the unmoving black ripple marks. We were within fifteen yards before he moved! An incredibly lazy but efficient movement, so smooth that it left almost no mark on the surface. The great block of head simply lowered and raised the tail, which slipped down and out of sight. There was a pause, during which it seemed possible that there had never been anything there. Then, half a mile or more away, a geyser jetted up with such force that I wondered what would happen to a boat that happened to be in its path.

Sometime during the afternoon we were adopted by an albatross.

We mistook him for a glass ball when we first saw him, and steered over to scoop him up. By the time we were close enough to see that he was a large gray-brown bird with a white face, we had spotted three authentic glass balls in his area. We went after them, one by one, and the bird began to work with us. At first he seemed only to be getting out of our range. When we got too close, he would unfold his incredibly long wings, flap awkwardly up to an altitude where' he could maneuver, and then come down and reverse the folding process with his wings. Each time he settled it was near another glass ball, and we were the richer for his assistance.

Norris tried to feed him, but he didn't even deign to examine what was thrown to him. Neither did he let us out of sight.

Toward evening we spotted something that looked like "weather" ahead on the horizon: two patches of dull rainbow colors on either side of a rainsquall. The sea was a slate-colored mirror. Jack was beginning to mutter about the fuel we were using up and whether we could make it home if the calm kept up. It was time for the westerlies to catch up with us, but the breeze that was beginning to distort the mirror was easterly. It was not a good omen.

The rainsquall hit us after dark, and by morning of the tenth day we were heading directly into a wind that was listed on Jack's wind chart as O percent possible. We were still motoring and pounding against a stronger and stronger chop. Al, our albatross, was sticking with us, swooping and banking over the waves, like a small boy showing off. Sometimes his wing tips seemed actually to touch the water. "Look, Ma! No hands!" And when we had applauded a long sustained swoop with the right wing down, he circled around and made another pass to show that he could do it just as well with the left. Also, he caught fish and brought them back, settled down on a wave near our stern, and went through his comedy wing-folding act while juggling his catch into position for gulping. Our applause for this performance was dulled by envy. We were out of meat and had been fishing for two days without success. Plans were discussed for training Al to forage for us.

Our ship-to-shore radio began to bring us news of the Trans-Pac race from Los Angeles to Oahu. The Happy Hour broadcast was full of self-congratulatory accounts of record speeds being made on the unheard-of east wind that was making us so miserable. Jack and Benson were beginning to make two daily checks of the remaining fuel.

There were a few glass balls sighted on the eleventh day, but we didn't dare alter course for them. On the twelfth day it was quieter, and Al went back to spotting for us. We netted four.

By now we had lost all the northing we had to spare, and then some. The wind shifted to ENE, and we were making a zig-zag course that averaged out to something like 120 degrees. Our sleeping quarters again looked like padded cells. We knew enough to stay dry, but the problem about sleeping on the downside and getting pounded against the ribs remained. Also, we were back to the closed ports and the stale air. For the first time in many months it was possible to get chilled through on a night watch, although it was mid-July and we were slightly south of the latitude of San Diego.

In the late afternoon of the twelfth day, Benson buckled on his safety harness and secured himself to the mast and worked for over an hour trying to mend three broken sail ties *in situ*. If he felt any the worse for it, he didn't say so. But the next afternoon—the thirteenth—he had a bad leg cramp just as he was going on watch. He stood his two hours and could hardly walk away from the wheel.

"I'm not going to be able to take my night watch," he said, almost belligerently.

It took all of us a little while to adjust to this out-of-character behavior. Benson's next watch was six hours away. It seemed a little early to predict how a leg cramp would react to that much rest. Jack made no comment, but he changed the watch schedule so that each of the three left stood two hours on and four off.

There was a curious restrained resentment in the air. I found myself wondering why Benson didn't say more: explain, describe, elaborate, or ask for help. If anyone else had announced that he was *hors du combat*, Benson, as medical officer, would have intervened in some fashion, but none of us liked to invade his area of authority. I finally asked if he had taken a pain pill. He hadn't, so I dug out three codeine tablets I'd carried in my purse so long they were almost worn out. He took one of them meekly, and still made no comment of any kind.

By the next day we had been forced down to the thirty-second parallel, well south of Ensenada. Al was still with us and still catching fish. We still were not. There were less than a thousand miles to go, and Jack and Benson were calculating how much of that distance our fuel would carry us if we had to motor into the teeth of the wind. They agreed that we couldn't make it without some help from the wind or some extra diesel. We were in the shipping lanes, and it was possible that we might be able to beg or buy a few extra gallons. We forgot about ball spotting, and scanned the horizon for the mast or stack of a ship.

Benson finally broke down and admitted that since he had eaten my last tired codeine tablet he had been unable to get any sleep.

"Don't we have any pain-killers in the medical stores?" Jack asked. "I checked off that list when we stowed, and I thought we had a couple of hundred pills."

He was right. The bottle had never been opened and had got pushed back into the most inaccessible corner of the cupboards in the head. The medical officer had forgotten them in his hour of need, possibly because he was so unaccustomed to being in that sort of need.

By this time I was getting bolder about issuing medical advice and orders. I persuaded Benson to let me massage the sore leg. He refused to take off his jeans for fear he couldn't get them on again, with the boat pitching as she was. ("That leg is as stiff as a log," he said. "I can't bend the knee.") My attempt to massage the log was discouraging. Jack and I began to consult behind Benson's back.

Neither of us had ever heard of a leg cramp lasting this long. All suspicion that Benson was malingering had dissipated by now. He had tried (under sedation) to sit at the wheel for a short spell, and the pressure of the seat against the back of his thigh had been unbearable. Standing on the leg even for a few minutes brought on painful spasms. It began to seem possible that we had a really serious medical problem. We began to consult our medical library. Nothing described there fitted. And Benson caught us at the books and began doing his own research. He had eliminated the only comforting diagnosis (Charley horse) and was working his way into very alarming territory when I looked over his shoulder.

"Do you want to call Los Angeles and talk to a doctor?" I asked.

He looked so shocked that I was sorry I had spoken. Actually, I had very little confidence in the sort of medical advice one gets by telephone even ashore, and transmission by radio is hardly the equivalent of even the worst phone service on land.

"I really feel a lot better today," Benson said. "Last night it was rough for a while, but it's better now." But that was what he had been saying from the beginning. A stiff upper lip is not useful in dealing with a real problem. If he had been acting as medical officer, I didn't think he would have put up with that sort of childish heroics. But I didn't know how to switch the roles.

We got down to 31°35′ North latitude, before the wind shifted enough so we could sail a course of ninety degrees. It was not going to get us to Los Angeles, but at least we were not being driven any farther south. And we caught a magnificent big *mahi-mahi*, probably over twenty pounds, on a candy-bar lure, going about five knots.

There was plenty of meat to cut steaks this time, and we dipped them in egg and cornflake crumbs and pan-fried them. They were every bit as good as advertised. Apparently this is just one of the fishes that is not to be eaten raw.

For the first time I could remember, food failed as a morale builder. Everyone agreed that the fish was fine, and everyone went right on getting grumpier. We were beating into a headwind again, and bucking a chop. Jack and Norris were dog-tired, not only from standing watches minus two hours of sleep (which I was doing too) but also from assuming a whole list of chores that had formerly been Benson's. Sail changes, for example, had been accomplished by Benson and Norris, with Jack at the wheel, giving them orders. Now I held the wheel while Jack and Norris did the job. Jack was less tolerant of a fumble than Benson had been, so Norris was getting chewed out more than usual. He was getting fed up and looking for a scapegoat, and Benson—whose "dereliction" had started the trouble—was the obvious choice. He began to tease, and Benson, who was already fretting about his uselessness and looking for small punishments he could inflict on himself to expiate his guilt, was an easy mark.

Also, Benson was running out of patience and beginning to do bizarre things like suddenly shifting from pain pills to penicillin G, a move that indicated to me that he had selected one of the alternative diagnoses in the medical books, something really gory!

One particularly bad morning, Benson responded to Norris's baiting by trying to cook breakfast. He stomped around the galley like Long John Silver, cooking pancakes despite my well-advertised aversion to being waked in my airless berth by the stench of burning margarine. All he got as reward from the beneficiaries of this insanity was a crack about being able to stand a wheel watch if he could stand up to fry. I could have clobbered the three of them.

By nightfall he was goofier than ever, and insisted on sleeping on deck during my night watch. The purpose, presumably, was to be on hand if I needed help in trimming the sail, but the pills made him sleep too heavily to be waked. We were taking a lot of spray around the edge of the canopy, and I saw that he was getting drenched, despite his oilskins. I thought he ought not to get chilled, so I tried to pull one of the cushions over to shield him, without letting go the wheel. I nearly jibed, and woke Jack, who was quite properly infuriated. But neither of us could persuade Benson to go below.

Through all this gathering emotional storm, Al stayed with us. Sometimes he would be absent for most of the day, and we would suspect desertion. But as we assembled for Happy Hour, he would show up, make a few of his fancy banked turns, and disappear again. And he always checked in just before I went off watch at dawn.

By July 23 we had lost more northing, and were down to the latitude of Rosario and 128° 48′ West. What wind there was was from the east again (still unheard of in this place at this season according to Jack's chart). The sea was glassy again. We were motoring at the most economical speed possible (1300 rpm) and making about five knots.

Benson and I had a real quarrel. The trigger was another pancake atrocity. I had extracted a promise from him after the last one that he would wake me up and let me get out into the cockpit before the smell started funneling up into my berth, but he forgot. I had had about two of my four hours' sleep, which was not enough, when I waked up gagging. The combination of scorched cooking oil and righteous indignation was too much for my abraded tolerance mechanism. I stormed through the cabin and took the wheel for an unscheduled watch, exuding umbrage like a dust cloud. And Norris, who was doubtless responsible for this breach of domestic peace, rubbed salt (or burned grease) into the wounds on both sides.

After lunch, Benson got up the courage to work himself out of his jeans for the first time since his trouble began. He appeared on deck in shorts, and we could see the leg. It was appalling—a huge, purple-blue blotch from his groin to his knee on the underside of his thigh.

Jack asked me if I wanted to call a doctor in Los Angeles. I vacillated. It still seemed almost impossibly awkward, especially without Benson's cooperation. And I didn't think we could get that without really alarming him. (I could just hear him telling a doctor that it was "really quite a lot better" after we had spent hours getting through all the intervening barriers to communication.)

While I was trying to come to a decision, Jack tried to get through to his sister on other business, and discovered that this was one of the times we couldn't reach the marine operator in Oakland, so the whole question was moot.

As the afternoon wore on, we found ourselves in a field of what looked like floating cotton. Little blue jellyfish with a clear white wind vane on their backs: *Velella vulgaris,* or something very like them. We tried dipping for them, but they slipped through the wide meshes of our net. Finally, I stretched some cheesecloth across the frame and managed to bring up a few specimens. The bright blue tentacles were host to an exquisitely delicate type of violet snail. We began a new sort of collecting, pickling our catch in small bottles of alcohol to harden the shells and kill the occupants. (If they were left on the deck in the sun, the shrinking of the tentacles crushed the smaller shells.)

As darkness came on, the wind died completely. We reefed the main (to keep from breaking any more ties by slatting around) and dropped the jib. The boat was running on automatic pilot, so we had time to rest. There was a lot of joking (?) about amputation. Norris said that when gangrene set in it would be the captain's duty to take the leg off. Jack said it was the medical officer's job, and that if Benson decided to perform the operation he would only be responsible for signing as a witness.

The last calculation showed 450 miles still to go and almost no fuel in the tanks. Al checked in at sunset.

On the morning of the twenty-fourth, Jack got through to his sister by radio, but by the time he had finished his own business and was looking inquiringly in my direction, transmission was fading. I had been rehearsing a condensed version of Benson's symptoms which I was going to ask his sister to take down and relay to an appropriate authority, and I was going to try to set up an appointment call for the evening's good transmission hour. I knew Jack had not foreseen that we would run out of time before I got my turn, but I was angry anyway.

When the dipstick was dropped into the fuel tank at noon, it showed the same amount as the day before, despite the fact that we had motored almost continuously for twenty-four hours. Either a miracle or a miscalculation, but encouraging in either case.

Then we caught a fine big albacore on a Hansen spoon with a triple hook. We used the belly for *sashimi* and *poisson cru,* and steaked the rest. It was enough meat to see us to port—if we could keep moving in that direction.

Everyone was being so polite to everyone else that I had

the feeling we were on the edge of some truly awesome emotional chasm. I had got over my snit about the pancakes (thanks to Benson, whose gifts as a grudge-dissolver were unimpaired by his condition), but I still felt that it would take very little to drive me into tears.

We were all taking shots at ludicrously short intervals, although Norris pointed out at similar intervals that it was hardly likely we would miss our landfall going this way. (We had heard tales about people scraping bottom in the surf off Newport because they had got lazy about taking shots and missed all landmarks in a light haze that frequently shrouds the southern California coast.) I had finished *Ulysses* and there was nothing else to read. The Scrabble set was working at last, but under existing circumstances games seemed to me fraught with dangers that more than outweighed their usefulness.

Just before midnight, Norris, who was on watch, but not steering, came down and woke Benson. He had spotted the lights of a vessel some distance ahead and to port, and wanted advice on whether to approach it or give it a wide berth. Jack was sound asleep, and it seemed best not to wake him.

For a man with a wooden leg, Benson was out of the berth and on deck in an impressively short time. He had the spreader lights blinking and the boat heading straight for the lights of the other vessel before I could get myself up and sufficiently dressed to appear on deck. The vessel was blinking back at us, signaling that she had hove to and was waiting our approach.

It was calm enough for the lights of both boats to make wriggling pools of brilliance on the black surface of the sea, but not calm enough for a boarding operation. Benson's first "ahoys" had got Jack up. He was already negotiating an exchange of diesel for Johnny Walker Scotch.

"We can let you have ten gallons," said a voice from the darkness. "Could give you more except we're just starting out. Don't know how long we'll have to hang around here. You got a container?"

Jack said we'd toss one of the empty plastic jerry cans over, and the voice cautioned him to secure a line to the handle, in case of a miss. Benson tried to bring the *Aikane* alongside the

other boat—we could see the stern now, with the words "*Spirit,*
Seattle"—but as we got close, swells tipped us toward each other
and our mast nearly struck the tall tuna poles lashed upright
amidships on the trawler. He put the wheel over and started a
large circle designed to bring us across the *Spirit*'s stern. The
jerry can had landed safely and was being filled. The tricky
problem was going to be the delivery of the Scotch.

Our first pass across the stern was not close enough. On
our second, there was no one in sight to accept the bottle goods.
(Joe Smith, the skipper, was superintending the filling of the
jerry can from the *Spirit*'s reserve tanks, and the other hands
were bottling a couple of packages of cigarettes in an old Mason
jar.) Benson maneuvered us in so close that Jack was able to
reach over both our lifeline and the *Spirit*'s heavy rail and drop
the fifth of whiskey onto the deck without breaking it.

When Joe Smith *et al.* came out, we were one hundred yards
away, and they could hardly believe what they saw at their feet.

The line attached to the jerry can was tossed to us on the
next pass, and we hauled the full container through water that
floated it. But cigarettes don't float, and there was some tension
about that exchange. It worked, and everyone was as elated as if
we had just accomplished some miracle—which, of course, we
had in the sense that finding a floating gas dock in the middle of
the ocean is one.

"You run into any albacore?" Joe Smith asked.

We said yes, and he wanted to know how many. We said just
one.

"Just one? What the hell happened? You run out of the
school?"

"We don't know whether it was a school. All we needed
was one."

There was silence more eloquent than an expletive. We
couldn't see Joe Smith's face, but we could read it anyway. People who take one albacore and don't throw their hooks back in
are outside the experience of a man like Joe.

"You don't know if you were on the Banks, I suppose," he
said, a little shakily, I thought.

We didn't, but we were able to find out. It was the one
use to which all our careful tracking was ever put. By counting

back on Jack's big chart, we found that we had indeed caught our fish over the Erban Banks at a depth of 300 instead of 3000 feet. Joe Smith was encouraged by that, and said he'd be heading out that way in an hour or so.

By noon of July 25 we had only 300 miles to go. We could make it, motoring all the way, if we kept it down to 1300 rpm. The pressure was off in one sense, but now a new pressure was being applied.

A party was being planned ashore to welcome us home. Jack's sister wanted an Estimated Time of Arrival. Both a day and an hour! Since it was obvious that we were not going to make it on a weekend, and since most of the prospective guests worked through most of the day even in July, we were being urged to make port in the late afternoon—Tuesday, July 27, or Wednesday, July 28. (I was still too worried about Benson to fall into the spirit of party planning, but our chances of having a doctor on hand to examine him also depended on coordination of our ETA with some medical schedule.)

Calculating went on even while we were eating, and always achieved the same answer: it depended on the wind, which was still absolutely absent. Nothing you could plan on.

The weather was wonderful—for anything but sailing. The sun was hot as long as one was in it, but the shade was refreshingly cool. With neither pitch nor roll to contend with, Benson was getting some rest at last. (He had finally admitted that he could hardly sleep at all while we were bucking the chop because he had to hold on with both hands to keep from having to save himself from a pitch by using the injured leg.) There was still plenty to eat. Al was still with us. We were out of glass-ball and jellyfish country. On the shortwave we could hear albacore fishermen lying to each other about how poor the fishing was wherever they were. Several times people asked "Where's Joe Smith and the *Spirit*?" Apparently Joe was maintaining radio silence in the waters over the Erban Banks.

About noon on July 26, we sighted the mast of a sailing ship off our starboard stern quarter. She was gaining on us on a course roughly parallel to ours, not likely to pass close enough for a hail. Jack tried the radio and got through at once. The voice on the other end was that of the captain of the *Goodwill!*

She altered course and came alongside to ask if we had any diesel to spare. They were sixteen days out of Honolulu (compared to our twenty days out of Kauai) and had had almost no wind at all. All the diesel in the great tanks was long ago used up, and they were burning a combination of gasoline and motor oil.

There had been a doctor aboard the *Goodwill* when last we saw her, and I asked for him now.

"He stayed in Hawaii," said the captain. "Got a problem we can help with?"

I described Benson's condition as best I could, in spite of his interruptions to the effect that it was "really nothing" and/or "quite a lot better."

"We've got a man aboard with the same sort of thing. Ruptured blood vessel. All I'm doing is keeping him off it, propping the leg up, and feeding him aspirins."

The captain offered to take Benson aboard, assuming that he would make port in San Diego before we made Los Angeles, but Benson didn't want to go. There was, as Jack pointed out later, no reason to suppose that the *Goodwill* wouldn't end up worse off than we. When she ran out of fuel, she was going to have to wait for a lot bigger wind than we needed.

By 5:00 P.M. Jack had to make his decision about the ETA. He called his sister and told her Wednesday, the twenty-eighth. We would try to make it into the harbor mouth at 4:00 P.M. (We would have a hard time of it if we never picked up a wind or another floating gas dock, but he didn't say so.) He did make a point of reminding her to invite one of his friends who was a practicing physician and might have some problem about clearing that hour for purely social purposes.

At 9:00 P.M. a marvelous beam wind came up from the north-northwest. We climbed to five knots, and Jack cut the motor for the first time in days.

Al checked in with us about that time. It was too dark to see his face, but we recognized him by the fancy flying. It was good to know that he hadn't deserted us to follow the more glamorous

Goodwill. We began to think about inviting him to the welcome-home party. No one was going to believe him otherwise.

I did better than seven knots on my 2:00 A.M. watch, and by dawn (the twenty-seventh) we were clocking a miraculous nine knots, although the seas had built up. Jack began to make a new sort of calculation. If we were to give it all we had, we might make port by dark this very night! It would mean cancel-ing the party, but the alternative was heaving to somewhere and waiting for party time. An ignominious sort of finish to a great adventure!

We finally decided to stick with the party date, but to spend the "extra" time the wind was giving us anchored in the harbor of one of the Channel Islands. We could clean up the boat and ourselves and perhaps go ashore and hunt for abalone, this being one of the areas where they are supposed to be so abundant that one doesn't have to dive but can pick them off the rocks at low tide without an iron!

At a little before 10:00 A.M. we saw Santa Rosa Island off our port bow. We were heeled way over and doing over nine knots —the best time we had made on the whole trip. We could see San Nicholas Island to starboard, and Santa Cruz also to port, but farther away. Al was still with us, apparently enjoying the blow.

A small Navy plane came out and circled us, flying low and behaving as if it were trying to communicate something. Wel-come home, perhaps? Jack thought not. He tried to make radio contact, but got no answer on any of our frequencies. The pilot seemed to get discouraged, and took off toward Los Angeles.

Half an hour later, he was back, and this time we got the message. It was being yelled at us over a hailing horn, and came through in wind-torn snatches. ". . . present speed and course . . . your present speed . . . Maintain your present . . . your present speed and . . ." We were being instructed to maintain our pres-ent speed and course. Why, we didn't know. It was not a very pleasant welcome. Al didn't like it either. He disappeared.

The plane also disappeared, and Jack went below. A few minutes later he came back looking slightly embarrassed. He had consulted his chart of the coast and discovered that we were sailing through the Pacific Missile Testing Range. The Navy wanted us to maintain our present speed and course so they could calculate our position and miss us when they lobbed the next one over.

We didn't want to maintain that course. We wanted to fall off and get into the lee of Santa Rosa, possibly to anchor there. But we were afraid to do anything but what we were told. And if the wind slacked off? What then? It would be impossible to maintain nine knots. Would they blast us for insubordination?

We anchored for the night in Smugglers' Harbor on Santa Cruz, next to a big purse seiner from which we begged enough diesel to see us home even if the wind died. We didn't go ashore. Everyone was too tired. Especially me. Looking back over the last twelve hours of the voyage, I felt I had finally earned my spurs, or the nautical equivalent. It had been hard work, without enough rest between efforts. The wind had been the stiffest we ever encountered, and the seas not much tamer than those in the Alenuihaha Channel. No one had ordered me from the wheel because I was needed. I was the third man and indispensable.

I had also been pushed to the limit of my strength. Holding the wheel down hard to "maintain our present speed and course" had taken everything I had in the best muscular shape I had been in for years. But I had done it and I was proud of myself.

We spent a quiet and restful night—all except Benson, who had waited too long to take his pain pill, and thus established the fact that his leg was still in big trouble. We weighed anchor before dawn (entirely too early, as it turned out) and ran down the coast on a lovely reach, catching bonito and cleaning up the cabin. Most of the recently acquired flotsam, like the fifty glass balls of assorted sizes, was stowed under the cockpit benches. The dinghy contained the rest, discreetly covered with a tarp. There was still something of the *African Queen* about us, and we did not expect that anyone would mistake us for Sunday sailors.

Al had not checked in either at sunset or at dawn. Was it the screeching horn on the Navy plane that drove him off? Or the color of the water, which had changed from deep blue to green and then to red. There was a particularly bad siege of the plankton plague, killing fishes and poisoning shellfish all up and down the coast.

Also, the shoreline was depressing: hills scarred with fire-breaks and subdivisions, streaks and gouges of yellow against the dark blue. Beautiful beaches alternating with sewage plants, power plants, and oil fields. And over all, a black chiffon widow's veil of smog.

We tried to cheer ourselves up by deciding what to wear for the reception. I had only one clean garment—a short cotton muu-muu I had bought in Honolulu. Benson was wearing a red-and-black pareu; Norris got out his dark-blue-and-white one, but finally chickened out and got into the same wheat jeans and Banlon shirt he had worn when we left. Jack found a pair of clean white shorts and an almost clean shirt. It was not the way one would have costumed the finale of such a saga, but at least we covered the spectrum of possible adjustments between Poly-nesian and Californian culture.

We reached the mouth of the Playa del Rey harbor an hour and a half before we were due at the yacht club dock. There was nothing to do but tack back and forth, and wait. After a while Jack decided to go deliberately into irons so that no one had to work. We had hardly finished executing the maneuver when a real Sunday sailor came alongside to ask if we were in need of help. Obviously he thought we had crossed our sails in that nasty-looking way out of ignorance. We were too deeply in-sulted to explain.

At ten minutes to four, we unlocked the sails and started for the breakwater at the harbor mouth. As we made the turn into the channel, we met a crowd of boats of varied sizes—all coming to meet us! to bring us in!

Suddenly it was all enormously gala. I found our conch trumpet and began blowing my lungs out like a Polynesian fish peddler. Other boats blew their horns at us, but ours was loud-est. Greetings and questions from passing "stinkpots" were lost in the uproar.

Then it was time to drop the sails for the last time. Benson raised the dress flags, and Jack brought us in to the dock where the crowd was waiting. There was champagne instead of beer this time, and all sorts of beloved and familiar faces. I saw the doctor's among them, and he was the first man we took aboard.

While Jack was officially welcomed by the officers of the club and officially presented them with the greetings of the Bora-Bora Yacht Club, *et al.*, there was an informal medical consultation in the cabin. The verdict was phlebitis—a massive hemorrhage, probably caused by a muscle cramp so violent that it literally tore the leg apart in that area. The treatment we had given it was obviously adequate in that none of the clots had been dislodged and carried to other parts, but Benson had been running that danger all along. The treatment prescribed from here to recovery was complete immobility, hot baths, and some medication to speed the absorption of the clot.

We changed into clothes that would keep us warm in July in Los Angeles, and stuffed a laundry bag with other clothes and paraphernalia. For the first time ever, we slid the door boards of the *Aikane* into place and snapped a lock on the topmost. With a glass of champagne to cheer us, we headed into a new sort of navigational experience, one for which we had neither charts nor light lists: the freeways of Los Angeles in the evening rush hour, with expired driver's licenses in our pockets.

Aftermath
and Retrospect

It was several weeks—not until Benson had chased the last blood clot down to his ankle and out of sight, and we had collected our possessions and trophies from various lockers and holds, stowed them in a station wagon, and driven them to Oregon—before I had time to think about answers to the questions I had asked myself at the start of the voyage.

By this time they were less interesting than such bits of news as:

NORRIS, who had seemed to me the least affected by the sojourn in a different world, pulled up stakes and moved to Honolulu within a few weeks of our return.

JIM WILSON wrote Jack that the storm that blew us to Hilo tore up three of his sails and ripped a stainless-steel plate off the bowsprit of the *Elusive* as she came out of the pass at Uturoa. He had had to give up his intended trip to Papeete and take refuge in Huahiné for repairs.

JOE SMITH and the *Spirit* turned up at the fishing-fleet dock in Astoria, where we live. He welcomed us aboard as if we were old companions, and told us that the Scotch whiskey we had traded for diesel had been of use in a real emergency the very next day. Just about the time he had located "our" school of albacore over the Erban Banks, his first mate had a heart attack. Joe gave him the bottle to comfort and cheer him while they were hauling in fish.

"And we were doing great, too, till all at once the temperature changed and the fish stopped biting. There was nothing to do but take what we had in to Frisco and have a doc look at Bill's ticker. If I'd known how it was going to turn out, I could have given you folks all the diesel you wanted. But you never know. Maybe I was punished for being so stingy! Serves a man right!"

THE FLARE THAT WAS NOT FOLLOWED UP: The consensus of the best-informed opinion we could get was that it was either an illusion—a *folie à trois* that Jack initiated and Benson and I fell in with—or it was a warning from a surfacing submarine. One of the Coast Guardsmen in Hilo was of the latter opinion: "They don't take chances on colliding with something that they can't hear on their sonar." He didn't say who "they" might be, and we didn't think to ask until it was too late.

THE NOTE IN THE BOTTLE: We dropped champagne bottles with appropriate notes in them both times we crossed the Equator. Almost two years after the date of the first note, Jack had a caller in his Los Angeles office. It (the note) had been given by a native of the New Hebrides (who had picked it up near Swallow Island, 11° 17′ South, 166° 26′ East) to a young American member of a survey crew recharting the area. The bottle had drifted over 4000 miles.

The young man told Jack that some of the islands near Swallow are as much as twenty-five miles off their charted position. Our precautions about heaving to to avoid going on a reef in the darkness seemed less adequate in that perspective.

That sort of retrospect and the questions people continued to ask finally brought me back to my postponed assessment of myself and the experience. "How did you all get along with one another?" "Did you feel yourself outnumbered?" "Was there a problem about privacy for you? Because of you?" "Did you miss having another woman to talk to?" Those were the questions most frequently asked by other people. My own were harder to answer, and I postponed these as long as I could.

First of all, in my opinion we got along pretty well. Many people have told us that it was better than that, and reeled off the names of boats whose crews broke up in Tahiti or elsewhere for reasons of "interpersonal friction," or old friends who never spoke to each other again after they got home. I have tried to re-create in my mind the strains I felt and to imagine the others'. It is hard to gauge their intensity from this distance. One thing I am sure of: The strains were never equal. My worst times were not Jack's or Norris's or Benson's. Perhaps that is why we made out as well as we did: because there was always someone with enough "play" in his personality to adjust the balance.

I never felt outnumbered in the sense of being one against three. I often felt a split between the couple and the two singletons, which was not what I had expected. The greatest friction frequently had to do with the fact that Benson and I were linked in a way that left the other two out. I was sometimes conscious of it and made an effort to compensate, but I doubt that it was successful. The two unattached males not infrequently indicated by their behavior that they felt "orphaned," "unloved," and discriminated against.

I had no problem about privacy, nor did Benson and Jack. We had camped together enough times to have learned an etiquette that worked satisfactorily in a world where there were no doors on dressing rooms. It was harder on Norris. Until the trip from Kauai to Los Angeles, he was still asking me to be sure "not to look" when he struggled out of wet clothes and into dry ones. But before we got home, he too had relaxed into the "eye-dropping" routine.

I did miss the company of women, but not women in the abstract. I missed certain individual women, just as I missed certain individual men. There isn't the same division of spheres of interest at sea in a small boat as there is ashore. When everyone is involved in cooking, motor repairs, navigation, and radio operation, there is no such thing as "man-talk" and "woman-talk."

And what about the bet I made with myself? Had I "made it" as well as the men? Perhaps the verdict should have been rendered by an impartial observer, but who? None of the men qualified for such a role. Anyway, it was how I *felt* about my own performance that mattered—to me.

On the whole, I felt good. Within the limitations of my physical strength and abilities, I think I did as well as the men did within theirs. More important than this sort of pointless comparison is the fact that I got more chances to push myself to the limits of that strength and abilities than I would ever have had ashore. I learned that I could endure as long as anyone else aboard, and perform—not brilliantly, but adequately—in most of the necessary functions. I'll never make a first-class navigator, and no one will ever sign me on as deck crew for a race. But there were some very important things I could do well enough to make up for my deficiencies in plotting position and changing sails. I don't think I was an albatross (dead) around the *Aikane*'s neck.

Part of the reason for this smug self-estimate is the help the *Aikane* gave me. She was on my side from the start. She responded to my manipulations even when they were most inexpert. She kept me comfortable and secure as long as she was either of those things. We suffered together almost to the breaking point on the voyage north, and I was glad that both of us concealed our cowardice till it was beside the point.

But the larger share of credit for my success as a woman aboard must go to the men. Not so much for anything they did as for what they didn't do. I have no way of guessing how hard it was for them to live up to the bargain made at the start, but they did. I was never once imposed on as a woman, never "put down." I was granted no special favors and put in no special category. The one time I was ordered away from the wheel, it was half in joke. I knew that if I protested I could win my right —or my duty—to the wheel. The one area in which I was patronized and teased in the traditional way was that in which I was behaving like the traditional woman-who-can't-add. I went on the defensive and sulked because I couldn't seem to climb out of my rut on my own. But that too passed away.

And those minor exceptions define and clarify the basic conclusion I have reached after months of thinking about it: that the reason there were no problems about being a woman aboard was that the men aboard didn't make any. Whether this bears applying to other situations in which women find themselves, aboard or ashore, is for someone else to prove.

Sample Menus

(One week's: the second week out of last
shore port, Guadalupe)

Breakfast:
    Orange (1 per person)
    Bacon and fried eggs
    Toast
    Coffee

Lunch:
    Abalone chowder
    Matzohs
    Cold lobster salad

Supper:
    Fried abalone steak
    Spaghetti
    Canned pears
    White wine

Breakfast:
    Grapefruit (½ per person)
    Oatmeal with raisins (canned
      milk)
    Coffee

Lunch:
    Cold lobster salad
    Coleslaw
    Peanut butter and matzohs

Supper:
    Roast leg of lamb
    Rice pilaf
    Canned green beans
    Red wine

Breakfast:
    Orange (the last!)
    Eggs scrambled with salami
    Toast
    Coffee

Lunch:
    Tomato juice
    Sliced salami, matzohs
    Pickles, celery

Supper:
  Beef stroganoff
  Brown rice
  Beets
  Red wine

Breakfast:
  Fried flying fish and squid
  Toast (the last)
  Coffee

Happy Hour:
  Snacks
  Beer

Breakfast:
  Grapefruit
  Scrambled eggs on matzohs
  Coffee

Lunch:
  Cold lamb
  Raw cauliflower salad
  Milk

Supper:
  Leftover beef stroganoff
  Whipped potatoes
  Corn

Lunch:
  Soup (canned tomato and
    dried garden vegetable)
  Celery and carrot sticks
  Cookies and prunes

Supper:
  Lamb and rice casserole
  Beet salad
  Pickles
  Chocolate pudding
  Red wine

Breakfast:
  Pancakes and syrup
  Grapefruit (the last)

Lunch:
  Leftover casserole (reheated)
  Leftover lobster salad
  Matzohs
  Pears

Supper:
  Canned ham
  Spaghetti
  Asparagus (cold) and
    mayonnaise
  Red wine

Breakfast:
    Eggs and salami
    Matzohs
    Coffee

Happy Hour:
    Bloody Marys
    Nuts and olives

Lunch:
    Leftover ham and spaghetti
    English muffins
    Cream cheese and jam

Supper:
    Cold pork loin
    Sauce (mustard and sour
      cream)
    Mashed potatoes
    Green beans (cold), French
      dressing

Ship's Stores

Edibles

   Oranges and grapefruit—1 case, mixed
   Lemons and limes—½ case, mixed
   Potatoes—20-lb. sack
   Carrots—20-lb. sack
   Cabbage—6 large heads
   Cauliflower—2 heads
   Celery—6 large bunches
   Eggs—1 case (12 doz.)[1]
   Bread—4 loaves, wrapped and sealed in plastic bags
   English muffins—2 packages, sealed

DRIED FOODS
   Oatmeal—6 boxes (too much)
   Grits (instant)—2 boxes
   Powdered milk—6 large boxes (8 qts. in each)[2]
   Powdered chocolate—2 large boxes
   Pancake mix—4 boxes, assorted blends (not enough)
   Cake mixes—12 boxes, assorted
   Flour—2 5-lb. sacks
   Sugar—2 5-lb. sacks
   Salt—12 individually wrapped medium-size boxes
   Matzohs—12 boxes, each wrapped in plastic bag
   Finn Crisp—2 boxes (could have used more)
   Cold-water biscuits—1 box (could have used more)
   Rice—5-lb. sack of instant white; 5 1-lb. boxes of instant brown
   Spaghetti—10 lbs. stored in plastic jar

[1] Each egg dipped in mineral oil.
[2] Whole milk is better than skim milk.

Potatoes—10 8-oz. boxes of flakes
Green peas (split)—5 lbs.
Lentils—5 lbs.
Mushrooms—5 packages
Cookies—12 boxes, individually wrapped (needed more)
Chocolate and other puddings—12 boxes
Raisins—5 lbs.
Prunes—10 lbs.
Figs—2 lbs.
Soups—30 packages: onion, green pea, beef, mushroom, chicken
Onions—minced 4 boxes (2 packages in each)
Gelatin—large box of unflavored, in individual envelopes
Coffee (instant)—10 large jars [3]
Tea—1 lb. green; 1 lb. black, 1 box spiced black
Cream—4 bottles, medium sized (irreplaceable in islands)

CANNED GOODS: MEATS
Bacon—24 1-lb. cans
Hams—6 approximately 3-lb. size (*not* the refrigerated type)
Tongues—6 approximately 1 lb.
Pork loins—10
Corned beef—6
Luncheon meats—6 cans
One-dish emergency meals
  1 can of Swedish meatballs
  1 can of chicken and gravy
  1 can ravioli
  2 cans spaghetti and meatballs
  1 can chili and beans
  1 can roast beef hash
  1 can corned beef hash
  6 cans cheese rarebit (also used as sauce)

CANNED GOODS: VEGETABLES
Asparagus—2 cans (white)
Beans (green)—6 cans
Beans (kidney)—6 cans
Beans and chili—2 cans
Beets—6 cans (sliced and julienne)
Carrots—2 cans

[3] A mistake: more small jars would have preserved flavor better.

Corn—6 cans (assorted styles)
Garbanzos—6 cans
Onions (Dutch style)—2 cans
Sauerkraut—2 cans
Tomato juice—12 large cans
Tomato sauce—12 large cans
Vegetable soups—12 cans (black bean, cheddar cheese, mushroom, tomato)[4]

CANNED GOODS: FRUITS
Orange and grapefruit juice—1 case large cans
Pears—1 case
Applesauce—2 cans (could have used more)
Pineapple—1 can
Fruit salad—2 cans
Lemon, lime, and orange juice—2 cans each

CANNED GOODS: MISCELLANEOUS
Milk (evaporated)—1 case, 24 cans
Cream sauce—4 cans
Hors d'œuvres:

Olives	Smoked oysters
Nuts	Anchovies
Pâté de foie gras	Anchovy paste
Camembert cheese	
Brie cheese	

MEATS [5]
Salami—San Francisco style, 6
Filet mignon (frozen)—3 lbs.
New York steaks (frozen)—2 thick
Lamb—1 5–6-lb. leg
Beef stew meat (frozen)—3 lbs.
Pork steak (frozen)—2 lbs.
Chickens, cut up for frying (frozen)—2
Ground sirloin (frozen)—1½ lbs.
Ground sirloin (not frozen)—1½ lbs.

IN JARS AND BOTTLES
Catsup—3 bottles

[4] Usually used for sauces.
[5] Stored in refrigerator.

Chili sauce—3 bottles
Cheese spreads—6 jars
Honey—2 1-lb. jars
Jam—6 large jars, assorted
Mustard—2 large jars
Peanut butter—6 pint jars, assorted
Pickles—4 large jars, assorted
Salad and cooking oil (corn)—3 qts.[6]
Syrup—3 qts. (not enough)
Vinegar—2 qts. red and white [7]

MISCELLANEOUS
Cheese—10 lbs. wrapped in wax paper and plastic
Cream cheese—2 large packages (refrigerated)
Sour cream—2 pints (refrigerated)
Margarine—24 1-lb. packages
Baking powder—1 can
Cornstarch—1 package (in plastic bag)
Cornmeal—1 lb.
Crumbs, etc., for frying—4 packages
Crisco—1 small can
8 large chocolate bars (not enough)
1 canned fruitcake

SPICES
Pepper—1 large jar, black, medium grind
Paprika—1 small can
Mustard—1 small can
Curry powder—1 can
Mole powder—1 can
Tarragon—1 jar of flakes
Marjoram—1 jar of flakes
Oregano—1 jar of flakes
Cinnamon—1 large can
Garlic salt—2 jars
Garlic powder—1 jar
Horseradish—1 bottle
Soy sauce—1 qt.
Worcestershire sauce—1 bottle

[6] In French islands, we restocked peanut oil.
[7] Restocked in French islands.

Capers—3 bottles
Vanilla—1 bottle (not used)
Bouillon cubes—10 packages
Bouillon granules—2 jars
Salad-dressing mixes—12 packages

WINES AND LIQUORS

WINES
6 gals. mountain white
6 gals. mountain red

BEER
6 6-packs of tall cans
8 bottles of "specials"

HARD LIQUOR
1 qt. high-proof Demerera rum
2 qts. brandy (for medicinal use)
1 qt. bourbon [8]
3 qts. each, vodka and gin

PAPER GOODS AND SOAP

PAPER
Toilet tissue—20 rolls
Paper towels—4 large rolls (not enough)
Paper napkins—approximately 700 (restocked in Tahiti)
Paper plates—100 (hard to restock)
Plastic cups—100 (hard to restock)
Tissues—6 large boxes
Aluminum foil—4 rolls

SOAPS, ETC.
3 large bottles Joy [9] for dishes
3 large bottles of Wisk for laundry

---

[8] We bought Scotch, very cheaply, in the islands.
[9] Brand names are mentioned because there is a great difference in the way detergents react to salt water, which we had to use. Wisk did not do wonders, but the other two did.

3 large bottles Lux for bath and shampoo in salt water
6 large cans scouring powder (plastic containers)
12 bars Ivory soap
1 bar Lava soap
1 can Scat
2 cans deodorant spray (for the head)

GALLEY EQUIPMENT

Pressure cooker—3-qt. size
Teakettle
Heavy cast-iron skillet
Heavy cast-aluminum pot (4-qt.) with cover
Long cast-iron skillet (low edge) covering two burners
Thermos bottles: 1-qt. size; 1-pt. size
3 aluminum saucepans, 1-, 2-, and 3-qt. sizes
Hibachi

Wooden cooking spoons and forks
Knives in a fixed holder
Plastic dishes, cups, glasses, etc.
Stainless steel flatware, with wooden handles
Plastic bags, tough plastic jars with screw-on lids

MEDICAL SUPPLIES

MEDICINES

1 jar (100) salt tablets
2 bottles (100) Dramamine tablets (for seasickness)
3 boxes Ducolax suppositories (for constipation)
3 bottles (100) tetracycline (broad-spectrum antibiotic)
100 Allbee with C vitamins (1 per person per week)
1 bottle Cheracol (for cough)
2 boxes Coldettes (common cold relief)
1 nasal inhaler (common cold relief)
1 large bottle Parapectolin and paregoric (for stomach cramps)
1 large bottle (200) Darvon capsules (pain relief)
1000 aspirin tablets (pain relief) (too many)
100 tablets Empirin with codeine (cough and pain relief) (not enough)

1 tube neomycin ointment (for cuts)
1 tube zinc oxide (for skin rash)
2 bottles Titralac (acidity)
1 small bottle sleeping pills (never used)
Eyedrops—Isophren ¼% in methyl cellulose
1 bottle Kaopectate (diarrhea)

FIRST-AID SUPPLIES

1 can First Aid spray (disinfectant)
2 pairs surgical gloves
scalpel, surgical scissors, tweezers
sterile suture material and needles
1 can anesthetic spray
Dental mirror and packing instrument, filling material
Ace bandages, 2″ and 4″
6 rolls nonallergic adhesive tape
2 jumbo boxes of Band-Aids, all sizes and shapes
1 box square, Telta-covered pads
Telta bandages for burns
2 rolls bandage, each, 1″, 2″, and 3″
1 large box cotton balls
1 box Q-tips
1 box Kotex for compress pads
Sling material (for broken arm)
1 can B.F.I. powder

MISCELLANEOUS

1 jar Vaseline
Hot-water bottle (also used for ice bag)
Enema bag
2 oral thermometers
1 large bottle Lubriderm
6 bottles insect repellent [10] (We used 6-12; very good.)
1 large can medicated talcum powder
1 bottle Halazone tablets (water purifier)

[10] We didn't take any rubbing alcohol or any iodine; we could have used both, in combination, for *no-no* bites.

Index of Recipes

General Index

Because the crew of the *Aikane*—the author and her husband, Janet and Benson Rotstein; Norris, world traveler; and Jack, the owner of the craft—appear on virtually every page of the story of *Woman Aboard,* they are not listed in the Index. The story is their index. Page numbers in italic indicate illustrations.